What is Citizenship?

What is Citizenship?

DEREK HEATER

Polity Press

First published in 1999 by Polity Press in association with Blackwell Publishers Ltd.

Reprinted 2002, 2005

Polity Press
65 Bridge Street
Cambridge CB2 1UR, UK

Polity Press
350 Main Street
Maldon, MA 02148, USA

ISBN 0−7456−2229−1
ISBN 0−7456−2230−5 (pbk)

A catalogue record for this book is available from the British Library.

Library of Congress Cataloging-in-Publication Data
Heater, Derek Benjamin.
    What is citizenship? / Derek Heater.
      p.   cm.
    Includes bibliographical references.
    ISBN 0−7456−2229−1. — ISBN 0−7456−2230−5 (pbk.)
    1. Citizenship. I. Title.
JF801.H433 1999
323.6—dc21   99−19927
                                                CIP

Typeset in 11 on 13pt Adobe Caslon
by Graphicraft Limited, Hong Kong
Printed and bound in Great Britain by Marston Book Services Limited, Oxford

This book is printed on acid-free paper.

For further information on Polity, visit our website: www.polity.co.uk

Contents

Preface   vii
Acknowledgement   viii

Introduction   1

1 The Liberal Tradition   4
   Origins • Citizenship and capitalism • Marshall's analysis •
   Marshall: influence and judgements • Social citizenship and
   neo-liberalism • Two additional elements • Citizenship
   rights at the turn of the century • The problem of rights
   in practice

2 The Civic Republican Tradition   44
   Major thinkers • Purpose of citizenship • Style of
   citizenship • Qualities of citizenship • Role of the citizen •
   Forming the citizen • Revival and arguments • Adaptations
   for today

3 Who Are Citizens?   80
   Legal definitions • Equality or elitism? • Feminist
   perspectives • Citizenship as nationality: origins •
   Citizenship and nationality synthesized • National citizens:
   made or born • Multiculturalism

Contents

4 Multiple Citizenship 115
The idea of multiple citizenship • Parallel citizenships •
Federal constitutions • The European Union • Sub-state
citizenships • The idea of cosmopolis • World citizenship
identity and morality • World law and the citizen • World
governance and the citizen • Pros and cons

5 Problems and Resolutions 155
Inherent problems and tensions • Current issues • The
roles of education • Connections and essence

References 181
Select Reading List 187
Index 189

Preface

Yet another book on citizenship needs to be justified. This is simply done: among the great outpouring of works on the topic during the past decade or so, it is difficult to find a succinct analysis of the subject-matter. David Held recognized the gap, invited me to try to fill it, and he and his colleagues at Polity Press have been of great assistance in seeing the task through to completion. I am also grateful for the comments of two anonymous readers of the manuscript. My wife, too, deserves my usual thanks for uncomplainingly being drawn away from her interest to listen to mine. But, of course, none of these can be thought responsible for the judgements I have made about the content and general approach of the book nor for any errors that it may contain.

I must add two explanations. One is that the book perhaps reflects my own greater interest in the academic disciplines of history and politics rather than sociology, though I have striven to present what I believe to be a reasonable balance. The other is that, although the material is presented in summary form and will, it is hoped, find favour with students, what follows is not just a 'textbook'. I have attempted in places some interpretations by clustering material into patterns, which will add, I trust, both to the understanding of this complicated topic and to its intrinsic interest.

Derek Heater

Acknowledgement

The author and publisher wish to thank Pluto Press for permission to reproduce extracts from T. H. Marshall and Tom Bottomore, *Citizenship and Social Class*.

Introduction

The title of citizen (*citoyen, citoyenne*) was adopted by the French revolutionaries to pronounce the symbolic reality of equality: the titles of
aristocratic distinction were expunged. The Russian revolutionaries went
one better by replacing even the title of Mr (*gospodin*) by the uniform
title of citizen (*grazhdanin*). Today citizenship is a commonly held
status throughout the world, though, true, the title has not persisted;
so equality, at least in theory, in principle and in law, might seem pervasive. But explaining that equality – how it has evolved; its variegated
elements, including rights and duties; the civic identity it provides;
and how far the practice so often falls short of the theory – all this is
a much more complicated business than the bland statement of the
generalized principle of equality might suggest.

Yet, however difficult the concept of citizenship may be, the effort
of comprehension is especially necessary now. For we are at present living
through an age that for good reasons considers citizenship of cardinal
significance. However, as a consequence of this recognized importance,
academic enquiry has uncovered the extraordinary complexity of its
history and present condition to aid our more accurate understanding.

There have been other ages of heightened consciousness of citizenship, often associated with particular states. Fifth to fourth-century BC
Athens, first-century BC to first-century AD Rome, late medieval Florence, late eighteenth-century America and France spring obviously to
mind. The present interest is different: it is virtually global in its extent.
How, then, to explain the fascination the subject currently holds? It

1

derives from the confluence of a number of events and concerns in the 1980s and 1990s.

First, in the established liberal democracies the emergence to political and doctrinal dominance of the New Right in the US and UK threw into question the validity of 'social citizenship'. By social citizenship is meant the provision of welfare state benefits as a *right*. It is a right that was conceded in order to ensure a greater equality for citizens than would be the case if untempered market forces of employment and wages were allowed to prevail.

Secondly, partly because of accelerated human migrations and partly because of enhanced and politicized awareness of ethnic differences within states, the fact that almost all states are multicultural in demographic composition has become an issue related to the definition of citizenship as civic identity.

Thirdly, and closely related to this development, ethnic, cultural and national consciousness have brought about either the loosening or the actual fragmentation of polities hitherto thought of as nation-states. What does it mean, for example, to be a Canadian citizen if one thinks of oneself primarily as a Québécois, or an Israeli citizen, if a Palestinian Arab? In potentially fissiparous conditions like these only a stable or strong government could hold a national citizenship in place. In the Soviet Union and Yugoslavia that stability and strength failed; and the assumed nation-states disintegrated. Furthermore, it was a consciousness among a critical mass of the population of the need and the opportunity to claim an effective citizenship that wrought these changes.

But, and moreover, these states had been autocratic regimes, many of whose successor governments sought to rebuild their political systems, this time following the liberal democratic blueprint. And so, fourthly, they have needed to construct fresh constitutions and ways of conducting public life which could give reality to the legal and political rights of citizenship that had not been thoroughly enjoyed under Communism. Nor were the ex-Communist countries alone in striving to make this transition: South Africa and the states of sub-Saharan Africa and Latin America that had endured but shook themselves loose from military dictatorships, have passed through similar experiences of improving the meaning of citizenship for their people.

2

Fifthly, we are becoming increasingly conscious that for large numbers of people throughout the world the idea of citizenship is still hollow and meaningless, deprived as they are of virtually all its attributes.

Sixthly, the validity of the nation-state is itself being put in question. Uniquely, at the sub-continental level, the European Union has created a new, legally defined category of citizenship, namely, of the Union. Meanwhile, economic developments and environmental worries have revived the ancient concept of cosmopolitan citizenship, the awareness of being a citizen of the world and the imperative need to behave and to be encouraged to behave as such. These trends are part of the increasing recognition that citizenship is a multiple rather than a singular feeling and status.

Citizenship in our complex times reflects this complexity. Its elements derive from manifold sources, influences and needs. To analyse them is, inevitably, to oversimplify and to exaggerate the separateness of the component parts. However, this is the route to understanding and therefore this is the task upon which we now embark.

1

The Liberal Tradition

Origins

Something of an oversimplification it may be, but it is most helpful to easy comprehension – not to mention quite fashionable – to distinguish between two traditions and interpretations of the nature of citizenship. These are the civic republican style, which places its stress on duties, and the liberal style, which emphasizes rights. Now, despite the former's origins in classical antiquity and therefore its longevity, it is the liberal form that has been dominant for the past two centuries and remains so today. It is therefore fitting to start with the liberal tradition, postponing consideration of civic republicanism to the next chapter. Compared with the republican variant, liberal citizenship is much less demanding of the individual. It involves a loosely committed relationship to the state, a relationship held in place in the main by a set of civic rights, honoured by the state, which otherwise interferes as little as possible in the citizen's life.

Liberal citizenship was the offspring of the liaison between revolutionary upheaval and contractarian natural rights theory, Great Britain playing the role of midwife. True, it was the French Revolution that first established the principle and practice of citizenship as the central feature of the modern socio-political structure, but it was the British (including, crucially, the American) experience over one-and-a-half centuries prior to 1789 that laid the foundations for the transition from a monarch–subject relationship to a state–citizen relationship. Paradoxically, the actual terms 'citizen' and 'citizenship' were rarely used in the

4

liberal sense in the English-speaking world. Yet the English Civil War and its aftermath, the political theory of John Locke, and the seizing of independence by the American colonies and their transmutation into the United States were all absolutely vital to the evolution of the liberal mode of citizenship and citizens' rights.

A citizen has the right to vote: Colonel Rainborough declared in 1647, 'I do think that the poorest man in England is not at all bound in a strict sense to that government that he has not had a voice to put himself under' (see Wootton, 1986, p. 286). A citizen also has a right to just treatment by the law: the first Habeas Corpus Act was passed in Britain in 1679. In about this year Locke wrote his *Two Treatises of Civil Government* (though they were not published until a decade later, in 1690). In the second of these Locke influentially expounded his theory of natural rights, that every man should have the free and equal right 'to preserve . . . his life, liberty, and estate' (Locke, 1962, s. 87). The American revolutionaries adapted this formula to 'life, liberty and the pursuit of happiness', and the French, to 'liberty, property, security, and resistance to oppression'. These rights are God-given; but it is the function of the state to ensure their protection. We therefore step from generalized natural rights, which individuals have *qua* human beings, to specific civic rights, which are assured by the state to individuals *qua* citizens. Hence the dual title of the French Declaration – of Man and the Citizen.

The distinction could be telling, as Marx recognized. The rights of man are negative, allowing the individual to pursue his own, personal life, not committing him to a life as a member of a community, a citizen. Marx cites Art. 6 of the French Declaration, which defines liberty as 'the power of doing anything that does not harm others', and he continues:

> The freedom in question is that of a man treated as an isolated monad and withdrawn into himself . . . none of the so-called rights of man goes beyond egoistic man . . . namely an individual withdrawn behind his private interests and whims and separated from the community.
>
> *('On the Jewish Question', in McLellan, 1977, pp. 53–4)*

The rights of the citizen, on the other hand, have a more defined, positive character. For example, the French Declaration and the American

Bill of Rights (the first ten Amendments to the Constitution), finalized within weeks of each other in 1789, concentrated particularly on a range of legal rights such as freedom of speech and conscience, equality before the law, presumption of innocence, trial by jury (see French Declaration Arts. 3–11; Bill of Rights, Arts. 1, 5–9).

Another feature of citizens' rights considered to be crucial in these early days of defining liberal citizenship was the right to property. Locke firmly established this principle. He declared quite trenchantly that 'government has no other end but the preservation of property' (Locke, 1962, s. 94). The language of the Declaration of Rights is even more forceful, asserting that the right to property is 'inviolable and sacred' (Art. 17). Ownership of property was not only a right, it was, as a universal practice, a requirement for the basic political right of citizenship, namely the right to vote. For instance, even in Massachusetts, hub of the rebellion against the British government, the franchise was restricted in *c.*1790 to the owners of real estate worth $12 a year or any property with a capital value of $240. The political crises of the late eighteenth century threw up the issue of universal manhood suffrage, a cause persistently supported, for example, by Thomas Paine. But the mystique of property was too powerful for its implementation yet. Not until the 1820s did some American states lead the way.

How, then, may we characterize the concept of liberal citizenship in these emergent years? It is an important question because the consolidation of the basics from roughly Locke to the French Revolution provided a legacy which still shapes our assumptions about citizenship in our own times.

First, the individual remains an individual. The acquisition of citizenly status does not necessitate abandonment of the pursuit of self-interest. Public and private spheres are kept distinct, and citizens are under no obligation to participate in the public arena if they have no inclination to do so. Nor have citizens any defined responsibilities *vis-à-vis* their fellow citizens. All are equal, autonomous beings, so that there is no sense that the state has any organic existence, bonding the citizens to it and to each other. Citizens have the odd duty to perform, it is true – mainly the payment of taxes – in return for the protection of their rights by the state. But there is only a slight change of heart, a weak sense of identity, no necessary pride in thinking oneself into the station of citizen. Citizenship largely means the pursuit of one's private life and

6

interests more comfortably because that private life is insured by state-protected rights. In short, therefore, the extrapolation of the rights of the citizen from the rights of man may marginally have adapted, but by no means transformed, the individual from Marx's 'isolated monad'.

If the liberal citizen is expected to feel only a limited obligation to the state, *pari passu* the state is expected to impinge on the citizen's life in only a feeble way. This is the second feature of liberal citizenship as laid down from the late seventeenth century. The state is useful to the citizen as, in Locke's striking image, a 'nightwatchman'. And if any government oversteps its limited powers and interferes in its citizens' activities to the detriment of their life-styles, or, conversely, fails in its protective function, then the citizenry has the right to rouse itself from the quiet pursuit of private affairs and rebel, as the American colonists did in 1776.

And what, we ask thirdly, are these private affairs that the citizen must be allowed independently to pursue? It is the accrual of wealth. Is, then, liberal citizenship a political expression of capitalism? Yes; but the relationship is, in fact, much more complicated than that.

Citizenship and capitalism

We cannot say categorically that the evolution of modern liberal citizenship would have been impossible without the emergence of a capitalist market economy and an accompanying, increasingly powerful, bourgeois class. For one thing, pressure for the legal and political rights that were conceded by the three revolutions in England, America and France was spearheaded as much by a lawyer-dominated professional class as by entrepreneurial capitalists, perhaps even more so. Nevertheless, the decay of a feudal or quasi-feudal society and its supersession by a market economy did introduce changes that were, if no more, at least conducive to the emergence of a liberal form of citizenship. (Henceforth, in this chapter, let us take 'liberal form of' for granted.) Three kinds of change may be identified.

1 Pre-capitalist society was based on personal subservience – vassal to lord, apprentice to master, subject to prince. In contrast, the free exercise of individual initiative is the very essence of capitalism. Similarly, citizenship grew by the extraction of rights for the individual.

7

Feudalism →	Capitalism →	Citizenship
Individual subservience	Individual initiative	Individual rights
Hierarchical society	Permeable class structure	Civic equality
Provincially fragmented economy	Open access to markets	National identity

Figure 1.1

2 Feudal structure was socially hierarchical. As the Victorian poet Cecil Frances Alexander unequivocally expressed the distinction between rich and poor: 'God made them, high or lowly, / And order'd their estate.' Capitalism, in contrast, requires social fluidity. Class divisions, it is true, are inevitable – middle class and the lower orders; but not caste rigidity. Initiative, to refer back to our first kind of change, required the partitions between classes to be permeable. The concept of citizenship took this alteration to the logical conclusion of equality of status. A citizen is a citizen is a citizen: no differentiation.

3 *Ancien régime* society was, to modern minds, unbelievably provincially fragmented. Economically, that is; not to be confused with the modern convenience of devolution. Internal customs barriers, even provincially distinct measurements of weights and capacity, were anathema to the capitalist's essential requirement of free and open access to markets. The integration and solidification of the nation-state, so essential for the capitalist, made way for citizenship as national identity.

The foregoing interpretation is simply tabulated in figure 1.1. One feature of this transformatory process was the alteration in the relationship between civil society and citizenship. In the Middle Ages citizenship meant being a privileged inhabitant of a city or other municipality, and the status tended to be accorded to members of corporate bodies such as guilds, that is, the component organizations of civil society. The growth of capitalism and the revolutionary changes wrought in Europe from the late eighteenth century undermined this localized and fragmented political role of civil society, and citizenship became attached to the national instead of the municipal sphere. The individual's communal identity was therefore bifurcated.

Marx, in fact, takes an extra step and argues that the collapse of the old structure also destroyed the sense of commitment which had made civil society such a co-operative network. 'The shaking off of the [feudal] political yoke', he explained, 'entailed the shaking off of those bonds that had kept the egoistic spirit of civil society fettered' (McLellan, 1977, p. 56). In so far as this analysis is valid, it means that citizenship in the modern, broader sense could alone provide a feeling of communal togetherness (stiffened, of course, by the ideology of nationalism).

One further introductory point on this matter of the relationship between capitalism and citizenship: we have a picture of a movement from a hierarchical to an increasingly egalitarian society as the rights of citizenship became democratized. But we must examine this picture more closely because, lurking there, is the counterbalancing economic inequality induced by unfettered capitalism. This is how Bryan Turner has explained this 'progress': 'The growth of modernity is a movement from de-jure inequalities in terms of legitimate status hierarchies to de-facto inequalities as a consequence of naked market forces where the labourer is defined as a "free" person' (Turner, 1986, p. 136).

So, in various ways and with outcomes not all necessarily an advance on what had been left behind, capitalism facilitated the emergence of liberal citizenship. But the connection has not been a one-way process, it has been reciprocal; for citizenship, in turn, has supported capitalism. We have already seen how prominent in the list of citizens' rights as drafted in the early years was the right of property ownership. In times of political upheaval this was a comforting formula for the middle classes. For instance, even the French Declaration of Rights of 1793, formulated by the radical Convention on the eve of the Terror, reiterated this right. The nervousness of the wealthy in the face of social and political upheaval provides another consideration, too: the damping down of civil discord by the broad concession of civil (i.e. legal) and political rights in practice affords a welcome calming of these fears. What is more, the middle classes benefited not just in this indirect manner. Chronologically it was they, not the working classes, who first had access to and made use of these civil and political rights of citizenship.

Nevertheless, the relationship between capitalism and citizenship has by no means been all mutual cosiness. In some circumstances citizenship has been threatening to capitalism and capitalism has been hostile to citizenship. The basic question has then arisen whether the state can ever, or indeed should ever, be a neutral observer when the interests of capitalism and citizenship are in collision.

One must, naturally, recognize that the state has an obligation to protect its citizens. How far does this extend? In practice, the state has often intervened on behalf of the citizen by curbing the absolute freedom of the capitalist to maximize his profit. This intervention has taken two main forms. One is by regulating the market by laws, for instance, against the formation of cartels and monopolies. The other is by increases in taxation on higher income and heritable wealth in order to fund welfare and educational services for the mass of citizens. For, particularly in the twentieth century, the belief that citizenship embodies social as well as legal and political rights has taken hold. Consider one illustration of this. Even in the Reagan–Thatcher era, when the Republican administration in the USA and the Conservative in the UK pursued quite radical neo-liberal free-market policies, the amounts spent by the governments on health and social security still increased. From 1979 to 1984 in the UK expenditure on health rose by 16 per cent and on social security by 26 per cent; from 1980 to 1984 in the USA expenditure on health rose by 38 per cent and on social security by 12 per cent. Taxation inevitably increased.

The capitalism–citizenship coin, however, has another side: the threat posed by capitalism to citizenship. We must not forget that the citizenship model presents a state composed of citizens of equal status, equally enjoying their rights and relating to the state by virtue of those rights and concomitant duties. Capitalism weakens this egalitarian political structure by giving primacy to economic relationships.

New class divisions open up, separating the wealthy entrepreneurs from the general populace, a gulf condoned by the liberal virtue of individual enterprise. For the successful, profit in the market place, not civic loyalty, gives social identification. For the rest, they are consumers of products and services, not citizens in the proper sense. *The Citizen's Charter* published by the British Conservative government in 1991 lets the capitalist cat out of the civic bag: the text refers in a number of places to 'customer' and 'client' as if these were synonymous with 'citizen'. The danger is that if citizenship is perceived as a set of rights to protect the individual *qua* consumer against some of the problems

10

exposed by a private or privatized economy, then the need to preserve and improve the core rights of real citizenship will be lost to sight.

Marx, as one would expect, portrayed the hostility of capitalism to citizenship in the starkest of terms, as embedded in the very nature of the state. According to his interpretation, the modern state is a bourgeois state, the expression and protector of bourgeois interests. It follows that the state is incapable of resolving the conflict between capitalism and citizenship because it is not itself a disinterested party. Citizenship as a status and a value is therefore in reality nothing more than a sop, a cloak for the citizen's impotence: 'political man is only the abstract fictional man' (McLellan, 1977, p. 56).

If there are two apparently contradictory arguments – that capitalism and citizenship are mutually supportive and mutually antipathetic – what conclusions can be drawn? There are two options.

The first is to settle for the view that the relationship is shot through with ambivalence. The modern state (certainly since the collapse of Communism) – swayed but gently by the doctrinal differences between moderate Left and Right political parties – juggles as best it can with guaranteeing both profit-making for the businessman and -woman and a measure of welfare and education for the general citizenry. In addition, there are two quite valid but different interpretations of the relationship between civil and political rights on the one hand and social rights on the other. One interpretation declares, following Marx, that the existence of civil and political rights is of little use for the majority of citizens if a reasonable life-style is not sustained by the allocation of social rights. The contrary interpretation is that, in fact, civil and political rights are, and historically have been, an essential set of levers for extracting those necessary social rights. More on this relationship between kinds of rights later.

The second option to adopt in the face of the fundamental contradictory arguments is to plump for one of them. This is a fairly common practice; and the case that is considered the stronger is that the ethic of capitalism and the ethic of citizenship really are incompatible. Liberal economics cannot cohabit with liberal politics without falling out over the issue. To quote Bryan Turner again:

> The societies of western industrial capitalism are essentially contradictory and there is an ongoing dynamic relationship between citizenship and

11

the inequalities of the market place. The dynamic feature of capitalism is precisely the contradiction between politics and economics as fought out in the sphere of social citizenship.

(Turner, 1986, p. 12)

The same conclusion has been expressed more pithily in the following words: 'it is clear that in the twentieth century, citizenship and the capitalist class system have been at war' (Marshall and Bottomore, 1992, p. 18). They were written by T. H. Marshall in the most famous single work to have been composed on liberal citizenship, *Citizenship and Social Class*.

Marshall's analysis

In 1949 Marshall, then Professor of Sociology at the London School of Economics and Political Science, delivered that year's lectures in Cambridge in commemoration of his namesake, Alfred Marshall. He published these lectures in expanded, essay form in the following year. *Citizenship and Social Class* has correctly been described as a seminal work and therefore deserves a generous allocation of space in this chapter. The present section provides, simply, a bald summary. There follows a brief review of the essay's influence and some of the judgements it has prompted from the many commentators who have responded to it since its publication. The section after that delves into recent debates concerning citizenship and social class including the concept of social citizenship, in particular from the neo-liberal standpoint; and these are issues which can hardly avoid cross-referencing to Marshall's work. So intertwined are these matters that there will inevitably be some slight repetition across these sections and the first two sections of the chapter also: this will at least reinforce the fact of the interconnections. We start, then, with a précis of Marshall's essay.

In one of his papers Alfred Marshall had argued the possibility of the progressive amelioration of the condition of the working class through economic and educational improvements in order to reach the life-style of what he called a 'gentleman'. T. H. Marshall draws the implication that 'We can go on to say that the claim to enjoy these conditions is a claim to be admitted to a share in the social heritage, which in turn means a claim to be accepted as full members of the society, that is, as citizens' (Marshall and Bottomore, 1992, p. 6).

The basic thesis is that, although economic inequalities can never be completely ironed out, 'the inequality of the social class system may be acceptable provided the equality of citizenship is recognised' (p. 6). By the 1940s this compatability of citizenship with class had become so ingrained that 'citizenship has itself become, in certain respects, the architect of legitimate social inequality' (p. 7). Marshall set himself four questions: (1) 'Is it still true that the basic equality can be created and preserved without invading the freedom of the competitive market?' (2) What is the effect of the coexistence of socialism and the market? (3) 'What is the effect of the marked shift of emphasis from duties to rights?' (4) Are there 'limits beyond which the modern drive towards social equality cannot, or is unlikely to, pass'? (p. 7).

Marshall then enters into a historical survey. He starts by defining his tripartite analysis of citizenship into civil, political and social, which has been so widely adopted:

> The civil element is composed of the rights necessary for individual freedom – liberty of the person, freedom of speech, thought and faith, the right to own property and to conclude valid contracts, and the right to justice. . . . By the political element I mean the right to participate in the exercise of political power, as a member of a body invested with political authority or as an elector of the members of such a body. . . . By the social element I mean the whole range from the right to a modicum of economic welfare and security to the right to share to the full in the social heritage and to live the life of a civilised being according to the standards prevailing in the society.
>
> *(p. 8)*

For the modern development of these rights in Great Britain (and Marshall confines his study to Britain), he stresses their separateness and assigns an approximate, though overlapping, period for each: civil (in which he incorporates the economic right to work) – eighteenth century; political – nineteenth century; social (in which he incorporates the right to education) – twentieth century.

Marshall was mainly interested in the third, social, type of rights because, as he explains, 'my special interest is in [citizenship's] impact on social equality' (p. 17). He dates the modern development of these rights to the provision of elementary education in the nineteenth century. But he identifies an apparent paradox from a much earlier period. This is the emergence of the egalitarian principle of citizenship in its civil guise from the late seventeenth century contemporaneously with the development of socially inegalitarian capitalism.

Marshall clarifies the problem by distinguishing between legally entrenched feudal class divisions and modern economically differentiated classes. With the former citizenship is incompatible; with the latter, compatible. More:

> civil rights were indispensable to a competitive market economy. They gave to each man, as part of his individual status, the power to engage as an independent unit in the economic struggle and made it possible to deny to him social protection on the ground that he was equipped with the means to protect himself.
>
> *(pp. 20–1)*

But civil rights have limited value if unaccompanied by social rights:

> if you . . . explain to a pauper that his property rights are the same as those of a millionaire, he will probably accuse you of quibbling. Similarly, the right to freedom of speech has little real substance if, from lack of education, you have nothing to say that is worth saying, and no means of making yourself heard if you say it.
>
> *(p. 21)*

Civil and, later, political rights in the eighteenth and nineteenth centuries were, in fact, equal only in principle, not in access, for several reasons, notably class prejudice and economic influence. These impediments to equality have gradually waned, though economic barriers to access to the law remained forbidding in Marshall's time.

The development in the course of the eighteenth and nineteenth centuries of the notion of citizenship effected important changes. It introduced 'the conception of equal social worth, not merely of equal natural rights' (p. 24); it gave 'a direct sense of community membership based on loyalty to a civilisation which is a common possession' (p. 24), including national patriotism; and in both its political and its civil forms it came to pose a threat to capitalism. Of great importance was the use by trade unions of civil rights to extract social rights by the method of collective bargaining. 'Trade unionism has, therefore, created a secondary system of industrial citizenship parallel with and supplementary to the system of political citizenship' (p. 26).

In the fourth section of his essay Marshall reaches the heart of what he wished to say, namely the issue of social citizenship in the twentieth century. For long, the alleviation of poverty was unassociated with any consideration of rights. Then:

> A new period opened at the end of the nineteenth century, conveniently marked by Booth's survey of Life and Labour of the People in London and the Royal Commission on the Aged Poor. It saw the first big advance in social rights, and this involved significant changes in the egalitarian principles expressed in citizenship.
>
> *(p. 28)*

Economic changes also were eroding class distinctions and were gradually producing a more integrated and egalitarian society. This led to a desire for full equality. 'These aspirations have in part been met by incorporating social rights in the status of citizenship and thus creating a universal right to real income which is not proportionate to the market value of the claimant' (p. 28).

One of the problems associated with legislating for social rights is how 'to combine the principles of social equality and the price system' (p. 31). The most common solution is for the state to guarantee 'a minimum supply of certain essential goods and services . . . or a minimum money income available to be spent on essentials. . . . Anyone able to exceed the guaranteed minimum out of his own resources is at liberty to do so' (p. 32). But there are problems in the details of administering such a system. The main point to grasp is that

> The extension of the social services is not primarily a means of equalising incomes. . . . What matters is that there is a general enrichment of the concrete substance of civilised life, a general reduction of risk and insecurity, an equalisation between the more and the less fortunate at all levels. . . . Equalisation is not so much between classes as between individuals within a population which is now treated for this purpose as though it were one class. Equality of status is more important than equality of income.
>
> *(p. 33)*

However, benefits of social citizenship, such as education and health, are concerned with the quality of life, which means that these rights of the citizen cannot be precisely defined or legally enforced. Nor is it possible to determine with any precision what is or will be affordable by the state. A crucial distinction therefore arises in the sphere of social rights concerning those faults in the system for which the individual citizen can obtain redress and those where only government intervention (central or local) for society as a whole can effect a remedy. In the latter case, the social rights of the individual may have to be subordinated to the rights of the community: housing, town-planning and education are obvious examples, where there has not been equality of provision, whatever the intentions.

In the case of education, the post-1944 system aimed at a citizenly right to equality of opportunity. However, in practice, the system channelled individuals into particular kinds of jobs determined by their schooling and with little chance of job mobility in later life. Inherited privilege was weakened by the selective educational system, but a new 'hierarchy of groups' was consolidated (p. 39). And so,

> through education in its relations with occupational structure, citizenship operates as an instrument of social stratification. There is no reason to deplore this, but we should be aware of its consequences. The status acquired by education is carried out into the world bearing the stamp of legitimacy, because it has been conferred by an institution designed to give the citizen his just rights.
>
> *(p. 39)*

Turning now to the relationship between citizenship and capitalism, there is an inherent conflict between the system of status of the one and of contract of the other, between social justice and market price. A study of the trade unions highlights the distinction because they have acted out an anomaly by creating 'a sort of secondary industrial citizenship' (p. 40). Citizens' rights are just that – rights; they are not matters for bargaining. A living wage is a social right, yet trade unions have bargained for this goal. But if trade unions base their claims on the principle of citizenship, they should balance their demand for rights by a sense of duty: unofficial strikes are incompatible with this position.

16

More importantly, the idea of a fair wage raises the question of wage differentiation between jobs and their relative status. Consequently, as with education, jobs become classified into a hierarchy. In practice, the social concept of status becomes entangled with the economic pressures of the market price for the needed workforce, and national wage standards with the principle of individual incentive.

In conclusion, Marshall identified three factors that have affected social structure:

> First, the compression at both ends, of the scale of income distribution. Second, the great extension of the area of common culture and common experience. And third, the enrichment of the universal status of citizenship, combined with the recognition and stabilisation of certain status differences chiefly through the linked systems of education and occupation. The first two have made the third possible.
>
> *(p. 44)*

The issue of status differences is important. Marshall concludes that such distinctions are compatible with citizenship so long as they do not cut too deep and are not hereditary.

The matter of the duties of citizenship is also important, partly because they are not so clearly understood as rights. How, for example, can one impress upon the citizenry the obligation to work and to work conscientiously? Devolution of the expected discharge of duties to the local community or workplace might be a solution.

Finally, social inequalities have become more acceptable because of the levelling effects of the welfare state and other devices which have widened the distinction between money income and real income. In any case, Britain *c.*1950 featured many socio-economic paradoxes, such as the relationship between citizenship and social inequality; yet with tolerance they could be abated and lived with.

Marshall: influence and judgements

> There is a good case to be made that the most significant contribution to social and political theory made this century by a British sociologist is 'citizenship' and that it was made by the very English T. H. Marshall.
>
> *(Colin Bell, on jacket of Bulmer and Rees, 1996)*

This is the considered judgement of one British academic. More epigrammatically, Ralf Dahrendorf has rated the lectures as 'one of the gems of social analysis' (Bulmer and Rees, 1996, p. 35). Recognition of Marshall's signal contribution to the study of citizenship has burgeoned since the mid-1980s. He has been honoured by the institution of a series of memorial lectures at the University of Southampton and his work has been the subject of a remarkable amount of commentary, development and criticism. The main focus of this exegesis has been his *Citizenship and Social Class*, though his subsequent work on the topic (notably in *The Right to Welfare and Other Essays*, 1981) has also been embraced in many of these analyses.

Why the fame? His two principal assertions – that citizenship contains three elements or 'bundles' of rights, and that social citizenship is a vital underpinning for the other two – were simple, illuminating insights encapsulating much truth. In particular, few commentators on citizenship rights before him thought to add social to the political dimension of citizenship. True, Marshall's predecessor Leonard Hobhouse is an important exception to this statement, but he exercised much less influence. Marshall's eminence derives not just from the quality of his work but also from its clear relevance in Britain to the post-war creation of the welfare state and the problems and doubts surrounding these social institutions and provisions in the 1980s and 1990s.

Nor has Marshall's fame and influence been confined to his native land. His arguments that citizenship contains three elements and that social citizenship is a vital underpinning for the other two, especially civil citizenship, have become very widely accepted. For example, two Canadian scholars, W. Kymlicka and W. Norman, have described *Citizenship and Social Class* as 'The most influential exposition' of the 'postwar conception of citizenship-as-rights' (Beiner, 1995, p. 285). And when in the mid-1990s a British research project undertook to identify the 'hallmarks of citizenship' imprinted in the laws and practices of the member states of the European Union, the published findings used the threefold division explicitly acknowledged as being derived from Marshall (Gardner, n.d., p. 9).

On the other hand, Marshall has by no means been spared from criticism, as is only to be expected. After all, no one, no matter how distinguished, is immune to failings, either by the tests of his own time or retrospectively. (Even so, to balance this observation, it should be noted that some of Marshall's critics have themselves been the subject of academic counter-attack.)

A survey of the critical judgements on Marshall reveals a formidable list of identified faults. These may be clustered into five categories: that his study was temporally and geographically too myopic; that his notion of citizenship was too exclusive; that his vision was too optimistic; that his triad of rights was too simplistic; and that his interpretation was too unhistorical. (For an alternative classification of criticisms, see Faulks, 1998, pp. 41–52.) However, despite this range of apparent failings, covering both detail and the core of Marshall's thesis, some of the commentary has overstepped the boundary into unfairness. The remainder of this section is accordingly devoted to an analysis and judgement of these five points. A review of this critical work is, indeed, worthwhile not merely for the light it sheds on Marshall's interpretation, but also as an informative commentary on the liberal version of citizenship, particularly in England.

First, Marshall's myopia. He delivered his lectures in 1949. The Beveridge Report (1942), the Butler Education Act (1944) and the creation of the National Health Service (1946) seemed at this time to have laid firm foundations for a welfare state second to none in the world. In his enthusiasm for these achievements Marshall, so his critics aver, underestimated the perhaps tentative nature of the social citizenship which he saw the welfare state as consolidating. He gave no thought to the possible future need to advance the social element in the citizenly status, let alone defend it against retrogression.

Furthermore, if his model of an evolutionary tripartite form of citizenship was intended for general application, he was culpable of ignoring not just all other countries, but even the relationship of England with the rest of the United Kingdom. As to Britain, if civil rights had been as solidly established in Northern Ireland as in England, the 'troubles' that burst out in 1968 might have been averted. And even a superficial survey of other countries reveals wide variations in the phasing of and manner in which citizens' rights have been won, a matter which will be discussed later.

Secondly, the exclusive nature of Marshall's picture of the development of citizenship. Most noticeably, it is centred on the achievement of male citizenship: his pattern falls apart if the experience of women is incorporated. Marshall describes the position of women in the nineteenth century with regard to civil rights as 'in some important respects peculiar' (p. 12). Only by making this rather ungracious concession to the fact that the condition of half the population invalidated his sequence of civil rights as *preceding* political rights could Marshall pretend to sustain his evolutionary thesis. After all, women were enfranchised in 1928, yet not until 1990, for instance, were they automatically taxed separately from their husbands. Only very gradually have they approximated to a position of civic equality with men. By casting his discussion of citizenship in relation to class differences, Marshall omitted the differences between the sexes which cut across class divisions.

But women are not the only group who have failed to keep pace with Marshall's historical design of the gradual achievement of full citizenship status. Still today many people are in reality only partial citizens: members of racial and ethnic minorities, the very poor 'underclass', and the various individuals who are incapable for one reason or another of complete 'self-determination' (children, the mentally incapable, the elderly infirm). Such people clearly cannot participate on equal terms with the rest of the community in the enjoyment of a common civic culture as Marshall envisaged citizens able to do; yet he makes no reference to the possibility of some individuals being citizens in only a second-class or partial sense.

Thirdly, Marshall's optimism. This accusation has several strands. He is charged with assuming too readily – caught up as he was in the general enthusiasm for the welfare state – that progress in social rights would continue. It has even been suggested that his optimism was an expression of his naïvety. Looking back from a standpoint in the 1990s, critics can indicate a number of features in British history during the second half of the century which have counteracted the egalitarian thrust of social citizenship described by Marshall.

Society has not become more homogeneous and egalitarian in socio-economic terms. A number of reasons have been presented as having contributed to this disappointment of Marshall's hopes. Education has not yet become a means of providing equal opportunities for all. Nor are the social services, including health, equally accessible to all. Capitalism has been more resistant to the spread of social citizenship than Marshall allowed for. And the state has not been neutral, as he implied, in the citizenship *v.* class competition for the distribution of resources.

For instance, because of government policy the gap between rich and poor in Britain actually widened to a marked degree in the 1980s. In short, if the creation of the welfare state was something of a social revolution, Marshall can be interpreted as not allowing for the resilience of the old regime or the counter-revolution of the neo-liberalism of the New Right.

So far, what we have been reporting are lapses in the detail of Marshall's handling of his subject-matter. What we must now go on to consider are the attacks that penetrated to the very heart of his explanatory schema. The fourth count is that his plan of a triangular shape to citizenship was overly simple. This criticism can itself be broken down into three sub-divisions.

Basically, it is argued, citizens' rights do not neatly fall into three compartments; and to try to force them into this pattern is misleading. A number of proposals for sub-dividing, reallocating content and adding to the categories have been made. The most cogent criticism is that the category of civil citizenship really contains two quite distinct sets of rights. One of these is the right of *individuals* to pursue their own interests – the bourgeois establishment of equality before the law and of market rights such as the freedom to trade and make contracts. The other is the right of acting to achieve *collective* aims, notably through trade unionism – what Marshall calls 'economic civil rights'. The first entailed a confrontation with the state; the second, with the state and employers.

Another weakness detected in Marshall's tripartite pattern is his failure to recognize that social citizenship is different in kind from the political and, especially, civil varieties. Civil citizenship establishes rights *against* the state; social citizenship establishes rights *provided by* the state. Social citizenship consequently involves expenditure and hence taxation on a considerable scale. But taxation invades civil rights in their capitalist form of the sanctity of property. So, civil and social citizenship, which in Marshall's scenario are complementary components, are in fact potentially at loggerheads.

And there is yet another problem with the idea that citizenship comprises three sets of rights: the simplicity of the pattern ignores the differences between entitlements and provision, between formal and substantive rights. Entitlements are the rights which in *theory* citizens should have; provision is what in *practice* citizens are allowed to have.

Marshall was more interested in defining the former rather than the latter. Similarly, he was more interested in substantive citizenship, involving *what* citizens could expect in the way of rights, than he was in formal citizenship, involving *who* had the right to be citizens – a matter that proved difficult and contentious in the face of pressure for immigration from other Commonwealth countries.

We come finally and fifthly to the accusation that Marshall's sequential pattern of civil followed by political followed by social citizenship does violence to the historical facts; a serious charge given that Marshall had originally been a trained and practising historian. Related to this concern are other opinions that his understanding of the relevant historical processes also left something to be desired.

The trouble with Marshall's phases is twofold: it is too neat for Britain and it is not applicable to some countries at all. In Britain, the real pattern was much more confused and overlapping. Even discounting the exclusion of women from his pattern, critics have listed what they hold to be unfortunate exceptions to his periodization. His allocation of the achievement of civil rights to the eighteenth century ignores the very important struggle for trade union rights in the nineteenth. His allocation of the achievement of political rights to the nineteenth century underplays the lateness of the concession of full manhood suffrage – 1918. And his allocation of the achievement of social rights to the twentieth century underestimates the value of the old, admittedly paternalistic, system of employment and poor relief which persisted into the eighteenth century.

When one turns to the development of citizens' rights in other countries, one may note two examples where critics have pointed out that social rights preceded civil and political rights. One is post-1871 Imperial Germany. There, Bismarck introduced social insurance schemes in a politically authoritarian state. The second example is the strength of social rights in the post-1945 Soviet bloc prior to the acquisition of civil and political rights consequent upon the collapse of Communism.

Not only has it been suggested that Marshall's sequential pattern is faulty, the very notion of a smooth evolutionary process has been challenged. By portraying the development of rights in tidy stages – political rights from a platform of civil rights, political rights then in turn providing a platform for achieving social rights – Marshall obscures the historical reality of conservative resistance at all times and the often intense struggle necessary to overcome this resistance. (Could not the anthem of the American Civil Rights movement 'We shall overcome' have been sung in Britain?) Nor are causes and connections evident in Marshall's narrative. What conditions were propitious for the extraction of rights? What was the role of war? What was the role of the economic health of the country? He does not say.

Moreover, the struggle to achieve citizenship rights cannot be adequately understood merely in terms of the relationship between citizenship and social class. Different groups and individuals have campaigned for rights without necessarily acting for or against class interests. As one British academic has stressed, 'The very meaning of particular rights cannot be adequately understood if the range of concerns and pressures which have given rise to them is not properly grasped' (Held, 1989, p. 200).

Thus the case against Marshall. What, finally, can be, indeed has been, said in his defence? Let us run through each of the five arguments in turn.

First, the accusation that he was too myopic. The suggestion that the development of citizenship in other countries did not accord with the British pattern is fair only if we assume that Marshall's objective was to frame a universally valid typology; but it is by no means evident that this was his intention. Similarly his focus on a perspective taken in his own time was to a certain extent deliberate and almost inevitable: he was not equipped with a crystal ball. Furthermore, the scope of the essay was constrained by its origin as a series of lectures, so that the work is very brief with little room for fine detail. Marshall should not therefore be criticized for not doing what he did not or could not have chosen to do in the circumstances.

Secondly, the charge that he was too exclusive. It may be only a partial defence, but Marshall was of his age in paying scant attention to women and none to the other groups he has been criticized for ignoring. These marginalized people have only recently made themselves politically visible through protest and thus become the subjects of concern. In the case of ethnic minorities, of course, they existed in only tiny numbers in Britain in 1949.

Thirdly, the opinion that he was too optimistic. This is simply unfair. Marshall ended his essay by a clear warning that the balance between class and citizenship was precarious: 'It may be', he said, 'that some of the conflicts within our social system are becoming too sharp for the compromise to achieve its purpose much longer' (p. 49).

Fourthly, was he too simplistic? This too is rather unfair. He was painting with a broad brush. Others have wished to add to or rearrange the detail. But Marshall's triptych has remained firmly established as a most useful mental visual aid to comprehending the complexities of the citizenly status and condition.

Fifthly, the claimed lack of historical understanding. This accusation is partly the result of selective reading of his text. Careful study reveals many provisos, including a clear admission that his periods do overlap (pp. 10, 13). However, the most powerful accusation has been the assertion that his account of the acquisition of rights is too bland, that he does not tell his readers about the history of struggle. This is a complicated issue. It is not true that he totally ignores the histor-ical struggles for citizenship in Britain, for he does make occasional references (e.g. the role of Wilkes, pp. 10–11). Also, we have seen that Marshall describes citizenship and capitalism as being 'at war' in the twentieth century. On the other hand, later on in the essay he admits that his use of this phrase was 'too strong' (p. 40). Moreover, in later works he wrote of the emergence of an amicable democratic-welfare-capitalism 'hyphenated society'. The presentation of this concept counters his critics from the other flank who have pounced on his 'at war' as a distortion of the relatively pacific character of Britain's citizen-ship story compared with that of some other countries. As with so many of the criticisms, it is a matter of nuance.

What cannot be gainsaid is that Marshall's essay and the toing and froing of praise and criticism have made an indelible impression on our understanding of the liberal style of citizenship. In particular, no one is now able to ignore the element of social rights – even though (or perhaps, rather, because) there has arisen within the liberal tradition itself, in the form of the neo-liberal New Right ideology, a fundamental questioning of its status in the citizen's portfolio of rights.

Social citizenship and neo-liberalism

Paradoxically, the liberal style of thinking about citizenship has produced both the assertion that citizenship in its fullest sense is impossible

24

without social rights and the argument that the development of social rights has actually undermined citizenship to a significant degree. And so it came about that by the last two decades of the twentieth century the social liberalism of the first of these interpretations coexisted with the neo-liberalism of the second. Particularly in the USA and the UK this situation generated debates, often conducted at a high temperature, in both the academic and policy-making arenas. (Strictly speaking, there are differences of detail between New Right, neo-conservatism and neo-liberalism, which need not detain us.)

The reason for this internecine doctrinal warfare in the liberal camp is that the fundamental liberal civic principle of the freedom and autonomy of the individual has been extrapolated in two distinct ways, both grounded in unproven hypotheses. These hypotheses concern the connection between social citizenship on the one hand and civil and political citizenship on the other. Social liberals of the Marshall school have believed that indigence impedes the citizen's full use of the civil and political status; the welfare state is therefore necessary to raise the relatively poor to a condition in which they can enjoy the citizenly condition of full autonomy, freedom and participation. Neo-liberals take the contrary view that autonomy and freedom are stripped away by the welfare state, reducing the citizen to a condition of dependency on the 'nanny state'.

Two influential thinkers who set the tone for the New Right policies of Reagan in the USA and Thatcher in the UK were F. A. Hayek and Robert Nozick, both of whom stressed the need to protect the individual's negative freedom against the power of the state. In the words of Hayek, socialism was 'the road to serfdom', the title he gave to a book he published in 1944.

The neo-liberal antipathy to social citizenship finds expression in a number of constituent arguments, both pragmatic and ideological. We may start with the key assertion that the underlying objective of social citizenship, namely, the shaping of a more equal society, is a forlorn hope for the simple reason that people are inherently unequal: this fact of human nature should be accepted; the state should not try to tamper with it. Indeed, attempts at state intervention have in practice not worked. Huge sums of money have been expended in western countries on welfare provision, yet, as St John said, 'The poor always ye have with you.'

But the task of levelling up is more than otiose, it has decidedly deleterious effects. Because the social liberal promise of a bettering of the life-style for all the poor is impossible of achievement, the realization of this fact could well lead to social discontent among those with disappointed expectations. And the more the egalitarian principle of citizenship is broadcast, the deeper will be the resentment.

Alternatively, the welfare state system may foster a weak-willed docility, as the poor lapse into a resigned acceptance of their inferior condition – or fecklessly allow themselves to lapse, in the view of the harder of the New Right. Because of the very existence of state-provided social security, these 'partial' citizens lose all self-esteem and consequently any initiative for self-improvement to full citizenly status. One of the results is actually to *increase* poverty because of the lack of incentive to work. One of the reasons advanced in the neo-liberal case for this impoverishment of the human spirit, leading to material impoverishment, is the extensive and daunting impersonal bureaucracy with which the welfare state is managed.

In turn, this bureaucracy has to be funded; and so, together with the costs in the form of cash payments and services for welfare, health and education, the total bill is so large that a substantial proportion of GDP must perforce be allocated to meeting it. Drawing money from taxpayers for this purpose has, to the neo-liberal mind, two infelicitous effects.

One is that personal wealth is diverted from its potential use for improving the country's economy. The other effect is to foreclose individuals' choices by taking their wealth and directing them to the state-provided welfare, health and education services. Free and autonomous citizens should be able to keep that portion of their income and spend it how they judge best for themselves and their families. What is more, because of the earlier argument that there can be no end in sight to the social liberal's programme of raising all to a notional full citizenship status, there can be no calculable ceiling to the required tax burden for reaching that chimerical goal.

Finally, there is the moral issue, which takes the neo-liberal reasoning to the heart of the citizenship ideal. This is the immorality of accepting rights – in this case social rights – without honouring reciprocal obligations. To put the matter curtly: it is unethical to expect hard-working citizens to meet their *obligations* to pay a high rate of tax in order that listless citizens shall enjoy their *rights* to social welfare payments. Those rights should be conditional, not automatic, be earned through evidence of genuine attempts at self-improvement.

Thoughts along these lines were expressed in the 1980s and 1990s by Thatcherite politicians and policy-framers. Keith Joseph, Mrs Thatcher's mentor, dismissed the whole concept of egalitarianism. He wrote:

> The aspiration to equality may be elevated, but the reality of equality is grubby and unpleasant. In the name of an ideal which promises what it cannot give, it is necessary to embark on a continual process of mutual inspection and assessment, to give institutional form to every mean resentment, to require every man to justify those respects in which he is happier than his fellows.
>
> *(Joseph and Sumption, 1979, p. 121)*

In deliberately more vulgar tone, Norman Tebbit told the unemployed to get on their bikes and look for work. New Right 'think tanks' also issued papers to provoke radical thinking. One, compiled by the Social Affairs Unit, was meaningfully entitled *Breaking the Spell of the Welfare State*.

However, the true home of the New Right has been the USA. Unlike politicians or the drafters of papers who seek their implementation as government policy, philosophers can afford the luxury of truly radical thought. In publishing *Anarchy, State, and Utopia* in 1980 Robert Nozick allowed himself to enjoy this luxury. The right of the individual to natural freedom, he argued, is paramount. The state must not be permitted to intervene and thus abridge that right except for the purpose of utmost necessity like policing. A minimalist state is all that is warranted. The negative right of freedom against the state is justified; a positive right to 'social freedom', whereby individuals make claims against others and the state to provide them with social services and education is, in contrast, not justified. The corollary, of course, is that the whole welfare state edifice should be dismantled: to mix metaphors, the social rights leg of Marshall's tripod should be cut off and citizenship become properly bipedal.

But complete amputation has not found favour as a practicable policy even among the most diehard Reaganites. Slimming-down and alternative administrative regimes have been considered preferable. For example, in the fiscal year 1982 approximately 20 per cent was cut from the Food Stamps and AFDC (Aid for Families with Dependent Children) budgets.

Of the adaptations to welfare administration, the idea of 'workfare' has been the most widely canvassed: work in return for welfare. This idea was expounded by Lawrence Mead in 1986 in his *Beyond Entitlement: The Social Obligations of Citizenship*, where he declared that 'work must be treated as a social obligation akin to paying taxes and obeying the law' (Mead, 1986, p. 82). The position is this: welfare payments are not absolute entitlements; for the able-bodied they are conditional on entering paid employment or job-training schemes. In practice, in the USA, 'workfare' was patchily implemented by the New Right government of the 1980s and showed patchy results.

Not surprisingly the New Right/neo-liberal arguments and policies have been subject to considerable adverse commentary, in terms both of the morality of their premises and their supposed practical benefits. The unleashing of market forces has undermined the equality and fraternity of citizenship. At its best, the policy has exacerbated the polarization of social classes, the selfish rich at the top, the despairing poor at the bottom. At its worst, it has led to a siege mentality in some countries – literally, as the wealthy live in ghettoes defended against the criminalized underclass by means of high walls, barbed wire and private security guards.

Furthermore, as a British academic, Norman Barry has logically observed, 'To prevent the corruption of the welfare system and reduce the dependence of individuals on it, would require an array of positive duties by the individual towards the state which are inconsistent with the liberal idea of citizenship' (Plant and Barry, 1990, p. 65). And so, ironically, in order to preserve its essential character of rights and freedom, distinct from the civic republican style of duties and freedom, liberal citizenship could end up looking remarkably like the classical alternative.

Two additional elements

The history of the liberal style of citizenship has been dominated by the story of establishing the principle of citizens' rights in the component spheres of civic life, and the struggle to achieve their enjoyment in practice. However, our narrative so far regarding the elements of liberal citizenship is not entirely complete. Rights have the prospect of being added to; and rights should have the expected complement of duties.

Thus, to the civil, political, social and economic rights of Marshall's classic formulation we must add the newly claimed environmental rights. In the parlance of some commentators these are perceived as 'third-generation' rights, supplementing the 'first generation' of civil and political rights and the 'second generation' of social and economic rights. Concerning the need to incorporate duties in the citizenly formula, the liberal stress on rights has often appeared somewhat lopsided. Rights are what citizens take out of the civic system; should they not, in return, put something in? Surely citizenship is not a selfish idea. Obligations, duties, loyalties – in short, civic virtues – must be part of the vocabulary. These, then, are our two addenda for this section: environmental citizenship and citizenly virtue in the liberal vein.

The need to posit an environmental element to citizenship has emerged recently in response to very obvious problems. Yet, at the same time, the concept itself presents many difficulties; it does not sit easily in the framework of liberal citizenship. Environmental citizenship relates to the quality of life. Rather like social citizenship, it is not easy, compared with the civil and political varieties, to define exactly what the rights in this sphere should be or to legislate for their protection. How does one pin down the right to a pleasing, supportive and justly enjoyed environment? Yet these conditions are already denied to some people and are under threat globally. The list is familiar: air, water and noise pollution; meteorological perils such as erosion of the ozone layer and global warming; and resource depletion due to climate change, industrialization and population increase.

By placing the individual *qua* citizen in a relationship to these issues we are expanding the very concept of citizenship beyond its traditional boundaries. In a literal geographical sense, of course, in that many of the forms taken by the forces of environmental degradation cannot possibly be constrained by the national frontiers within which the role of citizen has usually been acted out. There is also a subtler difference between environmental citizenship and the more established elements, a difference which suggests that it should be considered virtually *sui generis*. A British writer explains:

29

The concept [of citizenship] is formulated to deal with the relationship between the individual and the community within human society, but the fundamental issue addressed by green politics is the status of nature as separate and distinct from human society. Does nature have *rights* and if so, then how are they to be articulated and represented in a discourse on social citizenship. In more realistic terms, how are the 'rights of nature' to be protected against incursion and violation by human society?

(*F. Steward, in Andrews, 1991, p. 73*)

And to cap the peculiarity of environmental citizenship, it is in actual constant tension with some other features of the citizenly concept and status: of that, later.

Citizenship accords rights. What, then, are the rights of environmental citizenship? We may identify them as being of two kinds – individual and global. But they are all tentatively held and must be understood as being often objectives rather than achievements, disputed rather than universally agreed. A few examples will show this. It can be argued that an individual has the right not to be subjected to the noxious effects of passive smoking in the workplace or to offensively rowdy music from neighbours. On a planetary level it can be argued that all people have the right of access to clean water.

In addition, more than has usually been the case with liberal citizenship, environmental citizenship imposes obvious responsibility on the individual – it behoves the citizen to protect the environment. In merely human terms, let alone the rest of life-forms, this obligation holds for the sake both of the present community as a whole (including global humanity) and of future generations. In asserting the rights of posterity, the environmental case that the present generation is merely a temporary user of the resources of nature echoes Burke's basic political principle, expounded in his *Reflections on the Revolution in France*:

Society is, indeed, a contract [he declared]. . . . [But] it is not a partnership in things subservient only to the gross animal existence of a temporary and perishable nature . . . it becomes a partnership not only between those who are living, but between those who are dead, and those who are to be born.

(*See Buck, 1975, p. 51*)

In their alert awareness of their environmental obligations, citizens may therefore take as a warning slogan the words of the Roman jurist Gaius (who, it happens, contributed to the ancient concept of citizenship), and by so doing prevent at all costs being responsible for *damnosa hereditas*, a ruinous inheritance.

This responsibility, moreover, requires not merely the negative behaviour of refraining from spoliation, but active participation in preventing others from causing harm. And so environmental citizenship joins hand-in-hand with political citizenship. In truth, single-issue political action for environmental causes has frequently been a more popular form of citizenly participation than multi-purpose 'political' politics. Opportunities abound through the existence of myriad pressure groups, operating at every geographical level, from local preservation societies to Greenpeace. Furthermore, motivation is high: it is a matter of preservation and destruction, of health and illness; it is a matter of life and death. Egoism chimes with altruism.

Even so, there are tricky incompatibilities. We should outline three. First, the assertion of an individual's or group's rights may be an infringement of another's. The right to breathe clean air is a denial of another's right to smoke. The right of deforestation of the Indian foothills for much-needed agricultural land produces disastrous flooding in Bangladesh, destroying the right to a home, to life itself even. Secondly, the planet has finite resources and a finite capacity to absorb pollutants. Yet hundreds of millions of pathetically poverty-stricken people have a right in all conscience to a better life; so how can the rights of nature be protected and the earth sustain the massive demands for such improvements?

And thirdly, there is an inherent contradiction in placing the environmental agenda in the citizenship package at all, certainly in its liberal form. It has truly been said that 'The world's economy and earth's ecology are now interlocked – "until death do them part"' (MacNeill et al., 1991, p. 4). But the world's economy is a capitalist economy; and liberal citizenship was born of capitalism. The civil rights of liberal citizenship have, as a consequence, been in part devised to protect the freedom of the market, a feature, as we have seen, especially beloved of the neo-liberals. How, then, can civil citizenship, which favours exploitation of resources, coexist with environmental citizenship, which insists on their prudent conservation?

The role of responsibility and duty in the theory of environmental citizenship is more evident than in the earlier components. Indeed, the relative neglect in the liberal tradition of duties and, generally, the whole politics of morality has occasioned some concern, especially when compared with the stress laid upon duties and virtue by the alternative, civic republican tradition. Nevertheless, as the American academic Stephen Macedo has thoroughly demonstrated, the republicans by no means have a monopoly on civic virtue. His *Liberal Virtues* is an invaluable corrective and his case therefore requires due consideration here.

Macedo's argument runs as follows. Freedom, which, after all, is the very essence of liberalism, does not mean a free-for-all: it requires vital moral qualities in the citizen to prevent this abuse. He lists these as: 'tolerance, self-criticism, moderation, and a reasonable degree of engagement in the activities of citizenship' (Macedo, 1990, p. 2). Essentially, enjoying freedom involves a readiness to uphold and preserve it, and implies an acceptance of the freedom of others. Expressed negatively, apathy and intolerance are the vices abhorred by liberal civic virtue. Apathy is unacceptable because the very basis of modern representative government is the critically necessary vigilance of the citizenry (often by the news media on their behalf) to ensure the proper, that is, efficient, just and uncorrupt, running of the system.

Macedo's argument thus far relates to the citizen behaving as a civically moral individual. However, above and beyond this level, he argues, lies a morality of community in the liberal tradition that is founded on the two principles of impersonal justice and reasonableness (that is, the authorities giving reasoned explanations for their judgements and actions). Good citizens, it follows, are those who monitor all branches of government in order to extract reasons for decisions and to ensure that they are not partial in their implementation.

The good citizen's sense of morality may also justifiably prompt activities of protest. If citizens judge that government actions are misguided, are harmful to the common good and are impervious to change through constitutional channels, then, by the tenets of liberal virtue, civil disobedience is more than permissible, it is a responsibility. The citizen's freedom and autonomy, in accord with the principles of liberalism, lead via conscience to this conclusion.

What, then, are the essential characteristics of liberal virtues? First, what they are not. Macedo is quite firm: 'Quiet obedience, deference, unquestioned devotion, and humility, could not be counted among the liberal virtues' (Macedo, 1990, p. 278).

Of the positive qualities, three are prominent. One is moderation. The motto written on the temple at Delphi – 'nothing in excess' – was perhaps written by an ancient Greek liberal! No fanaticism, no extremism – for these breed intolerance. And the liberal citizen understands and accepts the plurality of society, a condition that demands toleration, lest society plunge into communal or civil discord. Citizenly virtue must therefore incorporate an attitude of live-and-let-live; it requires the cultivation of empathy. People as individuals or as groups are different, but they are all fellow citizens and should be respected as such. This is not, however, a fantasy of paradisiacal harmony: disagreements and tensions unavoidably arise in any society. What the virtues of liberalism expect is the amelioration or resolution of these differences, not by coercion, but by reasoned persuasion.

Liberal citizenship may, then, be interpreted as the responsible enjoyment of civic rights. This is all very well in theory, but how widely available are such rights in practice in the world today?

Citizenship rights at the turn of the century

During the course of a few years either side of 1990 a remarkable concatenation of events transformed the world's political complexion. Authoritarian governments collapsed; liberal democracy seemed triumphant. In a number of Latin American and African states constitutional governments replaced military and civilian dictatorships; the apartheid regime in South Africa surrendered; and the Communist forms of totalitarianism disappeared from Europe in virtually simultaneous puffs of emancipatory smoke. In states with autocratic styles of government civil and political citizenship is to all intents and purposes a farcical façade. Therefore, as liberal democracy became not only the almost sole legitimate form of government, but also more widely established in practice, so citizenship burgeoned as a status with greater reality than ever before.

One computation of the expansion of liberal democracy over the globe gives the following figures for the number of countries that can be counted in that category over the past two centuries – 1790: 3,

1919: 25, 1975: 30, 1990: 61 (Fukuyama, 1992, pp. 49–50). To a certain extent, of course, such figures derive from superficial criteria of classification; nor should we necessarily accept the questionable thesis of the author listing these figures that the trend they so vividly demonstrate is irreversible. Nevertheless, it cannot be denied that a greater proportion of the world's population had become citizens in a fuller sense at the end of the twentieth century than even two decades earlier.

Can this vague observation be clad in some detail? Citizens' rights are sometimes accorded by individual laws and sometimes by particular articles of a constitution (the right to vote and stand for public office, for example). Even so, the best starting-point for assessing what citizenship rights do exist is to examine the lists which usually form a prologue to or distinct part of constitutions. For, by deciding to preface the articles of the Constitution by a Declaration of Rights, the representatives at Versailles in 1789 set a precedent. With the framing of a new constitution – following a change of regime, a revolution or independence from colonial rule – it has become commonplace to adopt this practice. What do these lists of rights tell us about the legal/constitutional position of citizens today?

Let us consider first some general observations about the rights listed in modern constitutional documents, with a more detailed treatment of the South African Bill of Rights. Secondly, some comments about citizenship rights in practice. One explanatory footnote, however. Although the 1789 French Declaration made the distinction between 'man' and 'the citizen', we shall not, generally, be drawing this distinction here. There are, in truth, difficulties involved these days in identifying sharp differences, a matter that will be discussed in chapter 5.

The following extract from a British publication of the 1990s provides a useful checklist of what are reckoned to be the basic rights and duties of the citizen at the turn of the century:

(i)   Civic [sic, i.e. civil] rights and duties
      freedom to reside and to travel, including the right to a passport and to diplomatic protection;
      rights of liberty of the person and freedom of expression, the right to own property, the right of justice and other fundamental rights;
      duties to pay taxes, perform military service, do jury service;
      right to legal redress, etc.

(ii) Political rights and duties
       right (and sometimes duty) to vote;
       right to stand for public office;
       freedom of speech (in political context), etc.
(iii) Social and economic rights and duties
       right to employment;
       right to social security (welfare benefits, unemployment benefits,
       health benefits, pensions, etc.)
       rights . . . to expect standards of service and performance from
       public servants and nationalised industries, such as transport, the
       health service, etc.

(Gardner, n.d., pp. 8–9)

Constitutional documents nevertheless vary very considerably in the ways they treat the rights of citizens. Some lists are far longer than the seventeen brief articles of the 1789 French Declaration: the Indian Fundamental Rights consist of thirty-five articles and the South African Bill of Rights has thirty-nine, for example. Furthermore, the exposition of each of the rights is often more detailed. To take the rights of property, admittedly an extreme case: the South African article on the rights of property is sub-divided into nine sections, and the Indian stretches to five pages. There are two reasons for these changes over the past two centuries.

One is that the whole concept of citizens' rights has expanded. Thus, the Preamble to the Constitution of the French Fifth Republic reaffirms the 1789 Declaration, then 'further proclaims as most vital in our time the following political, economic and social principles'. These include, for instance, the right to strike, that could not have appeared in 1789. Social and economic rights, naturally, are far more prominent in modern documents than in the earlier.

Another reason for the expansion of the lists of rights derives from the historical circumstances of their compilation. As a consequence, items appear in one country's document which one would not expect to find in others'. Citizens' listed rights, in other words, are sometimes an amalgam of generalized, virtually universally accepted basic rights and those that the drafters of the rights judged important to stress because of particular conditions.

A few examples. Because of the specially degrading form of inequality in India, namely 'untouchability', Art. 17 of the constitution declares: '"Untouchability" is abolished and its practice in any form is forbidden.' The general articles pronouncing equality, it was felt, had to be supplemented by this specific assertion. Similarly, the French pronouncement of equality had to be supplemented in the Constitution of the Fourth Republic (carried forward to the Fifth) because it had been a falsehood for women, who were denied the vote until after the Second World War. Thus, the first of the 'further principles' was the statement that 'The law guarantees to women equal rights with men in all spheres.' Turning to the German Basic Law, it may at first seem strange that it was necessary to include a reference forbidding forced labour (Art. 12(3)) – until one remembers the use of this device during the Nazi regime. Akin to this example is the background of apartheid in South Africa, hence the incorporation in its Bill of Rights that 'No one may be subjected to slavery, servitude or forced labour' (Art. 13).

Indeed, if one wishes to study the provision of citizens' rights as conceived at the end of the twentieth century, there can be few documents that present a better subject for a case-study than the South African Bill of Rights. There are several reasons for examining this catalogue of rights as an exemplar.

One is that it is a particularly up-to-date interpretation of rights: it was promulgated, as Chapter 2 of the Constitution, in 1996. Secondly, that Constitution was constructed for the express purpose of drawing a firm line under the era of apartheid – to replace a system that was a frank and blatant denial of citizenship for the vast majority of the country's people with a state composed of citizens of equal rights. Thirdly, as a consequence of the memory of the apartheid regime and the determination completely to expunge its principles and practices, the Bill of Rights covers the subject of rights with conspicuous thoroughness. The constitution is, indeed, the most liberal in the world. Fourthly, the very arrangements for its careful drafting involved widespread consultation, itself a recognition that the whole population was, indeed, endowed with the basic status of citizenship. An Explanatory Memorandum attached to the Constitution summarizes the process:

> the process of drafting this text involved many South Africans in the largest public participation programme ever carried out in South Africa. After nearly two years of intensive consultations, political parties represented in the Constitutional Assembly negotiated the formulations contained in this text which are an integration of ideas from ordinary

citizens, civil society and political parties represented in and outside the constitutional Assembly.

These national discussions threw into sharp relief the most controversial of the rights proposed by many members of the Constitutional Assembly, especially members of the predominantly black African National Congress (ANC). Two of the most contentious were whether the Bill of Rights should apply 'horizontally' as well as 'vertically', and whether social and economic rights should be incorporated as well as the obvious civil rights. Neither was an easy or straightforward matter, and the arguments reveal the universal difficulty of comfortably embracing all possible rights of citizenship in such a document.

A quotation from the Chief Executive of the South African Institute for Race Relations on the first of these issues explains the problem:

> The ANC has frequently reiterated that the only way to prevent 'privatised apartheid' is to outlaw it through the Bill of Rights – in technical jargon, by making the Bill of Rights apply 'horizontally' so that it regulates not only the behaviour of the state but also private relationships. Some opposition MPs acknowledge that there may be problems in giving the state such extensive powers, but they fear being branded racists.
>
> *(Kane-Berman, n.d.)*

In other words, although citizenship involves citizenly behaviour between individuals, it may well not be prudent and practicable, even if politically pragmatic, to enshrine this ideal of civic virtue as a state-enforceable constitutional right.

The second controversial question was encapsulated by one commentator in the question: 'is the right to be housed as much a right as the right to free speech?' (Pakendorf, 1995). The proposal that a full slate of social and economic rights should be included was opposed, like the opposition to 'horizontal' citizenship, on the grounds that it would invite, indeed necessitate, excessive state intervention. Another cogent argument was based on the fundamental principle that an unenforceable law brings the legal system into disrepute. To quote the South African commentator already cited, 'why include something as a right which the state cannot deliver, thus making a mockery of the Bill of Rights and expose the state to endless litigation as people demand their guaranteed rights?' (Pakendorf, 1995).

In the event, both matters were resolved by incorporation into the Constitution. Art. 9(4) states that 'No person may unfairly discriminate directly or indirectly against anyone. . . . National legislation must be enacted to prevent or prohibit unfair discrimination'; whilst Arts. 23–9 provide extremely comprehensive lists of social and economic rights.

Naturally, the South African Bill of Rights contains all the expected civil rights that one finds in comparable enactments in other states. However, it is a specially noteworthy document for including a number of additional articles illustrative of the recent tendency to expand the scope of citizens' rights.

In many states some political rights are placed in the body of the Constitution. In contrast, in South Africa, the rights to form and participate in political parties, to regular and fair elections, to vote and hold public office are accorded the greater prominence and sanctity of incorporation in the Bill of Rights (Art. 19). Also unlike most declarations or bills of rights (with certainly the important exception of the Indian Fundamental Rights), the rights to property are spelled out in very great detail (Art. 25), a corollary, as indicated in the text, of 'the history of the acquisition and the use of property' (Art. 25(3)(b)). And so, 300 years after Locke's stress on the rights of property, we again find the topic fully displayed, though, in the South African case, in great practical complexity.

Related to property rights is the specific social right of housing, which occasioned some doubt during the consultation process. But, there it is, together with an overt obligation placed upon the state: 'Everyone has the right to have access to adequate housing' (Art. 26(1)); 'The state must take reasonable legislative and other measures, within its available resources, to achieve the progressive realisation of this right' (Art. 26(2)). Also affecting a person's everyday life, of course, are labour relations. The Bill of Rights is of interest on this subject for its conscious balance, specifying the rights of employers as well as employees (Art. 23).

However, what are particularly significant are the articles relating to the environment (Art. 24) and health care, food, water and social security (Art. 27). Each is brief but provides clear evidence of matters that are, or will become, pressing down-to-earth issues for ordinary citizens especially in countries with historical and geographical conditions like South Africa's. One cannot pronounce a more basic right

than 'to have access to . . . sufficient food and water' (Art. 27(1)(b));
and again, as with housing, the state is required to take reasonable
action to ensure this right. On the environment, 'Everyone has the
right (a) to an environment that is not harmful to their health or well-
being; and (b) to have the environment protected, for the benefit of
the present and future generations' (Art. 24).

Throughout the Bill of Rights are several matters where the drafters
were perfectly aware that, in conditions as they obtained at the time,
the rights could not be guaranteed without further government action.
They therefore deliberately wrote into the appropriate articles specific
requirements in order to underscore these obligations. We have already
noted this feature of Arts. 26 and 27. Similar obligations were inserted
into rights of property (Art. 25(5) and (9)); access to information
(Art. 32(2)); and just administrative action (Art. 33(3)).

Promises were clear and expectations were raised with the enactment
of this Bill of Rights. Not for the first time in history (e.g. 'Untouch-
ables'), promises were slow to be fulfilled, expectations were disappointed, and the reality of citizenship fell grievously short of the theory.

The problem of rights in practice

The existence of citizens' rights in the form of their enshrinement in a
constitutional document is a most imperfect index of the existence of
rights in practice. In a number of states, it is true, there is now a fairly
close correspondence between the enunciated rights of citizenship and
the rights enjoyed in practice – the countries of western Europe, for
example. However, taking the world as a whole, there are many exceptions. We may identify four variants. These may be summarized as:
rights effectively denied; rights not defined but mainly available; rights
defined in distorted form; and rights defined but difficulties in practice.
Illustrations of each of these categories will clarify them.

Although most states now have some form of representative political institutions and give at least lip-service to the principle of rights, a
few still adhere to social and political arrangements which pre-date
these relatively modern innovations. Some Middle Eastern states do
not provide the basic political right to vote, for example. There is no
franchise in Bahrein, Oman or Saudi Arabia, and women are not

enfranchised in Kuwait or the United Arab Emirates. Far more common, of course, have been authoritarian regimes in Asia (e.g. China, Burma, Indonesia) and Africa (e.g. Zaïre, Nigeria, Uganda) where civil rights have been denied and political opposition has not been tolerated. In such states either constitutions provide limited rights or, more often, have been suspended. Worse, millions of people still even suffer the most degraded non-citizen condition, that of slavery.

Our second category has been famously (or notoriously) illustrated by the lack of a written constitution or bill of rights in the United Kingdom. The practice of defining the constitution and rights in an explicit document effectively emerged with the revolutionary events in North America and France in the late eighteenth century. And when countries in subsequent years experienced revolutionary or other cataclysmic changes, it has become a common habit to produce similar statements.

But Britain escaped such events and thus avoided the necessity to frame a definitive constitutional document. The 1689 Bill of Rights does not count: its purpose was to weaken the arbitrary power of the king *vis-à-vis* the political elite and Parliament. Parliament, indeed, came to be accepted as the sovereign authority. Moreover, the British population have been, technically, subjects of the monarch; they are not citizens, the collective source of national sovereignty. Consequently, their rights derive from sundry enactments and, significantly and negatively, what Parliament has not forbidden – Britons have legally enjoyed residual liberties, not citizens' rights. None the less, these freedoms are in truth substantial: for centuries Britons were justly proud of their liberties compared with those of many of their continental neighbours.

And yet, uneasiness about this rather vague and increasingly anomalous situation grew from the late 1980s. Therefore, although doubts about and opposition to a bill of rights persisted, they were to some degree circumvented by its proponents securing the passage of the Human Rights Act in 1998, which would incorporate the European Convention of Human Rights into British law. This Council of Europe document, to which Britain was already a signatory, would henceforth serve the purpose of a yardstick of rights in British courts. Nevertheless, Parliament remained sovereign and Britons were still not fully-fledged citizens.

Even so, better to have a condition of muddle on paper, in which most individuals enjoy significant freedoms and rights in practice, than for individuals to be pronounced citizens, but where their rights are reflected to them by the distorting mirror of an ideologically framed constitution. Although it was substantially amended in 1977 and did not survive the upheavals of the Gorbachev era, the Soviet Constitution of 1936 is such a perfect example of this contrivance that the temptation to cite it here cannot be resisted. Chapter 10 (much extended as Chapter 7 of the 1977 Constitution) contained the list of citizens' rights and obligations, covering all the expected topics, with the stress, inevitably in a Communist document, on social and economic rights. But – and there are two sizeable buts – the careful wording of the articles ensured that what was given by one phrase was permitted to be taken away by another; and the chances of citizens upholding their rights in the courts depended not so much on the law as on the political climate. Two examples will help to clarify these points.

The Soviet authorities did make commendable efforts, fluctuating naturally according to economic circumstances, to honour the rights to health, welfare, education and employment. Yet even here there was a catch. As one British authority explained in the 1970s:

> peasants, who still form nearly half of the labour force, are not included in the category of 'workers and employees' and are therefore not normally covered by social insurance. Yet this does not, in Soviet law, give the collective farm peasant (the peasant on a state farm is an employee) a right of action in the courts to enforce his 'right' as a citizen under article 200.
>
> *(Schapiro, 1977, pp. 90–1)*

Our second example concerns Arts. 125 and 126 (Arts. 50 and 51 in the 1977 Constitution), which guaranteed all citizens freedom of speech, freedom of the press, freedom of association and meetings, and freedom for street processions and demonstrations. But ... These freedoms were guaranteed 'in conformity with the interests of the working people and for the purpose of strengthening and developing the socialist system' and 'In conformity with the aims of building communism' (Arts. 50 and 51, 1977 Constitution).

Just how determined the Soviet authorities could be to block even these constrained rights was infamously demonstrated in 1966 by the trial, conviction and sentencing to terms of hard labour of the writers Sinyavsky and Daniel. Their crime was to have written a political satire on the Soviet Union. Even the proviso of Art. 125 of the 1936

Constitution was too weak to damage their defence, so they were charged under Art. 70 of the Criminal Code, which forbade 'anti-Soviet propaganda'. And just to make sure for the future, a new criminal law was designed to make it an offence to publish 'false information which slanders the Soviet state'. In what sense could Soviet writers wishing to comment on historical, social, economic, legal or political matters be considered citizens with civic rights?

Russia also provides a vivid example of the ways in which the reality of citizenship falls short of legal/constitutional prescription, our fourth and most common category. This phenomenon may be considered under three headings: lack of civic virtue, problems relating to political rights, and lack of social and economic rights.

We have seen that, although the modern trend in citizenship theory harps on rights, virtues such as a sense of responsibility and some civic participation have not been ignored. Since the Soviet system, despite its borrowing of the liberal concept of rights, was a conscious rejection of the liberal-capitalist system, it is not surprising that here we find an even greater assertion of citizens' duties than in western democracies. It is no accident that rights were listed in the 1977 Constitution in a chapter entitled 'The Basic Rights, Freedoms and Duties of USSR Citizens'. Furthermore, there is considerable anecdotal evidence (apart from propaganda) of Soviet citizens proudly and conscientiously performing their duties.

But even the Russian soul, amazingly resilient as it has proved to be through the injustices and hardships of many centuries, can bear only so much. How could one expect a civic spirit to survive the squalid chaos of the Yeltsin regime of political vacillation, mismanaged privatization, non-payment of wages, spiralling inflation and obscenely self-enriching mafia? The exhortation in the 1977 Constitution that 'It shall be the duty of a citizen of the USSR to combat embezzlement' (Art. 61) must have rung cynically hollow two decades later. One academic has written of the 'radical alienation of Russians': 'Feelings of citizenship, involvement in public affairs, have not increased following the fall of the Soviet system with its repressive apparatus, as many had taken for granted, but have diminished drastically' (V. Schlapentokh, in Ichilov, 1998, p. 28).

The values, in both senses of the word, of liberal democracy are hard to learn and appreciate. Even in countries with less cause than

42

Russia to be sceptical about the advantages of discarding an authoritarian regime, political citizenship is not necessarily accepted as a valued political right. This is the experience, for instance, of a number of Latin American states. Opinion poll figures in Argentina provide manifest evidence. After the transition from military dictatorship to constitutional government in 1984, voting was made mandatory. In 1991 9 per cent of the sampled electorate declared they would not vote but for that requirement; in 1997, the figure had risen to 51 per cent.

At the heart of this kind of apathy (or positive alienation) is the understandable perception of hundreds of millions of people throughout the world about what their priorities should be in the range of putative rights with which they are endowed as citizens. If newly provided political rights cannot in practice be used to win sorely needed economic rights – which are, after all, most individuals' prime concern – two outcomes are possible: rebellion or a resigned feeling of inefficacy. The latter reaction leads on to disappointment, turning to despair, and mounting crime. At the end of the twentieth century, South Africa appeared, sadly, to be descending down this route. Despite the glowing promises of the Bill of Rights regarding economic changes involving some redistribution of wealth, as a distinguished journalist recorded: 'Any visitor can see that South Africa, nearly four years after the ANC's election victory, still looks like a white man's country, with white bosses in charge nearly everywhere' (Sampson, 1998). And crime was endemic.

A chasm of unbridgeable magnitude separates the impoverished masses from the super-rich in many countries, most notoriously perhaps in Russia. These are class-ridden societies, whether the term is used or not. Marshall famously asserted that 'the inequality of the social class system may be acceptable provided the equality of citizenship is recognised' (Marshall and Bottomore, 1992, p. 6). In the world at the turn of the twentieth century, this is surely not a tenable proposition. Perhaps, therefore, the status of citizenship should be stripped back to its original civil and political content, discarding the social and economic rights which so often cannot, dispiritingly, be honoured. The alternative to the liberal tradition, namely the civic republican style of citizenship, which is based on civil and political ideals, might have pertinent lessons from which we can learn.

2

The Civic Republican
Tradition

Major thinkers

Although liberal interpretations of citizenship have in the main shaped
our current civic style, the alternative civic republican tradition has a
far more venerable lineage, and retains its relevance. Moreover, many
of the really significant thinkers who have written on the subject of
citizenship adhered to the civic republican mode. Because a few of these
deserve more than a passing mention, their particular contributions will
be outlined in this section. First of all, though, a word of explanation
about the use of the term 'civic republican'. By 'republic' is meant a
constitutional system with some form of sharing out of power to prevent concentrated arbitrary and autocratic government; and 'civic' means
the involvement of the citizenry in public affairs to the mutual benefit
of the individual and the community.

Sixth- to fourth-century Sparta and Athens and Rome's half-
millennium of Republican rule set the scene. Of all the classical political theorists and historians who wrote about citizenship as defined by
and experienced in these states, Aristotle and Cicero each typified his
age, expounded the subject thoroughly and exerted a great influence
on subsequent thinkers. We should start, therefore, with the citizenship practices of ancient Greece as commented upon by Aristotle.

Sparta and Athens at the pinnacle of their fame are the archetypes of
opposed political principles – stern authoritarianism and free democracy.
Yet as exponents of the classical institution of citizenship, they were really
not so very far apart. Indeed, it is instructive to view Spartan citizenship

as 'an intensification of the Athenian notion of public service' (Riesenberg, 1992, p. 8). Both of these city-states were proud of their citizens' commitment to their civic duties, though whereas Athens is famed for the ready participation of her citizens in governmental and juridical functions, Sparta is renowned for the selfless devotion of her citizen-soldiers.

How does this background relate to Aristotle's treatment of the subject of citizenship? The topic features as part of one 'book' (III) of eight in his *Politics*, and appears in a few relevant passages in the *Nicomachean Ethics*. In the *Politics* he explains the great variety of practices at different times in history and in different states, leading him to declare that 'The nature of citizenship . . . is a question which is often disputed' (Aristotle, 1948, 1274b). However, Aristotle was not only a political scientist, he was a political theorist as well: he therefore also expressed his views on what citizenship ideally should be.

What, then, is particularly characteristic about Aristotle's conception of citizenship? Size of population is important for him. The body of citizens should be sufficiently compact as to enable them to 'know one another's characters' (Aristotle, 1948, 1326b). Only by means of this intimacy could the necessary communal bonds of true fraternal citizenship – 'concord' – be tied. Athens, where he spent just over half of his life, exceeded his absolute maximum (its citizen population has been computed at about 40,000). Another of his ideal characteristics of citizenship, for which in fact Athens did provide an apposite model, was that citizens should 'share in the civic life of ruling and being ruled in turn' (Aristotle, 1948, 1283b). There is no room for apathy: citizens are expected to be publicly active.

But the crucial requirement was that citizens must be possessed of and display *aretē*, goodness or virtue. By this Aristotle meant fitting in, in social and political behaviour, to the style of the particular constitution of the *polis*. In a sense, therefore, civic virtue was for Aristotle a relative quality. Even so, a basic moral calibre was essential in whatever *polis*: the good citizens were those wholly and efficiently committed through thought and action to the common weal. Moreover, by living such a life the citizen benefited himself as well as the state: he became a morally more mature person. There was, indeed, no other way of becoming a fulfilled human being because, Aristotle asserted, 'man is by nature an animal intended to live in a polis' (often translated simply as 'a political animal': Aristotle, 1948, 1253a).

45

Two problems arise from this conception of *aretē*. One is that men who must work full-time for a living cannot have the leisure to study or participate fully in public affairs; so, although in some city-states such men were enrolled as citizens, it was difficult for them to be good, 'proper' citizens. Aristotle's model citizenry was a leisured, propertied elite. The second problem concerns those who, although by all other criteria are citizens, are deficient of the ideal virtuous qualities. After all, good citizens are not born. Aristotle was fully aware that good citizens are the product of education. He was convinced that the state provision of education is absolutely essential, and admired Sparta as being almost the only *polis* to undertake this responsibility. Not that he at all approved of the concentration on the physical and militaristic training as prescribed for the Spartiates (citizens): he believed firmly that the moral qualities required of good citizens would be attained through the character-forming influences of aesthetic education.

Aristotle provided the classic exposition of the civic republican form of citizenship. From him the ideal was passed on through Zeno, the founder of Stoicism, to Roman thinkers such as Cicero. And although Machiavelli and Rousseau do not overtly mention Aristotle, there can be little doubt that, through the deep study of classical writers that dominated Renaissance and eighteenth-century education and literature, they did absorb his teaching. Absorption does not necessarily mean total acceptance, of course. For instance, Cicero, while admiring Aristotle's stress on morality, rejected his elitist definition of citizenship, even though he wrote primarily to remind the Roman oligarchy of their state's honourable tradition of civic virtue.

Cicero lived in disturbed times – he was 62 when Julius Caesar was assassinated. Nor did he personally escape the turmoil, for he was a lawyer, a politician and, by philosophical conviction, a Stoic. Moreover, he lived by his beliefs.

> Nature [he wrote] has implanted in the human race so great a need of virtue and so great a desire to defend the common safety that the strength thereof has conquered all the allurements of pleasure and ease.
>
> But it is not enough to possess virtue ... the existence of virtue depends entirely upon its use; and its noblest use is the government of the State.
>
> *(Cicero, 1959, I.1–2)*

46

And as he lived by his beliefs, so he died by them, paying the ultimate, bloody price for his civic moral standards. On the death of Caesar, Cicero warned against the danger posed to the Roman Republic of the power being amassed by the contemptible Mark Antony, the very antithesis of Cicero's concept of a virtuous citizen. Caught in flight from Antony's agents, he was murdered and his severed head and hands were sent to Mark Antony and his wife.

Cicero's education had given him a splendid foundation for thinking about citizenship: he studied political theory in Athens and law in Rome. Unlike Aristotle, however, he made no consolidated statement on the subject, but rather incorporated scattered references in a number of works, both treatises to persuade the reader and oratory in his professional forensic craft of swaying juries. A rough distinction needs to be made, indeed, between Cicero the lawyer and Cicero the moral philosopher. *Qua* lawyer he defended the legal right of individuals to Roman citizenship according to the rules; *qua* philosopher he was concerned to counter what he perceived as the laxity of the ruling class in his own times by inducing a stiffening of its civic moral fibre.

It is in this latter role that Cicero is of the greater interest to us. For it was his staunch commitment to the Stoic ethic that gave his interpretation of citizenship its weighty influence. Basing his arguments on this demanding philosophy, Cicero explained that man must use his gifts of speech and moral and rational thought for virtuous actions. If a citizen, by withdrawing into the ease of a private existence, denies his fellow men, his community and his state the benefit of his conscientious involvement in public work, he is betraying his nature as a social animal.

Only the higher ranks of Roman society, of course, had the opportunity to commit themselves really fully to public service; as a consequence, the responsibility of living the life of a good citizen fell most heavily upon them. Thus, Cicero asserted in *De Officiis* (*On Duties*) that

> a worthy and truly brave citizen, and one who deserves to hold the reins of government, will shun and detest [civil dissensions, tumults and civil wars;] and will give himself so to the service of the public, as to aim at no riches or power for himself; and will so take care of the whole community, as not to pass over any part of it . . . [and] will rather part with his life itself, than do anything that is contrary to the virtues I have mentioned.
>
> *(see Clarke, 1994, p. 49)*

47

Through the exposition of his high moral principles and his clear, elegant prose, Cicero remained the most influential of all moral philosophers in Europe down to the nineteenth century. His influence was especially marked in Renaissance Italy. Here an awareness of the ancient practice and ideal of citizenship was also enlivened by the study of Roman historians. Among these, and of incomparable stature, was Livy, who had laboured for forty years to produce his *History of Rome from its Foundation* in 142 'books'. The first ten of these were used by Machiavelli as a platform on which to muse about the nature of politics, including citizenship. This work is *The Discourses on the First Ten Books of Titus Livius*.

Like Cicero, Niccolò Machiavelli was disturbed by the turbulence of his times, viewed from the perspective of engagement in public affairs – in Machiavelli's case as minister, diplomat and soldier for the city-state of Florence. Following military defeat and a change of regime, he was dismissed from office, imprisoned and tortured. On his release, he retired to the exiled sanctuary of his farm some miles south of the city. There, in the evenings, closeted in his study, he settled to a new life as a writer. And in so doing he gave a new impetus to the civic republican conception of citizenship.

Machiavelli was a realist, or pessimist if you will. His studies and experience led him to believe that violence and war are more common than peace, that despotic government is more common than republican, and that corrupt and self-seeking behaviour is more common than good citizenship. Yet good citizenship is essential for sustaining a militarily secure state and a republican form of government; indeed, citizenship is possible only in a republic. But for Machiavelli good citizenship had necessarily to be of a hardened, tougher moral fabric than even the classical writers had commended.

And so, as with Aristotle and Cicero, civic virtue is central to Machiavelli's thinking on citizenship. However, his use of the word *virtù*, though conveniently translated as 'virtue', carries many overtones quite absent from the English word. Of its rich content, one of Machiavelli's recent English editors lists:

> Courage, fortitude, audacity, skill and civic spirit. . . . *Virtù* is the quality of mind and action that creates, saves or maintains cities. . . . 'Civic

spirit' is probably the best simple translation – if by 'spirit' one means
spirited action.

(Crick in Machiavelli, 1998, pp. 58–9)

How are such men made, men with this crucial though, in Renaissance
Italy, all too rare quality of *virtù*? By an education steeped in a vigorous
civic religion, Machiavelli believed. Here lies the difference between
pagan Rome and Christian Italy, he argued, the one strengthened by
the virtue of stout-hearted manliness, the other weakened by the virtue
of Christian humility.

The good citizen, effectively educated in the precepts of *virtù*, must
lead an active life, whether civilian or military. In civilian life the
citizen must take a positive interest in public affairs and, above all,
refrain from according priority to a private life of wealth, luxury and
ease over a commitment to the general public good.

But it is the role of the citizen as soldier that Machiavelli especially
emphasizes. Military service provides the discipline necessary to con-
vert the naturally wicked man into a virtuous, patriotic citizen; and
patriotic citizen-soldiers will serve the state so much more effectively
than mercenaries. Politics and military organization are, in fact, to
Machiavelli's mind, interrelated. In the *Discourses* he declares that where
military discipline 'does not exist, there can neither be good laws nor
anything else that is good'. The truth of the necessity for this discipline,
he explains, 'is apparent on every page of Livy's history' (Machiavelli,
1998, III.31, p. 491). Only by deploying its citizens as soldiers aggress-
ively can the republic ensure that its citizens as civilians can enjoy the
benefits of a stable polity.

Machiavelli and other Renaissance thinkers revived the classical concept
of citizenship and when, in the eighteenth century, a new intensification
of classical studies came about, the writings of the Italian political theorists reinforced the civic republican message. According to an influential
thesis by J. G. A. Pocock, the political thinking which led up to the
American War of Independence and Constitution was largely coloured
by this shade of transmitted citizenship theory. As one student of American work in the field of political theory has succinctly stated: 'Pocock
sees Americans as the ultimate beneficiaries of a classical republicanism
recodified by Machiavelli' (Lutz, 1992, p. 100).

49

Be that as it may – for it is a disputed interpretation – there is no doubting the lively interest in civic republicanism in North America and western Europe in the eighteenth century. Jean-Jacques Rousseau is a very clear example. He read the works of Machiavelli, whom he described as a 'profound political thinker' (Rousseau, 1968, III.6n.), and his own ideas reveal close similarities to the Florentine's, for example, on the need for a civic religion and the military role of the citizen.

Rousseau's views on citizenship were drawn, however, from Plutarch rather than Livy, and from the history of Sparta as much as Rome. His early absorption in Roman history at his father's knee led him later to proclaim that 'I was a Roman before I was twelve' (see Rousseau, 1968, p. 10). Even so, it was the small-scale compactness of the city-state that he, like Aristotle, felt to be the best-suited context for an ideal polity: hence part of Sparta's attraction for him. He was also influenced by his admiration for the city-state republic of Geneva, where he was born: he signed *The Social Contract* 'J.-J. Rousseau, Citizen of Geneva'. He spent a varied life, mainly in France, settling in due course to writing on various subjects and in different genres, including work as a musicologist, composer, novelist, essayist, and – the work to which he was most committed – as a political theorist. In his political writing, especially *The Social Contract*, he gave considerable attention to the topic of citizenship.

Rousseau set himself the task of solving the basic conundrum: How can men subject themselves to government, which is necessary for security, while, at the same time, retaining their freedom, which is their moral right? His solution was the General Will. Through the exercise of virtuous decision-making, the sovereign people make judgements which benefit the whole community and then agree to abide by those outcomes. In behaving obediently individuals live as subjects of the state; in contributing to the formulation of the General Will they live as citizens. The state, comprising its citizens, operates as an organic whole:

Each one of us [he explained] puts into the community his person and all his powers under the supreme direction of the general will; and as a body, we incorporate every member as an indivisible part of the whole.
(Rousseau, 1968, I.6)

50

This is the meaning of the social contract.

These ideal arrangements, in effect a utopia, would not be easy to apply in eighteenth-century circumstances. Rousseau was forced to address this problem because he was asked twice to advise countries in difficulties, namely, Corsica and Poland. He saw that one of their needs was a boosting of patriotism, and suggested that, in these modern conditions, unlike those of classical antiquity, the bonding force could most effectively be provided by a sense of nationhood. Thus he wrote to the Corsicans: 'The first rule that we have to follow is national character: all people have, or should have, a national character; if it is lacking in this, it would be necessary to start by giving it one' (see Cobban, 1964, p. 109).

Rousseau was breaking the classical mould, and his fame and influence as a political thinker derive as much from innovative ideas as his continuation of tradition, probably more so. Yet his true self was surely happier in the old tradition. Seven years before he wrote *The Social Contract* and ten years before his work on Corsica he epigrammatically assured his readers that, 'The country (*la patrie*) cannot continue to exist without liberty, nor liberty without virtue, nor virtue without citizens' (see Cobban, 1964, p. 104).

Rousseau's political ideas (so unlike some of his other writings) had little impact before the French Revolution. Then they caught on. 'The law is the expression of the general will', proclaimed the Declaration of Rights (Art. 6). No one was a more pious disciple of Jean-Jacques than Robespierre. His ardent desire was to make France a nation of virtuous citizens. The difficulty was how to achieve this end. Rousseau advocated the moral force of education as the normal method; Robespierre was convinced of the educational morality of force in the abnormal times of crisis: virtue must be supplemented by the propagandistic use of terror – 'virtue without which terror is squalidly repressive, terror without which virtue lies disarmed' (see Rudé, 1975, p. 118). But, then, did not Rousseau insist that obedience to the General Will was the way to true freedom and that anyone who disobeyed it 'shall be forced to be free' (Rousseau, 1968, I.7)? If insistence on civic virtue had come to this, it was fortunate that the revolutionary era also opened up the alternative, liberal concept of citizenship which we have examined in the previous chapter.

Yet the civic republican version did not die. It was sustained in the nineteenth century alongside the new liberal interpretation by such

Purpose of citizenship	freedom; republican state
Style of citizenship	community – friendship, concord, fraternity; issue of property
Quality of the citizen	virtue, patriotism, judgement
Role of the citizen	civil and military duty/participation; watch on government
Forming the citizen	problem of motivation, education, religion

Figure 2.1

figures as Hegel and Tocqueville; while more recently its qualities have been recognized and attempts been made to use them as a counterbalance to the perceived defects of liberal citizenship. Accordingly, the distinguished writers in the classical tradition are not just of historical interest. They still have contributions to make to our own understanding of the basic principles of civic republicanism, to which we must now turn our attention.

By drawing upon the key thinkers and modern commentary upon them it is possible to identify five major features; though it must be understood that this teasing out is an oversimplification of a closely woven theory. These features may be tabulated, as in figure 2.1. Two brief notes before discussing each of these features in turn: (1) To avoid boring repetition, throughout the rest of this chapter 'citizen' and 'citizenship' are to be understood as referring just to the civic republican mode. (2) A. Oldfield's *Citizenship and Community* has been very helpful for some of the detail, though has not shaped the structure, of what follows.

Purpose of citizenship

All institutions must serve a purpose. A purpose may, however, be complex, it may be controversial, and its operation in practice may not live up to ideal expectations. In these, very common, circumstances theorists and commentators expound, elucidate, judge and defend. The objectives of citizenship have been clarified and promoted by such processes; and from this work we can derive a short definition which might run along these lines: The purpose of citizenship is to connect the individual and the state in a symbiotic relationship so that a just and stable republican polity can be created and sustained and the individual citizen can enjoy freedom. Thus, the individual can be truly free only in a republic; a republic can exist only through the support of its citizens.

'Man was born free, and he is everywhere in chains', Rousseau famously declared (Rousseau, 1968, I.1). How to resolve the antithesis? One way is by a revolutionary breaking of the chains of tyranny – the liberal way of asserting the citizen's rights, including the right to a private life free of state interference. But Rousseau did not want to break the chains; he wanted to make them legitimate, to achieve their mutation into a linkage that would provide mankind with a moral, positive form of freedom: the republican way.

Rousseau, whose work is a particularly good exemplar of the civic republican view of freedom, distinguished between natural liberty as freedom through the pursuit of self-interest, and civil liberty as freedom through the merging of self-interest with duty. He asserted this principle pungently in negative form while proclaiming its absolute primacy: 'To renounce freedom', he declared, 'is to renounce one's humanity, one's rights as a man and equally one's duties' (Rousseau, 1968, I.4). This kind of freedom is the prerequisite for a life of happiness and virtue; and it can be enjoyed only as a citizen – just look at the alternatives. In a polity devoid of citizenship, men are subject to the arbitrary will of others; outside a political structure (in a state of nature) men are subject to their own whims.

One is free in a republic because *qua* citizen the 'them and us' opposition of government and subject is dissolved. In Rousseau's theory this is achieved by his ingenious device of the General Will. The basic concept, however, was already present in the thought of Aristotle, who said, 'Liberty has more than one form. One of its forms [is the political, which] consists in the interchange of ruling and being ruled' (Aristotle, 1948, 1317b).

So, one of the purposes of citizenship is to secure freedom; the other is to underpin the republican state. What kind of polity is best suited to the effective discharge of this citizenly function? Two characteristics are especially desirable, perhaps essential. One is a mixed constitution, the other is compact size.

Citizenship does not imply democracy: this form of constitution is not conducive to stability, so many of the theorists argued. Citizenship produces the best kind of state, a republic, when that status operates through a constitution in which different forms are mingled. Aristotle established this desideratum. What he advocated was the avoidance of extremes – the golden mean of a mixture of aristocratic and democratic elements: 'it is clear', he asserted, 'that the middle type of constitution is best [for the *majority* of states]. It is the one type free from faction' (Aristotle, 1948, 1295b). He classified Sparta as such a state.

Machiavelli followed Aristotle closely. Strength and stability, he explained, had in the past derived from constitutions that shared the different forms: 'for if in one and the same state there was principality, aristocracy and democracy each would keep watch over the other.' Like Aristotle, too, he cited Sparta as a prime example, where the lawgiver Lycurgus 'assigned to the kings, to the aristocracy, and to the populace each its own functions, and thus introduced a form of government which lasted more than eight hundred years' (Machiavelli, 1998, I.2). Rousseau may appear not to align himself with this approach, asserting that 'Any state which is ruled by law I call a "republic", whatever form its constitution' (Rousseau, 1968, II.6). But his description of the working of the General Will gives a different picture. Although the citizen body is sovereign, it passes up to the magistrates the function of interpreting and implementing the General Will.

The purpose of citizenship therefore is to maintain the republican form of government, to prevent its degeneration. Each citizen, whether prince, magistrate, aristocrat or unprivileged, upholds that purpose in his own manner and by living his own particular role.

Now although the ideal republic is mixed in form of constitution, it must nevertheless be coherently knitted together. Citizens cannot hold the state in stable equilibrium if it is too unwieldy. We have already seen how concerned Aristotle was that a *polis* should not exceed its optimum size. Rousseau, too, again as already mentioned, wished for a small scale. Apart from other considerations, a small polity is essential for citizens to know each other as individuals and as a community and to have opportunities for participation. But how was this Aristotelian ideal to be translated into the modern world?

Montesquieu, in his *Spirit of the Laws* (1748), provided the solution: 'confederation' (*république fédérative*) combines 'all the internal advantages of a republican, together with the external force of a monarchical, government' (Montesquieu, 1949, IX.1). What is crucial is that the component republics preserve their happiness and probity. This device was found especially attractive to Alexander Hamilton, who contributed so significantly to the civic republican thinking in the American colonies/ USA. Tocqueville, also, in the nineteenth century, was convinced that the pyramidal structure of the United States – from township to state to federal government – successfully retained the republican style of active citizenship.

Nevertheless, citizenship can neither preserve freedom nor sustain the republican state if citizens do not live it in the republican style of a sense of community, of friendship and concord.

Style of citizenship

The republican style of political thinking places great emphasis above all on the necessity for the state and its citizens to be a community, an organic society, not merely a collection of individuals. Constitutions and laws, it is true, lay down the rules by which a group of individuals live together in a state; but constitutions and laws cannot by themselves make a community, only the propitious conditions in which a group can gel into a community. That gelling process requires the essential ingredient of social friendship and harmony.

It was Aristotle who analysed this idea particularly thoroughly in the course of his survey of different kinds of friendship in the *Nicomachean Ethics*. Here he makes the basic observation that 'friendship is an expression of community', and continues by claiming that all friendship associations 'may be regarded as parts of the association we call the state' (Aristotle, 1955, VIII.9). However, he felt the need to introduce a special word to distinguish the particular kind of friendship that exists at the state level, at least in well-ordered polities. This word, a sort of catchword among Greek writers for a century before Aristotle, was *homonoia*. It carried the dual meaning of peace between the city-states and social/political harmony within them: the antonym respectively of war and civil strife. The usual translation is 'concord'.

Aristotle explained its meaning, and extracts from his chapter on the topic provide the best way of understanding this concept so vital to citizenship.

> [Concord is] something more than agreement in opinion, for that might be found in people who do not know one another. Neither do we call it concord when people agree in theory about a speculative matter. . . . But we say there is concord in a state when the citizens agree about their interests, adopt a policy unanimously and proceed to carry it out. This implies that we have concord only where a practical end is in view – an important end capable of attainment by the interested parties . . . concord is . . . friendship between the citizens of a state, its province being the interests and concerns of life.
>
> Now this conception of concord is realized among good men, for such are in harmony both with themselves and with one another. . . . But bad men . . . want more than their share . . . [and] shirk . . . public service. . . . The result is discord.
>
> *(Aristotle, 1955, IX.6)*

What Aristotle is describing is a relationship of mutual respect and the active pursuit of common purposes between virtuous citizens. Citizenship connects the individual to the state, certainly; but it also connects individuals to each other. Citizenship is teamwork; citizenship is shared activity in a spirit of mutual goodwill.

How, then, have subsequent writers in the republican tradition interpreted this essential feature? Machiavelli believed communal harmony was part of the quality of *virtù*. However, whereas Aristotle recognized that concord in a *polis* was dependent upon the attitudes and behaviour of good men, Machiavelli held that the moral force of good laws and religion were essential to mould men to the harmonious style of civic life.

Rousseau, too, understood that, though concord is crucial, it does not appear spontaneously. One of the methods he advocated was the use of theatre, festivals and spectacles to imbue the citizenry with 'public fraternity', in the tradition of the ancients. No event designed to enhance fraternal concord was more impressive than the extraordinary part-spontaneous, part-staged Festival of the Federation in France, which reached its planned climax in Paris for the celebration of the first anniversary of the fall of the Bastille. Over a quarter of a million citizens converged on the capital from all parts of the nation. On the Champ de Mars the most incredible religio-theatrical-political spectacle was enacted. Yet, even more impressive, in a way, was the readily, joyfully, mobilized workforce to prepare the vast arena. The drama critic L.-S. Mercier wrote a few years later:

> There has perhaps never been seen in any people this astonishing and forever memorable spectacle of fraternity. . . . It was there that I saw 150,000 citizens of all classes, of every age and sex, forming the most superb picture of concord, of work, of movement and happiness which has ever been shown.
>
> *(see Kennedy, 1989, pp. 330–1)*

Not exactly what Aristotle had in mind. Indeed, one may wonder whether the excessively emotional stimulation of such an event is not a contradiction of his conception of a steady condition of concord. Is it not possible that the greater the need for exciting expressions of concord, the less true and secure is that style of citizenship in citizens' hearts in the long term? If citizens are properly endowed with the qualities required of that status, they will conduct themselves accordingly. What, we must therefore ask, are those qualities? However, before addressing that question, we must investigate the issue of property, the socio-economic environment in which it has been believed that those qualities are most likely to be in evidence.

First, the bare bones of the civic republican argument concerning property. Citizenship requires independence of mind, else manipulation or corruption will destroy its very essence. Citizens must therefore be socially and economically independent in order to be able to resist attempts at manipulating or corrupting their free political or juridical judgement. They must also be disinterested, be independent in the sense of having the capacity to be objective. Moreover, they must have enough time to allocate to their civic activities. Only owners of a reasonable amount of property can answer to this description. But the case goes even further. Because it is so difficult to identify who is likely to be a virtuous, active and conscientious citizen, as a rule of thumb, ownership of property was taken to be as good a practical index and guide as any.

Nevertheless, not all property is associated with civic virtue, only land. It is owners of land who have been thought to be a reliable and stabilizing influence, though admittedly this feature of the class was often said to relate to self-interest. The argument is that investment in land gives the owner a tangible stake in the state, a vested interest therefore in its preservation and strength. In the republican tradition, however, the matter of motive was of lesser moment than the source of the property. *Owning* wealth was a sign of virtue; *making* wealth was civically questionable. To adapt the slogan of the rebellious citizens of Animal Farm: landowners good, merchants bad.

But there is a problem in all this. By identifying civic virtue with landed wealth, the civic republican thinkers were praising and supporting *inequality* in the economic realm while, at the same time, advocating and promoting citizenship as a means to *equality* in the political realm. We appear still to be in the pages of Orwell's agricultural fairy tale: some citizens are more equal than others. Moreover, this contradiction was of more than theoretical concern, as some writers were aware; for extreme disparities of wealth can lead to usurpation of power by the rich and/or destabilizing discontent. Rousseau consequently concluded that 'the social state is advantageous to men only when all possess something and none has too much' (Rousseau, 1968, I.9n.).

Aristotle, as one would expect, also argued against extremes. Assuredly, he put his faith in landowners as against traders: 'The natural form . . . of the art of acquisition is always and in all cases, acquisition from fruits and animals,' he asserted; in contrast to 'retail trade . . . [which] is justly censured, because the gain in which it results is not naturally made [from plants and animals], but is made at the expense of other men' (Aristotle, 1948, 1258a–b). In political terms, 'the land should be owned, in our ideal state, by the class which bears arms and the class which shares in the conduct of government' (Aristotle, 1948, 1329b). The very wealthy, however, should not be dominant. It is the middle ranks who should dominate in order to achieve the best state, for they neither provoke envy nor are envious themselves. As a consequence, 'where the middle class is large, there is the least likelihood of faction and dissension among citizens' (Aristotle, 1948, 1296a).

The issue of the source of wealth in relation to citizenship occasioned particularly lively debate in Britain from the mid-seventeenth to mid-eighteenth centuries, a debate which, in turn, influenced political thinking in the American colonies. Britain at this time was, after all, not only one of the few states with effective representative political institutions, it was also one of the leading mercantile nations. In addition, Parliament was controlled by the landed aristocracy and squirearchy. From the years of the Civil War and Interregnum the questions of the possible reform of the electoral system and composition of the House of Commons and the balance of powers between the Crown and Parliament were hotly argued. By the early eighteenth century a group calling themselves the Commonwealthmen – a kind of radical wing of the reformist Whigs hostile to royal power – were speaking the vocabulary of civic republicanism. In particular, they presented the virtue of the landed interest as an essential counter to the power of the monarch exerted through patronage. England before the Conquest, they insisted, was a land of virtuous freeholders.

Daniel Defoe was one who turned his literary talents to supporting this political position. In a tract entitled *The Freeholder's Plea against Stock-jobbing elections of Parliament Men* he put the case against the trading class rather more pungently than Aristotle:

> to attempt to fill the House with mechanicks, tradesmen, stock-jobbers, and men neither of sense nor honesty, is tricking at the root, and undermining the nation's felicity at once; and 'tis a wonder the impudence of this attempt has not made them stink in the nostrils of the whole nation.
>
> *(see Dickinson, 1977, p. 115)*

So, if it is men of landed property who possess the necessary qualities to benefit the state through the exercise of their citizenly functions, we need to ask what those qualities were thought to be.

Qualities of citizenship

Who are the good citizens of classical tradition? Take two stories from Livy. First, about Lucius Junius Brutus, who played a major role in expelling Rome's tyrannical royal family and became consul in the new republic. Then his sons became involved in an abortive plot to restore the monarchy. Their father was presented with an appalling dilemma: as consul he had the responsibility of passing sentence and witnessing their flogging and beheading. He did not flinch from performing his

59

civic duty; even though on his face 'a father's anguish was plain to see' (Livy, 1960, 2.5). The second story concerns Cincinnatus, who, after a period of public service, lived modestly working his three-acre farm. A desperate crisis arose. Cincinnatus was offered supreme political and military power for six months. He defeated the enemy, and 'finally resigned after holding office for fifteen days' (Livy, 1960, 3.30). He then returned to his plough, turning his back on both power and riches. (Notice, by the way, as a reflection of the connection between land-holding and civic virtue, that Cincinnatus was a farmer.) Self-interest, however tempting, must give way to the higher, indeed supreme, re-quirements of selfless civic duty. That is the mark of the model citizen.

These stories are therefore exemplifications of civic virtue. Now, although we have glimpsed the concept of virtue in the separate bio-graphical outlines, a more generalized commentary will be helpful at this point. The Greeks believed that there were four particular forms of goodness: these were temperance, justice, courage and wisdom, or prudence. In this section two of these will be examined, namely, courage, to which may be added patriotism, and wisdom, in the sense of the quality of judgement. The Greek word *aretē*, the Latin word *virtus* and the Italian word *virtù* all, significantly, carry in their complexity the meaning of manliness. The very etymology of the Latin and Italian words reveals this, deriving, as they do, from the Latin *vir*, man. Civic virtue also implies successful assertiveness; indeed one authority has even suggested that 'The Greeks would have regarded Napoleon as a man of pre-eminent *aretē*' (de Burgh, 1953, p. 103 n. 3).

Civic virtue, whether as understood by Aristotle, Cicero, Machiavelli or Rousseau, was applied to a man who displayed martial patriotic devotion. Both Aristotle and Machiavelli made it clear, however, that 'pure' courage was hardly to be expected of the citizen-soldier. Aristotle explained that the soldier's courage, while positively inspired 'by the desire of a noble thing, honour', is also negatively prompted by 'the wish to escape reproach' (Aristotle, 1955, III.8). Machiavelli believed that the courage of the citizen-soldier was the product of military training and religious indoctrination. The virtue of courage was not, therefore, exactly altruistically self-motivated. Yet, once instilled, it led to the ultimate sacrifice for one's country.

This is what is entailed in being a citizen-patriot. As the Roman poet Horace, 'the educator of citizens', wrote: 'It is sweet and fitting to die for one's country.' Even so, just as courage needs the spur of influences outside the individual citizen's conscience, so patriotism needs deliberate cultivation. Rousseau believed that this process does, and rightly should, start at birth. 'Every true republican', he wrote, 'takes in with his mother's milk the love of the fatherland. . . . This love forms all his existence; he sees nothing but his fatherland' (see Oldfield, 1990a, p. 71). This patriotism nevertheless has to be constantly refreshed through the virtuous mores of the community and, particularly, through the messages transmitted by the civil religion which Rousseau thought so essential for the political health and success of the state. Machiavelli also believed that religion, and more especially military discipline, was required to keep up the patriotic spirit.

Tocqueville, however, held that such devices produced a synthetic kind of patriotism, bland and unreflecting. He made two significant points. First, he linked the sentiment with his fundamental observation of the USA as a state operating in several strata. American patriotism, he was convinced, was rooted in the township and the several states rather than the Union, because citizens could more readily identify with and participate at these levels. Related to this interpretation is his second point, his distinction between 'instinctive' and 'well-considered' patriotism. Citizenship involves making judgements about public affairs, and that reflective style of life should inform the citizen's patriotism as much as any other aspect of his civic role.

This last observation must be understood in context. When 'patriotism' is so often used today to refer to an individual's attitude towards his or her country *vis-à-vis* another – sometimes even with a xenophobic coloration – the common meaning, particularly prevalent in the eighteenth century, may be overlooked. For, although Machiavelli attached to the notion a quality of aggressiveness, this was due to his personal experience and political diagnosis: it was exceptional in the republican tradition. Patriotism normally meant conflating one's private interests with those of the state, without any necessary regard to its foreign relations. In Montesquieu's words, 'love of the laws and of our country . . . requires a constant preference of public to private interest, it is the source of all private virtues; for they are nothing more than this very preference itself' (Montesquieu, 1949, I.v.5). And so, when Dr Johnson declared patriotism to be the last refuge of the scoundrel, he was not denigrating that virtue; he was complaining that radicals of the likes of

John Wilkes were distorting it by claiming, falsely, in Johnson's view, that their reforming political agenda was for the benefit of their country.

Patriotism, therefore, has not just a military meaning; it has a civil one also. And if citizens are to exhibit their love for their country by ensuring the good health of its constitutional structure and its governmental policies, then they must be able to use the political faculty of judgement. For judgement is to the citizen-as-civilian as courage is to the citizen-as-soldier.

In considering the quality of judgement it is wise again to start with Aristotle. The reason is that he shows how this capacity is connected with so many other features of citizenship. These linkages start with concord. The passage on this concept quoted above does not, it is true, contain the word 'judgement'; nevertheless, the meaning is there. A different translation of a key sentence reveals this, rendering Aristotle's description of the use of the term 'concord' as 'when the citizens have the same judgement about their common interest, when they choose the same things . . .' (see Beiner, 1983, p. 80). Political judgement involves individuals contributing their wisdom and considered opinions on what is prudent action to the compilation of a collective view. This collaboration cannot take place in an atmosphere of enmity; it requires friendly discussion.

Judgement, therefore, is the outcome of deliberation. In defending the mass participation of citizens, Aristotle reveals this link:

> There is this to be said for the Many. Each of them by himself may not be of a good quality; but when they all come together it is possible that they may surpass – collectively and as a body, although not individually – the quality of the few best. . . . when there are many [who contribute to the process of deliberation] each can bring his share of goodness and moral prudence.
>
> *(Aristotle, 1948, 1281a–b)*

There is, however, little point in the citizen exercising his wisdom and understanding in order to formulate his contributory judgement if the process ends there. The whole purpose of exercising judgement is to forward the procedure of decision-making. Judgement leads to action, whether juridical, legislative or executive. It is part of the package of civic virtue, an essential component of which is action.

On the other hand, if citizens are to be encouraged to use their judgement in order to help shape decisions, can the calibre of their judgement really be relied upon? Despite Aristotle's thinking that the process of aggregation would produce a reliable outcome, Machiavelli and Rousseau were not so sure: Machiavelli because of his belief in innate human wickedness; Rousseau because of his belief in man's corruption following his emergence from the state of nature.

Oldfield summarizes Machiavelli's position thus:

> The political judgment of neither senate nor plebs is to be trusted on its own, that is, without support. Each needs to be checked by the other, or to be disciplined by religion and military codes. . . . [In any case, there are only] a few for whom attentiveness to civic good is the overriding consideration in all judgments.
>
> *(Oldfield, 1990a, p. 49)*

Rousseau wrestles with the tension between his democratic instincts and his lack of trust in the general populace. Listen to his intellectual tussling:

> How can a blind multitude, which often does not know what it wants, because it seldom knows what is good for it, undertake by itself an enterprise as vast and difficult as a system of legislation? . . . The general will is always rightful, but the judgement which guides it is not always enlightened.
>
> *(Rousseau, 1968, II.6)*

In other words, the General Will in the heart is not matched by the judgement in the head. Rousseau's solution is the availability of a 'lawgiver' to guide the translation of the General Will into detailed practical effect, in order to support a somewhat frail faculty of judgement, which is all that the citizenry can be expected to muster.

And yet, with all their doubts, neither Machiavelli nor Rousseau would deny that citizens should exercise their judgement, however assisted. For using one's judgement is part of the condition of being a citizen. It is a quality, however limited its supply at its best, that must be fed into the political system. In short, its exercise is a duty.

Role of the citizen

Citizenly duties are civic qualities put into practice. The whole republican tradition is based upon the premise that citizens recognize and understand what their duties are and have a sense of moral obligation instilled into them to discharge these responsibilities. Indeed, individuals were considered barely worthy of the title of citizen if they avoided performing their appointed duties.

The requirement has been justified on the most basic of grounds: no duties, no republic. If citizens are unwilling to fight for the republic, it will be overwhelmed by its external enemies; and if citizens are unwilling to contribute to the civil affairs of the republic, it will collapse into corruption and dissension, ultimately into an authoritarian, even tyrannical form of state. Direct involvement is essential. Rousseau, for instance, rejected both the practice of paying mercenaries to fight and the election of representatives to attend the assembly. If a community resorts to these devices, 'Thanks to laziness and money, they end up with soldiers to enslave the country and deputies to sell it.' He concluded that 'As soon as someone says of the business of the state – "What does it matter to me?" – then the state must be reckoned lost' (Rousseau, 1968, III.15).

Military service was a central feature of Greek citizenship. We know, for example, that Socrates was called upon to fight in two battles, the second when he was 45. A middle-aged philosopher of portly mien might seem an unlikely infantryman, but he acquitted himself well. A century later, the Athenian statesman Lycurgus (not to be confused with his more famous Spartan namesake) introduced a two-year course of compulsory military training.

Drawing lessons mainly from Roman history, Machiavelli was convinced that the citizen's military duty was paramount. A valorous and disciplined citizen-army would be generally beneficial to the 'tone' of the state, so different from the effects of professional troops. Regiments of mercenary ruffians, having replaced the cities' citizen-militias, which had been common in the Middle Ages, were wreaking havoc in Italy in Machiavelli's own day. In both *The Prince* and *The Discourses* he vented his hatred of mercenaries. Only citizen-soldiers would dutifully and loyally protect their state and keep it free: just look at the evidence of ancient Sparta and Rome and contemporary Switzerland, he advises Lorenzo di Medici, to whom he addressed *The Prince*. Rousseau gave similar advice, more aphoristically, when he addressed his *Considerations on the Government of Poland* to Count Wielhorski: 'Every citizen must be a soldier as a duty,' he wrote, 'and none may be so by profession' (see Shklar, 1969, p. 189).

Qua civilian, as distinct from soldier, the duties of a citizen would vary, naturally, according to the constitutional arrangements. The Athenian democratic system of citizens' duties to act as politicians/legislators in the *ekklēsia* (assembly) and as jurors in the courts of law is the classical model. Rousseau was especially keen on assemblies of the sovereign citizenry. Tocqueville thought jury service to be of prime importance, its frequent use acting to remind citizens that, 'they have duties toward society . . . [and] making [them] pay attention to things other than their own affairs' (see Oldfield, 1990a, p. 135). Participation in both juridical and political matters is, therefore, a fundamental citizenly duty.

There is also another political duty (and right), and this is to act as a watchdog on the government. As the Bostonian orator Wendell Phillips famously declared, 'Eternal vigilance is the price of liberty.' Aristotle gives 'the calling of [magistrates] to account' as one of the sovereign rights of the deliberative (i.e. legislative) element in the constitution. 'The election of magistrates, and their examination at the end of their tenure, are the most important of issues,' he declares (Aristotle, 1948, 1298a, 1282a). Rousseau, too, considers such a function to be vital. He allocates the task to 'the assemblies of the people, which [he says] are the shield of the body politic and the brake on the government'. He adds that consequently they 'have always been the nightmare of magistrates' (Rousseau, 1968, III.14).

An obvious question arises from this quite formidable list of potential duties: Can everyone be expected to have the motivation, commitment and will-power to act as a citizen in this complete way?

Forming the citizen

It is, in fact, quite a tall order. And that is because what is being asked is scarcely a natural human activity. The cynic may think that all virtue is a bit of an effort; civic virtue certainly is. It requires the acquisition of knowledge and the development of skills; it requires considering the interests of others, not just one's own, even preferring them. Maybe one's own true interests are identical with the interests of the whole community, as Rousseau, for example, argued, if the General Will is allowed to prevail. But even that insight is not easily understood and appreciated. Self-motivation being rare, it must accordingly be bolstered by techniques devised and provided by society itself. Some theorists of civic republicanism identified two as being especially efficacious: education for the young, novice-citizens, and a civil religion as an educative device for all.

On the matter of education, Aristotle's considered advice might seem contradictory. In the *Ethics* he states categorically that 'political science is not a proper study for the young' (Aristotle, 1955, I.3). Yet in the *Politics* he asserts that 'The citizens of a state should always be educated to suit the constitution of their state' (Aristotle, 1948, 1337aII). How, then, are we to explain this apparent discrepancy in relation to the motivation of citizens to live the civic life?

The answer lies in distinguishing two elements in the notion of civic virtue – moral behaviour and efficient performance of duties. Aristotle's prime concern was to advocate the state control of education in order, through a liberal curriculum, to produce a good man, the necessary framework on which to shape a good citizen. It was Plato, however, who expressed the idea with succinct clarity. He wrote:

> what we have in mind is education from childhood in *virtue*, a training which produces a keen desire to become a perfect citizen who knows how to rule and be ruled as justice demands.
>
> *(Plato, 1970, I. 643)*

Education for civic participation, on the other hand, as actually happened in Athens, was best undertaken as a practical exercise – on-the-job training. As Aristotle pointed out by analogy, 'You do not see men becoming qualified in medicine by reading handbooks on the subject' (Aristotle, 1955, X.9). But this was secondary to the education of attitudes.

And this order of priorities was picked up by eighteenth-century writers. Montesquieu, for instance, asserted that in a republic inspiring 'love of the laws and of our country ... ought to be the principal business of education' (Montesquieu, 1949, IV.5). However, it was

Rousseau who, like Plato, distinguished himself almost equally as an educational theorist as he did as a political theorist. His ideas are therefore particularly useful for our survey.

Yet Rousseau's treatment of education is ambivalent. Unlike his Greek predecessors he allows for a private style of education for personal development which has no civic purpose. Even so, his parallel views on education for citizenship do reveal a role for the educative process every bit as vital for the success of the ideal state as Plato and Aristotle envisaged. Parents themselves have a civic duty to introduce their offspring to the appropriate attitudes; and when the state takes over through the schools, the aim is 'to accustom [the pupils] in good time to the rules, to equality, to fraternity, to competition, to live in the sight of their fellow-citizens and to desire public approbation' (see Oldfield, 1990a, p. 71). At the same time, he was very alert to the limitations of education: human beings had enough elemental, natural resistance to being bent to the needs of political society to render civic education only a partial success. Other devices were needed to combine for the formation of citizens. Absolutely essential was a civil religion.

Religion may be, as Marx asserted, an opiate, numbing the critical faculties of the people; but for civic republicans it also has its use as a stimulant, helping to arouse citizens to a positive allegiance to the state. Governments as well as writers have been well aware of this. The policy of Augustus, faced with the task of pulling Rome out of the depressing turmoil that brought about the collapse of the Republic, provides an illuminating example. He restored the old gods, both Olympian and domestic and familial, to greater public consciousness by refurbishing decayed temples and shrines and reviving ancient ceremonies and rites. Also, although only posthumously deified, he encouraged belief that he and his family existed on a specially exalted, numinous plane. For example, an inscription has been found on the southern littoral of the Black Sea, displaying an oath of utter devotion and loyalty to Augustus and his descendants. This oath was sworn by all the local inhabitants, including resident Roman citizens, and names Augustus together with 'all the gods and goddesses' as a guarantor of the oath and the executor of the awful penalties for betraying it (see Stockton, 1986, p. 543).

Machiavelli, calling upon the evidence of an earlier age in Rome's long history, was impressed with the way in which the Romans managed their religious observances. He tells his readers that

> It was religion that facilitated whatever enterprise the senate and great men of Rome designed to undertake. . . . religion helped in the control of armies, in encouraging the plebs, in producing good men, and in shaming the bad.
>
> *(Machiavelli, 1998, I.11)*

The Romans, he explains, were fortunate in their pagan religion because, unlike the Christian focus on the afterlife, it provided the state with a powerful reinforcement of civic purpose. Worship of the Roman deities encouraged men to 'magnanimity, bodily strength, and [boldness]' (Machiavelli, 1998, II.2). It also had a vital educative role: unlike the debilitating effect of Christian education, the Roman cults upheld republicanism and liberty.

Rousseau had even firmer opinions on the relationship of religion to citizenship, partly from personal experiences. He thought atheism intolerable, Christianity 'bizarre', and clergy politically dangerous. His positive recommendations were for an overtly civil religion – the title, in fact, of Book IV, Chapter 8 of *The Social Contract*. This faith would consist of 'articles, not strictly . . . religious dogmas', that are 'sentiments of sociability, without which it is impossible to be either a good citizen or a loyal subject' (Rousseau, 1968, IV.8). Following closely Rousseau's prescription, Robespierre, his most earnest politician-disciple, attempted, albeit briefly and abortively, to establish such a civil religion in his Cult of the Supreme Being.

Tocqueville, in contradistinction to Machiavelli and Rousseau, accepted, indeed welcomed the civic good of Christianity. This form of religion, he believed, is an essential concomitant of liberty. It encourages a sense of community and therefore patriotism; it gives moral tone to the community. Above all, his belief in the positive, benign influence of religion enabled Tocqueville to temper his own fear of the political tyranny of the majority in a democracy. He identified these civic qualities in the Christian religion by his study of the history of the American colonies and the evidence of his own ears and eyes on his visit to New England. Writing particularly of the Puritanism practised in these states, he explained that 'Religion is considered as the guardian of mores, and mores are regarded as the guarantee of the laws and pledge for the maintenance of freedom itself' (Tocqueville, 1968, p. 55).

Many present-day Americans would no doubt say that they can feel comfortable with that. But how true would such agreement be of other countries? And what of the other principles of civic republicanism? These principles and ideals were, after all, laid down in states and societies so very different from our own. The relevance of the civic republican tradition for our own times must therefore now be examined.

Revival and arguments

From the late eighteenth century the civic republican interpretation of citizenship steadily gave way to the liberal. In recent years, however, interest in the older tradition has revived, partly because of perceived weaknesses in or objections to the liberal style, and partly because of the putative intrinsic values of civic republicanism.

Scholars and public opinion in the USA have led the way. Several explanations may be offered for this American interest. First, the American Revolution was partly inspired and sustained by the classical ideals, particularly during the war; and the shift in focus to the liberal stress on individual rights in the Constitution, some argue, changed the balance too radically away from feelings of obligation and community. On the other hand, and secondly, as Tocqueville reported, the structure is in place for realistic participation in public affairs: township and state could replicate something of the intimacy of the city-state if a greater proportion of citizens seized the opportunities. Thirdly, a strengthening of a sense of community and of responsibility to contribute to communal harmony is felt to be imperative in a nation with so many social problems.

One of the most distinguished of recent American scholars in the field of politics, Hannah Arendt, was convinced of the value of active citizenship as construed by the classical writers. She expressed her ideas on the subject most fully in *The Human Condition*, published in 1958. However, let us cite another work in which she expounds, as a telling link back to the revolutionary period, Jefferson's idea of the ward system of 'little republics'. Jefferson, she explains, claimed that he concluded '"every opinion, with the injunction, 'divide the counties into wards'"' (Arendt, 1973, pp. 248–9). Arendt sums up her reading of Jefferson and her own philosophy in the following words:

69

The basic assumption of the ward system, whether Jefferson knew it or
not, was that no one could be happy without his share in public happiness, that no one could be called free without his experience in public
freedom, and that no one could be called either happy or free without
participating, and having a share, in public power.

(Arendt, 1973, p. 255)

These words were first published in 1963, though her influence has
carried over the years. It was not, indeed, for another two decades that
work to resuscitate civic republicanism really got under way. Two features
of what is sometimes referred to as 'neo-republicanism' are of cardinal
importance and may be illustrated by quotations from two of the leading exponents. One is disillusionment with the American democratic
system: so few even bother to vote; even fewer participate politically
in any other way. Benjamin Barber describes this condition as 'thin
democracy':

'Thin democracy' . . . yields neither the pleasures of participation nor the
fellowship of civic association, neither the autonomy and self-governance
of continuous political activity nor the enlarging mutuality of shared
public goods – of mutual deliberation, decision, and work.

(see Sinopoli, 1992, p. 160)

The other feature of neo-republicanism derives from the criticism
that liberal citizenship has led to a weak feeling of community. The
belief that a restored sense of neighbourhood, or indeed national 'togetherness', is essential has produced the word 'communitarian' to describe
this thinking. Let us hear Michael Sandel on this view:

to say that the members of a society are bound by a sense of community
is not simply to say that a great many of them profess communitarian
sentiments and pursue communitarian aims, but rather that they conceive
their identity . . . as defined to some extent by the community of which
they are a part. For them, community describes not just what they *have*
as fellow citizens, but also what they are.

(see Dagger, 1997, p. 49)

We shall need to investigate communitarianism a little more in the
next section because civic republicanism and communitarianism are

not exactly synonymous. Our immediate concern here must be to discover the pros and cons of civic republicanism and its relevance for modern states, polities which are so different from those in which the ideal and practice were originally developed. The lists of pros and cons which follow must be read as a rough guide to the kinds of points raised by the defenders and opponents of civic republican citizenship. They do not indicate the different nuances in detail of analysis and argument of different writers on the subject. The material is presented rather in the form of two sets of 'highest common factors'.

To convey the case in favour of civic republicanism involves to a large extent a repetition of the ideas already analysed. Still, collecting them all at this point, then juxtaposing the contrary arguments, will, it is hoped, elucidate the debates that have been engaged in during the past two decades.

In itemizing the elements for the positive case, let us start with the proposition that no individual is self-created or self-sufficient. A person is an amalgam of genetic inheritance, autonomous will and social influences. That third element not only makes its imprint, its renunciation is unnatural. Hermits are rare, and Robinson Crusoe needed his Man Friday. Man is a social animal. But society needs rules and some form of government to make and administer those rules, even in the most primitive of communities. So man, being a social animal, cannot avoid politics. This is Aristotle's basic message.

Now, just as it is natural to live in a community with other humans, so it is natural to feel a sense of duty towards them – to members of one's family, to one's friends, to one's neighbours. And to one's local community, and to one's country? Civic republicans admit that stretching the circle of duties beyond one's intimate contacts does not come easily; but at least behaving as a citizen in this way is rooted in a natural attribute. Yet the performance of duties on behalf of the community and the state is much more than the expansion of a natural human feeling; it is a moral obligation. Individuals are protected by a stable, just and efficient state from relapsing into the mode of life memorably described by Hobbes as being 'solitary, poore, nasty, brutish and short'. Enjoying the benefits surely requires, in Michael Walzer's phrase, the payment of the 'dues of membership' (see Oldfield, 1990a, p. 160).

One of the most compelling reasons for the revival of the civic republican ideal has been, indeed, the conviction that too many people in western countries are not paying their dues; they are abusing the social security system, for example, and giving nothing in return. Such people are, in short, 'free riders'. The liberal form of citizenship tends to focus on individual freedom and rights. But there should be, in all conscience, some balance, however rough it might be, between freedom and rights for the individual on the one hand and commitment and duties to the community on the other. Without such a balance, civic virtue is submerged by selfishness.

A society of selfish individuals is, at its extreme, no society at all, nor does it have citizens, properly speaking – it is nothing more than an agglomeration of competitive units. And self-seeking competitiveness generates stresses and resentments that are the very antithesis of the republican vision of a harmonious, co-operative community, in which self-interest and the interest of the community are in some sense identical. Moreover, the concord of mutually agreed strivings and achievements minimizes anti-social behaviour and thus reliance on coercive policing for maintaining the peace. In addition, of course, when the individual citizen's commitment to the community is turned from sustaining internal harmony to the requirements of external security, the civic republican ideal expects unquestioning patriotism and self-sacrifice.

This concentration on the image of the citizen as part of an organic community – as a member of an orchestra, not one of a convention of soloists – is, even so, only part of the case in favour of civic republicanism. For the ultimate objective is to bring benefits to the individual. To be a citizen in this fashion, it is conceded, is not easy. So, by the educative assistance of school and religion, the individual is continuously supported in the bearing of the burdens of the civic status. Furthermore, and this is the real point, the effort brings inestimable rewards, not just of living in a harmonious society, but of becoming a fuller, more truly happy and moral human being.

The picture is assuredly an attractive one, and although composed of contributions from centuries long ago, may well fit the needs of our own times as readily as those of Aristotle, Cicero, Machiavelli and Rousseau. The civic republican ideal contains perennial values. Or is this the complete picture? Are there not weaknesses in the case, elements, indeed, that some might find positively distasteful? And can a citizen in the imperfect world entering the twenty-first century really slot snugly into the imaginings of perfection conjured in the minds of political philosophers?

Even the proponents of civic republicanism accept that their expectations are very demanding. Citizenship is not an easy life; it requires conscientious application. Most people lead a very full life with their family commitments, leisure pursuits and employment – above all, employment, for we are not Greeks with slaves to work for us. Yet the republican citizen must, in addition, allocate time, summon up the energy and generate commitment to an involvement in public affairs. It is obvious, however, that there is a limit to the elasticity of a person's life-style, and in order to accommodate active participation in public affairs something has to give. Serious questions arise from this requirement. How many individuals are prepared to make that adjustment? Is it fair and is it desirable that the demand should be made? If harmony and happiness are the intended outcomes of civic republicanism – as they certainly are – it can be plausibly argued that this infringement of private life would have precisely the contrary effect.

The direction of individuals into involvement in the public arena and mobilizing the resources of education and religion to this purpose smacks of paternalism. By incorporation into this kind of civic regime the individual suffers a loss of personal freedom, autonomy and the power of fully independent critical thought. So speak the opponents of the republican school, arguing that the prospect of true freedom, autonomy and judgement through the blending process of identification with the community is little more than a philosophical sleight of hand.

It would not be so bad if the civic republicans could interpret participation in public affairs more loosely and flexibly than has normally been the case. But theirs has been the grand design of citizenly participation in the politics of the state, the Aristotelian *polis*, naturally, being the model.

This has at least three unfortunate consequences. One is that citizenship properly speaking becomes an elite activity, the rest of the populace relegated to a merely nominal citizenly status. The reason for this is that normally only the well-educated and the adequately wealthy have the inclination and time to participate in formal politics. Secondly, this narrow definition of public participation excludes the whole broad range of civic society activities, such as pressure groups, trade unions, charities. In chapter 4 we shall see how important this non-political, or more properly quasi-political, realm of organized activity can be. It can and does embrace far more people in community participation than the arena of formal politics. The third unfortunate consequence is that, generally speaking, men find it easier and more congenial to involve themselves in formal politics while women find it easier and more congenial to involve themselves in civil society. It is unsurprising, therefore, that feminists are often aligned against civic republicanism.

Moreover, the spurning of civil society is not the only cause of feminist resentment. Civic republican citizenship has been an essentially male concept because it was devised by men for male-dominated societies; it would be anachronistic to expect otherwise. And one of its evident male features is the requirement to be possessed of the virtue of military valour.

All these represent the contrary arguments in a generalized way, with just a few allusions to present-day conditions. Oldfield has suggested that modern citizens lack all three prerequisites for acting in the republican manner; these are resources, opportunities and motivation. A cogent case can be made to support this contention. Few people have the resources of information, time and energy for effective political participation. Political affairs in the modern world are exceedingly complex and often technically difficult, especially in the field of economics, and so mastering this material in order to make informed, detailed judgements is difficult. It has even been argued that the mass media, particularly in the USA, by trivializing their news presentations, obscure rather than facilitate the comprehension of the major issues. And the more difficult and controversial the problems are, the more onerous will be the citizen's engagement with them – the more time-consuming the committees, sub-committees and meetings are likely to be for the citizen-participants convened to resolve them.

Even if a person were to be equipped with sufficient information, time and energy, most modern states are so large and centralized that penetration to and participation in 'high' politics are possible only for the few. Britain has been a notable example of centralized government, where, for instance, the affairs devolved to the parochial level are just that – parochial. Hardly what Jefferson had in mind for his 'little republics'.

Nor are the devices envisaged by the mainstream writers for motivating individuals to citizenly activity available in modern states. A

Rousseauean civil religion is scarcely a common feature. The 'secular religions' of Communism and Nazism have had their day, but, in any case, were not exactly epitomes of the virtues of republicanism! Islam remains a religio-political force, particularly in Shi'ite Iran and Taliban Afghanistan, but not at all replicable in western societies. The use of military discipline as an alternative for welding a collection of men into a community of citizens is no longer an option in a world of technically sophisticated professional armies. Even France, with a long tradition of conscription, has abandoned its military national service. That leaves the schools. There is a widespread belief that schools could and should educate their pupils to be good citizens. Defining precise objectives and methodologies is, however, very hard, and the effectiveness of what is being attempted is highly questionable. It is a topic to which we shall return in chapter 5.

One of the problems facing schools is whether they influence society or society influences the schools. If the customs and tone of a society – the French word *moeurs* is most appropriate – are antipathetic to a citizenship of republican style, schools are a weak force to counteract this attitude. Civic republicanism, in other words, relies for acceptance and efficacy on what Tocqueville called 'habits of the heart' (Tocqueville, 1968, p. 355). We must conclude, therefore, that there are many objections and difficulties surrounding any attempt to restore a civic republican mode as a strong feature of citizenship in the modern world, yet at the same time there is still a recognized hard-core value in the ideal. The key question to be addressed, then, is how to create the habits of the heart for its acceptance, appropriately adapted to present-day circumstances and conditions.

Adaptations for today

If republicanism is worthy of revival by adaptation, there are basically two approaches. One is to adjust the detailed precepts and practices to modern life; the other is to rethink the main components and their relationships to other, successful and relevant ideas.

Two examples follow of the first of these kinds of adaptation. One of the ways in which, in the classical tradition, the citizen displayed the virtue of service to the community at large was by membership of the citizen-army. The obvious method of translating this into present-day conditions is to mobilize young people instead for civilian community service. Many schools now incorporate opportunities for their pupils to undertake local community work, especially for the disadvantaged. In Britain, a national body, Community Service Volunteers (CSV), has organized full-time voluntary work for many thousands of young people, sometimes for long periods. However, the community service provided by non-school bodies like CSV attracts only a small proportion of the total population, by no means commensurate with the republican tradition of (military) service as a universal duty.

The need to provide for an up-to-date form of national service has been canvassed most prominently and persistently by the American academic Morris Janowitz. Two of his later works are significantly entitled *The Reconstruction of Patriotism* (1983) and 'The Good Citizen – A Threatened Species?' (originally published in 1985). His thesis is that the USA, from the Revolution to the Second World War, was well served by a dual system of civic education, through schools and military service, and that both these formative experiences have lost their efficacy.

He advocates a combination of military and community service to restore the civic health of the United States, not primarily as training, but as a means of creating 'civic discipline' and a concrete awareness of what community means. At the heart of the American problem of the perceived decay in standards of citizenship are the large numbers of unemployed or underemployed disaffected youth (a malaise not confined to the USA). Janowitz is therefore adamant that the scheme he advocates should not be distorted into a liberal interpretation:

> Most important, the forms of national service must be seen not as welfare programmes but as expressions of civic duty by those who actively participate. Those very conditions which can work to resocialize poor youth away from a dead-end existence depend upon national service not being an employer of last resort, a definition that is hard to escape unless participation is relatively representative of all American youth.
>
> *(Janowitz, 1988, p. 70)*

He admits that setting up such a network of opportunities, conveying this correct message, would be difficult.

In the year that Janowitz republished the essay from which this quotation has been drawn the governing Conservative Party in Britain launched its notion of 'active citizenship'. 'Public service may once have been the duty of an elite,' the Home Secretary Douglas Hurd explained, 'but today it is the responsibility of all who have time or money to spare . . . we are now witnessing the democratisation of responsible citizenship' (see Heater, 1991, p. 140). In elaboration, it was shown to be a pale shadow of republicanism. Citizens were adjured, for instance, to join neighbourhood watch schemes, school governing bodies and environmental protection groups. In contrast to the civic republicanism design of civic participation in the governance of the state, what was being commended was a Heineken view of voluntary work, designed to reach the parts of British society which will always be beyond state provision.

These proposals for voluntary service were, in fact, only touching the surface of the issue of renovating republicanism. Deeper thought has been given to the matter, however. This has mainly taken two forms. One is an attempt to amalgamate elements of both the liberal and the republican approaches, which we shall examine in chapter 5. The other is the burgeoning of communitarianism, which extracts from the republican tradition the concentration on a feeling of community and a sense of duty, though omitting from its programme the strand of direct political participation and, some argue, crucially, the central republican concern for freedom. Communitarian thinking, in the sense of the primacy of the community over the individual, has in the past been adopted by many across the wide spread of the political spectrum.

However, today the word has been appropriated by political theorists and politicians to define a socio-political position which was emerging in the 1980s. The word itself was, in fact, formally adopted by a small-group meeting of American social scientists in 1990. A number of very distinguished scholars in the USA have associated themselves with and worked on the concept of communitarianism, albeit with slightly different personal nuances of interpretation: they include Amitai Etzioni, William Galston, Alasdair MacIntyre, Michael Sandel and Charles Taylor.

Communitarians are, fundamentally, reacting against both the credo of liberal individualism and the interpretation of citizenship as the enjoyment of rights, which provides the political undergirding of that philosophical position. They are concerned that the trend in the liberal direction (particularly in the USA, their main field of observation) has progressed so far as seriously to undermine the tradition and values of community and responsibility. The balance between rights and responsibilities must be redressed. One vital way of achieving this is to reduce welfare expenditure; another is to restore family values. Communitarians also find confrontational politics uncongenial. All these threads in their thinking are tied together in their celebration of the community as a form of human grouping which is ideally suited for promoting co-operation, mutual care and fairness, and for resisting the dehumanizing weight of the modern political system.

Liberal citizenship is nevertheless so firmly embedded, certainly in western political culture, and has so much to be said in its favour, that it would be surprising if communitarianism had not come under attack. Critics have worried on academic grounds that communitarians have failed to proffer a clear definition of what they mean by 'community'. (Though Etzioni (1993, p. 160) has written of the 'supracommunity, a community of communities – the American society'.) However, whatever the precise meaning, their stress on communal bonding raises several problems.

Integration of a community involves an implied rejection of the 'strangers' who are not members. It also implies that all who are members have the same interests, yet that is not necessarily so: what about the interests of women compared with men, or of ethnic minorities compared with the cultural majority? The whole reality of multiple identity, indeed, would seem to be underplayed. Communitarianism also has the smack of an authoritarian firming up of the status quo, even a retrogression to some supposed more attractive age. Feminists are especially unhappy about this: 'family values', 'mutual care' – do these items on the agenda not foretell a retying of the apron-strings?

Even so, the communitarians' case for recognizing the value of community life and the need to stem the selfish abuse of liberal values has appeared sufficiently cogent to have been adopted by a number of politicians. The most influential writer to achieve this practical effect has been Etzioni. The titles of some of his recent books reveal the thrust of his work: *The Moral Dimension, The Parenting Deficit* and, of widest impact, *The Spirit of Community*. Etzioni diagnoses the imbalance between rights and responsibilities and the decline in the two-parent family, the decay of religious faith and the collapse of a sense of neighbourhood as afflications causing a serious distemper in western democracies. He deeply regrets the 'millions of latchkey children' and, echoing Tocqueville's 'habits of the heart', urges a 'change of heart' among citizens (Etzioni, 1993, pp. 56, 18). From an early position of academic sociological analysis, Etzioni has come to adopt the posture of a campaigner. Communitarianism is not just a set of principles, but a movement.

By *c*.1990 the doctrines of both the traditional Left and the New Right were discredited. As a consequence, politicians such as Clinton in the USA, Berlusconi in Italy and Blair in the UK, searching for some principles with which to clothe their scantily clad pragmatism, bought communitarianism off the peg. In Britain New Labour's policy statements have been replete with references to 'community' and 'responsibility': communitarianism has been the intellectual foundation of the 'Third Way'. In 1994 Gordon Brown declared that 'people must accept their responsibilities as individuals and as citizens, and community action should never be a substitute for the assumption of personal responsibility.' Three years later, Tony Blair stated: 'I am utterly convinced that the only way to rebuild a strong civic society for the modern world is on the basis of rights and responsibility going together' (see Benyon and Edwards, 1997, p. 335).

There may well be signal advantages in the communitarian vision. On the other hand, we have journeyed some way from the classical republican concept of the citizen. Where is the legal status? Where is political participation? If anything, we need today a broader, not a narrower definition of citizenship than even civic republicanism can offer. Being a citizen is now an extraordinarily complicated business, as the next two chapters will reveal.

3

Who Are Citizens?

Legal definitions

Where better to start an answer to our question than with law? It provides an authoritative framework; and it demonstrates the extraordinary confusion that is typical of the whole subject of citizenship. At least we can establish three basic points. First, international law recognizes that each state has the right to define who are or are not permitted to be its citizens. Secondly, legal definitions conflate citizenship and nationality (in the political, of course, not the cultural sense). And thirdly, there are two methods of defining nationality/citizenship, namely, *jus sanguinis* and *jus soli*. *Jus sanguinis* means citizenship by inheritance: at birth one acquires the citizenship of one's parents. *Jus soli* means citizenship by state territory: at birth one acquires the citizenship of the land where one is born.

These alternative modes of defining a person's citizenship may appear at first sight both commonsensical and simple; in practice, however, they are not as simple as they seem. *Jus sanguinis* raises several practical questions – what to do about children of mixed marriages, for example. *Jus soli* also raises various detailed questions. For instance, Argentina felt compelled at one time to specify that this rule covered birth in a legation or on a warship or in an international zone under the Argentine flag! Indeed, when one examines the regulations now in use, it is clear that most states, in order to cope with the practical complexities, operate a combination of the two modes. Having adopted such a policy, indeed, some states interpret their own guidelines with such wide discretion as

Born outside territory, of citizen parent(s)	
Unconditional attribution of citizenship	France, FRG
Conditional attribution of citizenship	USA, Canada, UK

Born in territory, of non-citizen parents	
Unconditional attribution of citizenship	USA, Canada
Conditional attribution of citizenship	UK, France

NB In 1998 the FRG announced a plan to change its citizenship law. See below.

Figure 3.1

Source: Brubaker, 1989, p. 104.

to render easy generalizations rather difficult. One interesting analysis, summarized in figure 3.1, shows the pattern for the USA, Canada, the UK, France and the FRG.

There can be few states with citizenship/nationality laws quite as complex as the United Kingdom's. Indeed, one eminent British lawyer has suggested that many of the provisions of the British Nationality Act of 1981 'are so obscurely drafted that they are unfit to be in the statute book' (see Commission on Citizenship, 1990, p. 76). The legislation is the combined muddled outcome of, initially, a history of confused British imperialism and, then, concern about a too numerous immigration of coloured people as being productive of racial tension. The 1981 Act defines five categories in the following order: British citizens, British dependent territories citizens, British overseas citizens, British subjects and British protected persons. The first of these alone carries the right of abode in the UK and full civic rights. The four other categories carry very limited rights, decreasing as we move down the list.

The production of a graded classification of this kind inevitably raises the question of the worth of the oft-repeated statement that the essence of citizenship lies in the principle of equality.

Equality or elitism?

The principle of equality cannot, in truth, be discounted in any consideration of the nature of citizenship. What we must grasp, however, is that beneath this ideal lies a tangle of reservations and contradictions. It is our task here to try to unravel these complications in order to discover how far in theory and in practice the basic proposition that equality is the very essence of citizenship can be held to be valid.

Equality – Pairs of Distinctions	
Among individuals with citizen status	Opportunity to acquire citizenship
Rights, entitlements	Responsibilities, duties, obligations
Civil/political rights	Social/economic rights
Rights in law	Discrimination in practice
Theoretical equality – basic but vague assumption	Positive discrimination – policy of levelling up
Rights on demand	Rights to opportunities
Same treatment (ignoring wanted differences)	Equivalent treatment (acknowledging wanted differences)
Numerical equality (discounting merit)	Distributive justice (recognizing relative merit)

Figure 3.2

A fundamental cause of these complications is the wide variety of meanings attached to the word 'equality' that are pertinent to the study of citizenship. The simplified table in figure 3.2 provides an indication of the different usages and interpretations, which are referred to in various places in this book. The pairs represent complementary sets or opposites which need to be distinguished from each other.

Because of its relevance in so many different ways, it is scarcely surprising that equality has been perceived as a powerful characteristic of citizenship. By taking two great defining periods of citizenship, namely fourth-century BC Athens and the late eighteenth-century North Atlantic world, we can easily recognize the strength of the equality principle. In the first era, the constitutional mechanism depended ideally, to repeat the words of Aristotle, on citizens being '*all* who share in the civic life of ruling and being ruled in turn', a system in which citizens are 'equals and peers' (Aristotle, 1948, 1274b, 1279a). In the second era, the assertion of civic equality derived from the ethical principle that all men are created and remain morally equals. It was a proposition which the American Founding Fathers considered to be too 'self-evident' to explain. And if individuals as human beings are by nature equal, then a political system that enshrines inequality is *ipso facto* unjust. (We may note in passing that the language and ideas of that age are replicated in the present-day Universal Declaration of Human Rights.)

After all, consider the alternatives: a hierarchical society of vassal and lord or of subject and monarch with an intervening aristocracy. These arrangements are ultimately based on the exercise of force from above, not on the will of the people below. In the monarchical age of the eighteenth century the question arose: How could a revolutionary change from royal power to popular will be justified? It was this shift in the basis of authority, the locus of sovereignty indeed, that the political thinkers who set the scene for the American and French Revolutions strove to achieve. And they secured the change through the device of a 'virtual' contract. Rousseau, to take a notable example, was utterly convinced that the concept of the social contract led inexorably to the principle of the equality of citizens.

> Whichever way we look [he wrote], we always return to the same conclusion: namely that the social pact establishes equality among the citizens in that they all pledge themselves under the same conditions and must all enjoy the same rights. Hence by the nature of the compact, every act of sovereignty . . . binds or favours all the citizens equally.
>
> *(Rousseau, 1968, II.4)*

The men of the eighteenth century also spoke in the same breath of freedom or liberty. Without examining here the very real problems of connecting equality with freedom, there can be no doubt that the two are intimately related in the notion of citizenship. Citizenship, equality and freedom were certainly intertwined in Athens in its democratic age. Equality involved not only the obvious rights of voting and holding public office; it also meant the freedom to speak one's mind in the Assembly. Moreover, in the modern world, do we not, in English, use the word 'enfranchise' – make free – for the process of equalizing citizens by conferment of the right to vote? Even more crucially, what price freedom if citizens do not enjoy equality before the law?

There is, finally, the root need for the principle of equality: that is, to sustain the quality and harmony of life in the polity. The operation of a society of citizens relies on their co-operation at least, their altruism and civic conscience at best. This frame of mind needs, above all, fairness, and people are treated fairly if they are treated with at least a rough measure of equality. Discrimination, abuse of power, grossly unjust distribution of wealth and resources corrode equality and destroy any atmosphere of fairness, with the result that the virtues of citizenship are soured into apathy and alienation. Such a deleterious outcome may affect minority groups as well as individuals. Members of ethnic or religious minorities can feel that they are truly citizens only if they perceive an underlying fairness in the social, legal and political systems.

The extension of the status of citizenship from the eighteenth century has indubitably involved a process of mass equalization, however unfinished that process might be. A greater proportion of the world's population now – and especially since *c.*1990 – are treated equally before the law, have rights to participate fully in the political arena and enjoy a modicum of state-provided welfare. In so far as there are blatant denials of these rights of citizenship, they are cause for frequent adverse comment as violating the principle of civic equality.

On the other hand, equal access to and enjoyment of the rights of citizenship have not always been acclaimed as desirable ideals. Let us look at three different kinds of argument: against equality as a delusion; against equality of access to the status; and against equality within the body of the citizenry.

The case against equality as a delusion, our first argument, was famously expounded by Marx in 1843 in his essay 'On the Jewish Question'. Modern middle-class man, he argued, has a dual identity. He is simultaneously a citizen and a bourgeois. As a citizen he is equal with others in the state and is endowed with rights attendant upon that status; as a bourgeois he pursues his selfish interests through the market mechanisms of civil society. Living in the bourgeois mode, individuals are anything but equal; yet this is the reality of life in a capitalist society. Living in the citizenly mode, individuals are legally equal; yet this is a spurious equality.

Our second case is the reluctance to give equal opportunities for acquiring the title of citizen. For long in the classical world citizenship was a status to be coveted, a privilege to be prized, therefore the possession of a worthy elite. In Greece it was commonly confined to property owners. The Romans, differing markedly from the Athenians, steadily opened the ranks of citizenship to an ever-widening number until, in the early third century AD, the title was available promiscuously to virtually all free men. But even a century before this, Tacitus tartly contrasted the current policy with that, 'Long ago, when the grant was rare and only made as a reward of valour' (see Sherwin-White, 1973, p. 258 n. 1): if the honour was so diluted, it was meaningless. For those who had earned it, its dilution was an insult; or, viewed from the position of the easily enfranchised, the grant could conjure up a response akin to Groucho Marx's in a different context – 'I don't want to belong to any club that will accept me as a member'!

In our contemporary world, we see the concern about and the effects of the watering-down of the status of citizenship in ways typical of modern times. Resistance to a too inclusive policy of naturalization is most often the result of a desire for a country to retain its national-cultural homogeneity. As a consequence, perhaps millions of would-be citizens are denied that status in the country of their choice. We shall return to this matter later. The mirror-image of this situation is most evident in the USA. Many immigrants see little point in becoming citizens because successive laws have steadily reduced the distinction between citizens and non-citizens in terms of rights. Benevolent legislation has thus severely weakened the incentive for naturalization. (Though not entirely, for 'Many thousands of pregnant Mexican women cross the border illegally each year, presumably motivated in part by the desire to confer American citizenship upon the newborn children by the simple expedient of bearing them on American soil' (Brubaker, 1989, p. 167 n. 7).)

And so, to our third argument: the felt need to 'grade' those who already have the legal status of citizen. There have been persistent attempts throughout history to retain an elitist quality for political citizenship by the device of ensuring that, while all citizens are equal, some are more equal than others. In the ancient world, as Rome extended her sway in Italy, but reluctant to concede full citizenship to the incorporated peoples, she invented *civitas sine suffragio*. By this device individuals had citizenship without the franchise, legal but not political citizenship. In modern times, the suffrage has in many countries been conceded with slow reluctance. In Britain, for example, it took six Acts of Parliament (1832, 1867, 1884, 1918, 1928, 1969) before all adults aged 18 or over were eligible for the vote.

Perhaps the most tense and detailed debates over the very concept of equality of political rights took place at the time of the drafting of the French Constitution which came into operation in 1791. It fell to the Abbé Sieyes to protect the state from the 'undesirable' effects of the proclaimed Revolutionary objective of equality. By introducing a modest wealth qualification for the franchise he divided the body of citizens into 'active' and 'passive', barring the latter from the right to vote. He justified the distinction by asserting that

> there are men who may be perfectly sound in the physical sense, but to whom all social ideas are remote, and who are hence not in a position to take an active part in the public weal. They should not be personally discriminated against: but who would dare to consider it wrong that they should be excluded to some extent, not, it must be repeated, from legal protection and public aid, but from the exercise of political rights?
>
> *(see Forsyth, 1987, p. 162)*

Sieyes's criterion of exclusion was indeed relatively humane compared with the 'second-class citizenship' – for this was the origin of the term – of American black people. Moreover, their inferior status extended beyond the political into the civil realm of citizenship. The contradiction of the equality principle, enshrined though it was in the Declaration of Independence, has never been more blatant. For three generations after this seemingly unambiguous statement – until Emancipation in 1863 – millions of Americans were not only non-citizens, they were not even free. And even the post-bellum Fourteenth and Fifteenth Amendments to the Constitution, which provided for equal civil and political rights irrespective of race or colour, were no guarantee against widespread discrimination and physical assault. The black man may then have been, in the words of Senator Sumner, 'Clad in the full panoply of citizenship', but the bitterly hostile whites in the Deep South tore that panoply from him with impunity for a century thereafter.

We may additionally note that Native Americans, subjected to a policy of virtual genocide in the nineteenth century, could scarcely be counted among the ranks of American citizens. Indeed, not until 1924 were they accorded automatic citizenship at birth.

So, does citizenship live up to its vaunted reputation as incorporating the principle of equality? As a concept and arrangement for relating the individual to the law, politics and social structure, there is no room for doubt that citizenship is more equitable than other socio-political relationships devised for large human groupings. What we must be on guard against deriving from this judgement is that citizenship has been or is ever likely to be enjoyed to the level of perfection that an ideal model might suggest. In practice, we should envisage a hierarchy of expressions or experiences of citizenship which blurs any pure equality (whatever that can possibly mean).

At the top of the ladder are the full and also active citizens, those, depending on the society we are examining, who have the most complete set of rights and who most fully discharge their civic duties. It is important not to forget the second element in this definition: if equality is good for rights it must also hold good for responsibilities. On the second rung down (to continue our metaphor) are the full but passive citizens, where we are using 'passive' not in Sieyes's sense, but in the sense of being apathetic about performing duties. Thirdly, there are the second-class citizens. These are the individuals who have the legal status of citizen but, because of discrimination, are denied full rights in practice. For the fourth level we may use the term 'underclass', which became fashionable in the 1980s. These people have the legal standing of citizens, but are so economically and culturally impoverished that they are in effect excluded from the normal style of social and political activity which the term citizen connotes. Fifthly, there are residents, sometimes referred to by the recently revived word 'denizens'. These are persons who are not nationals of the state in which they live; they are therefore not legally citizens and have no political rights, but nevertheless enjoy many civil, social and economic rights associated with citizenship.

However, all these categories cut across the biggest group of all, who have, since the very invention of the role of citizenship, been deprived of civic equality. This group, of course, is the female half of the population.

Feminist perspectives

Statements of bald fact sometimes hide small exceptions to that truth. Such is the assertion that in the ancient, medieval and early modern eras women were not, nor were considered ever likely to be, citizens at all.

Two examples will help to show that this was not universally true. The first is late fifth- to early fourth-century Athens. Although they were excluded from citizenship in the proper sense of the term, the matter of women's political interest, capacity and influence was certainly being aired. Aristophanes wrote two plays on the theme, namely *Lysistrata* (in which the women are peace-making heroines) and *Women in Parliament*. Some years later Plato, writing about his concepts of Guardian and Ruler classes in *The Republic*, had this to say: 'for the purpose of keeping watch over the commonwealth, woman has the same nature as man, save in so far as she is weaker'; and, of the elite Rulers, 'All I have been saying applies just as much to any women who are found to have the necessary gifts' (Plato, 1941, v.455 and vii.540). Though, true, the more commonly held contrary opinion was voiced unequivocally by Aristotle.

The second example is taken from the haphazard system of parliamentary representation in England in the Middle Ages and the early modern period. Candidates were often chosen by the constituency landowner(s); and because of the limited franchise this sometimes meant effectively nominating the MP. In the Middle Ages abbesses are known to have named representatives, and in the reign of Elizabeth I two women who 'owned' boroughs returned the MPs. Not until 1644 did the distinguished lawyer Sir Edward Coke lay it down that 'all they that have no freehold . . . and all women having freehold or no freehold should be barred from the electoral process' (see Fraser, 1984, pp. 259–60).

The reference to property ownership is crucial. As a virtually general rule two considerations precluded women from being citizens in the full sense until a century or so ago. One was that women could rarely legally own real estate, while the ownership of property was the precondition of the franchise. The other was that women were considered incapable of engagement in politics. Aristotle proclaimed the latter opinion with conviction: 'The slave', he declared, 'is entirely without the faculty of deliberation; the female indeed possesses it, but in a form which remains inconclusive [i.e. inoperative]' (Aristotle, 1948, 1260a). Furthermore, the prejudice of women's intellectual inferiority was later sustained for centuries in the western world by the views of the Christian churches. Women's emancipation had to overcome these two impediments, both legal constraints and psychological assumptions.

The rejection of even the very occasional opportunity for women to involve themselves in elections in England was paralleled on the continent from the Middle Ages to the sixteenth century by a gradual exclusion of women from forms of civil and economic citizenship which they had sometimes formerly enjoyed. This resulted particularly from the firming up of the guild system, which denied women membership. Not until the eighteenth century did women in some countries demand rights alongside men and start effectively to participate in political affairs, for it was not only the men who were enthused by and swept up in the radical and revolutionary atmosphere, especially in France and Britain. In 1792 the first thorough exposition of the feminist case was published; this was Mary Wollstonecraft's *Vindication of the Rights of Woman*.

Wollstonecraft was clearly wrestling with what has been referred to as her 'dilemma' – a dichotomy in her feminist aims which still burdens the minds and consciences of feminist writers. On the one hand, she insists: 'When I treat of the peculiar duties of women, as I should treat of the peculiar duties of citizen or father, it will be found that I do not mean to insinuate that they should be taken out of their families.' On the other hand, she asserts that 'in order to render their private virtue a public benefit, they must have a civil existence in the State, single or married.' How, then, faithfully to discharge the duties of the two personae? She tries to resolve the dilemma by declaring that a 'wife, also an active citizen' – notice the echo of Sieyes – 'should be equally intent to manage her family, educate her children, and assist her neighbours' (Wollstonecraft, 1975, pp. 155, 262, 259). The bias, even so, is more towards the domestic than the public role. But, as we shall ask below, is that citizenship?

In the nineteenth century concerns about the condition of women found expression in two main forms. One was the contribution of European socialist, including Marxist, thinkers. The other was the practical campaigning for women's rights, confined mainly to the USA, Britain and Scandinavia. But even in those countries, advocacy and achievement alike were slow, hesitant and piecemeal. Various objectives were defined: to promote female leadership for the achievement of moral reform; to open up much fairer educational and employment opportunities for women; to liberate married women from their legal subordination to their husbands; and to acquire full rights of political participation. The last two of these items are especially germane to any definition of citizenship and therefore warrant a little detail.

In his exposition of the English law and constitution in the mid-eighteenth century, Blackstone bleakly declared: 'By marriage the husband and wife are one person in law; that is, the very being or legal existence of the woman is suspended during the marriage or at least is incorporated and consolidated into that of the husband' (see Kramnick, in Wollstonecraft, 1975, p. 34). Naturally this 'civil death' of the woman on entering the marriage contract included the loss of any right personally to hold property. Not until 1882 in England was this particular position reversed.

However, male-dominated societies and institutions, including, of course, legislatures, were not always by any means sympathetic to improving the lot of women. The notable exception to this widespread male attitude was John Stuart Mill, who wrote *The Subjection of Women* in 1861 (though it was not published until 1869) and who, six years later, moved (unsuccessfully) in the House of Commons that the franchise be extended to women. Suffragist movements in Britain and the USA succeeded in publicizing their cause; but it was the contribution of women to the war effort during the First World War that effectively won them their rights – by the Nineteenth Amendment to the US Constitution in 1920 and by British Acts of Parliament in 1918 and 1928. Yet these changes had been preceded by reforms in New Zealand (1893), Australia (1902) and Norway (1913). In France, in contrast, where women proudly bore the title '*citoyenne*' during the Revolution and where Marianne is the symbol of national pride, women had ironically to wait until 1945–6 for political equality: 'equal rights with men in all spheres' was the formula written into the Preamble of the Constitution of the Fourth Republic. Meanwhile, in Switzerland, where the cantonal system had become a byword for (male) democracy, female suffrage was lengthily delayed until 1971.

However, the right to vote, albeit a basic civic right, needs to be supplemented by the representation of women in legislatures if they are to arrive at full citizenly stature. Except in the Nordic countries, women have been slow to seek and/or gain election. For example, in 1994 women accounted for 41 per cent of the Swedish Riksdag, compared with only 9 per cent of British MPs (though in 1997 the British proportion was doubled).

Some feminists, nevertheless, would not now place such heavy emphasis on civil and political citizenship. This is partly because the campaigns in these fields have been largely won; but partly too because the characteristic nature of their sex and their child-bearing function tends to focus women's attention on the social and economic facets of citizenship. Since the mid-1960s, indeed, a great deal of thought has been devoted to the feminist agenda. Or, rather, agendas; for the subject, even when viewed just from the perspective of citizenship, has generated a number of different interpretations of women's rights and needs. It is scarcely surprising that women became especially conscious of their condition of second-class citizens at this time; after all, so many individuals, groups and peoples with grievances protested and rebelled in 1968.

Three main strands of feminist thinking may be traced from the 1960s, sometimes referred to as the 'second wave' to distinguish the period from the nineteenth century. The first strand is liberal feminism, which derives its concern for women's freedom and individualism from the tradition laid down by the likes of Wollstonecraft and Mill. Secondly, socialist feminism takes its inspiration from Fourier, Engels and Marx, accusing the male-dominated family and economic production systems as the sources of women's suppression. Thirdly, we may identify radical feminism, which develops the socialist agenda by attacking the whole structure of society as patriarchal, that is, entirely determined by male interests.

These programmes therefore stretch across the whole spectrum from a reforming agenda to one that is veritably revolutionary. And behind

91

these sociological analyses lie the fundamental alternatives: Do women wish to be treated equally with men in the sense of the same, or in the sense of equivalence? However, most feminists would adhere to two basic principles. These are the cardinal importance of the quality of life and the artificiality of the distinction between the private and public arenas.

With regard to the specific matter of citizenship, a feminist's answer to two key questions will be coloured by her doctrinal starting-point. These questions are as follows. Should women continue to strive to be full citizens or ignore the status of citizenship and pursue their interests by other means? And should women seek to change the very nature of citizenship?

There are, therefore, many dimensions to the feminist perspective on citizenship. In the brief space available here, let us concentrate on four issues. These are: the problem of the male shaping of the citizenship idea; the differences between the male and female approaches to social and political matters; women's need for citizenship; and the need of citizenship as an ideal and a status for women's full incorporation.

The civic republican tradition of citizenship was built upon the assumption and practice that being a citizen is a uniquely male function. The whole ethos was antipathetic to women. One feminist writer has expressed this point forcibly:

> Founded by men, the modern state and its public realm of citizenship paraded as universal values and norms which were derived from specifically masculine experience: militarist norms of honor and homoerotic camaraderie; respectful competition and bargaining among independent agents; discourse framed in unemotional tones of dispassionate reason.
>
> *(Iris Marion Young, in Beiner, 1995, p. 179)*

Obviously, this citizenship style has been mellowed by the influence of the liberal tradition. Yet the attitude lingers. Doctrinaires of the neo-liberal school have stressed enterprise and self-help, but in reality, it is argued, this all too often means men having the opportunities to be enterprising and women having the responsibilities of helping those left uncared for by a weakened welfare state.

The basic problem, as feminist commentators have complained, is that the stereotype of bifurcated sexual roles is still deeply rooted. In the *polis* the man was the public being leaving the home to perform his civic functions; the woman was the private being, staying in the home to perform her domestic and familial functions. Moreover, traditional roles are reinforced by different natures. Women have the caring and emotional qualities suited to the private sphere; men have the competitive and rational qualities suited to the public sphere. So the argument has persisted down to our own times. Three feminist reactions flow from such traditions.

One is that the persistence of these practices and assumptions is wrong: women's domestication has developed over the centuries, not because they are less well suited to public life but because men have enforced this dualism of the public and the private. Following this protesting interpretation, women should demand change – by insisting that men share domestic duties and that the state and/or employers provide the facilities (e.g. crèches) so that women can be free to pursue public lives alongside men.

The second reaction is that these traditions are valid: women *are* different, biologically and psychologically – and, proclaiming their positive characteristics, they should proudly but determinedly require the system to be changed. But the change should not be along the lines of the first reaction, of enabling women to become full citizens in the conventional male sense. Rather, the whole concept and practice of citizenship should be adapted in order to accommodate a feminine quality. Such a programme would involve fudging the age-old distinction between the public and the private. This can be achieved in two ways: by recognizing that women's caring work is a category of citizenship as much as, say, involvement in party politics; and by enhancing the effectiveness of neighbourhood, civil society activities – which women already willingly and efficiently engage in – as a bridge between the public and private spheres of life.

Thirdly, the attitudes that citizenship has for most of its history been a male domain, and that women should properly be confined to the private area can even provoke the extreme response of rejecting citizenship as a status too distorted away from the female mode of life. Yet there are cogent arguments against the exclusion of women – enforced or voluntary – from the roll of citizens.

The first argument is simply stated. No one doubts that women have benefited in the past from the winning of various civic rights. As two authorities on the subject have stated, democratic welfare states everywhere would look very different if their development had not coincided with the growth of women's movements and women's acquisition of citizenship rights – political as well as social rights. By working with and within other political and intellectual currents of the time as well as by insisting upon their own unique contributions to society at large, they ensured that women's needs were incorporated into policymaking.

(see Lister, 1997, p. 169)

Nor would anyone deny that men still, generally speaking, enjoy a privileged position *vis-à-vis* women in most societies. But, continuing the argument, women would be well advised to persevere in their fight for greater civic equality – however one may wish to define 'equality'. The reason is that this policy is likely to bring more just rewards than the alternative, namely, a policy of isolation from the norm of citizenship and attempts at improvements through arguments for complete differentiation. Maternalism is not enough. Metaphors come readily to mind with images of unpalatable grapes and the severing of noses.

It is accepted that citizenship rights must be bolstered by more equal opportunities – and not only for women. Even in western countries, where the status of women has been incomparably improved over the past century – let alone African and Asian countries, where little progress has been achieved – further reforms can be easily envisaged. Much greater state provision of dependant-care (for children, the sick and the elderly) would afford many women the extra time and energy necessary for a fuller social, economic and political life. Devolution of more decision-making down to parish or ward level would enable and encourage more women to participate in public affairs. Obviously, women would gain from developments like these and become citizens in a fuller sense. But in addition society generally would enjoy the positive effects of their contributions.

In other words, the institution of citizenship needs a more complete association of women as much as women need to be complete citizens. This is the second argument against the exclusion of women from citizenship. Women have contributed much in the past and could contribute even more in the future. A paper by a European Union body, stressing the political need for women's full involvement in political processes, illustrates this position:

A balanced representation of women and men at all levels of decision-making guarantees better government. . . . [Women] have different values and ideas and behave differently. Increased participation of women in decision-making will create a new political culture and shed new light on how power should be exercised.

(see Lister, 1997, pp. 158–9)

One field in which women have displayed their caring, non-competitive nature has so far gone unmentioned in this outline, namely, concern for the environment. Although this is not, of course, to suggest that all men are unconcerned about 'green' issues, feminists have claimed a special interest in conservation at both local and planetary levels.

Maybe women are less nationalistically minded than men. Conversely, nationalism, as an ideology, has tended to view women as basically 'biological reproducers'. Nazism is a notorious example. Even the liberal British Beveridge Report cited as a major reason for introducing child benefits the need to encourage child-bearing lest the 'British race' suffer a perilous numerical decline. So, even when citizenship is identified with nationality, women have often had separate and distinct experiences from the male half of humanity.

Citizenship as nationality: origins

For two hundred years citizenship and nationality have been political Siamese twins. Before the late eighteenth century the relationship was much looser than we have been accustomed to assume, and the connection is loosening again in our own age as multiple and world citizenships become increasingly evident. Without delving too deeply into the historical pattern, let us just indicate how this adhesion occurred.

In the mid-eighteenth century four ideas central to our purpose coexisted in European political thought: cosmopolitanism, citizenship, patriotism and nation. The first three derived from the classical revival of the mini-renaissance of the Enlightenment – cosmopolitanism from the Stoic tradition; citizenship and patriotism from the civic republican. Cosmopolitanism was held as an unspecific feeling of the essential unity and harmony of humankind. Citizenship was an assertion of freedom from arbitrary power, and usually intimately bound up with patriotism, the sense of loyalty to and duty to defend one's state. A nation was a group of people speaking the same language and not necessarily synonymous with the population of a state.

An individual could think of himself as a cosmopolitan, a citizen-patriot and a member of a nation simultaneously as different identities yet with neither a sense of inner contradiction nor of a need for close bonds. There was nevertheless a loose linkage relating them all. Cosmopolitanism stressed the importance of the individual in the universal order and therefore connected to the civic ideal of a citizen's freedom and equality with his fellows. Patriotism was a crucial element in the republican concept of citizenship; indeed, it was widely held that true patriotism was impossible without the freedom that was guaranteed by the status of citizen. Nor was patriotism a necessary antithesis to cosmopolitanism as long as one honoured one's enemies and did not sink into rank pride and xenophobia. The concept of nation could also sit happily with cosmopolitanism; for the linguistic and cultural divisions of humankind were not deeply cleft antagonisms, merely expressions of the 'spirits' of the several nations (a term coined in France by Montesquieu and in Germany by Moser).

But not only could these four concepts live in concord with each other, they in essence together represented a mode of thought and feeling opposed to the autocratic and aristocratic political reality of the time – whatever some privileged propagandists might have averred to the contrary.

The word 'nation' was not, in fact, very commonly used until the mid-century. From then, however, it was to be heard with increasing frequency and with adaptations of meaning. Its development in France is especially instructive, where '*nation*' came to be synonymous with '*patrie*' and '*peuple*'. It connoted the unity of the French people and its territory, fusing the classes and provinces. In their battle with the monarchy the privileged and politically ambitious *parlements* used '*nation*' in contradistinction to '*roi*': they claimed to stand for the interests of the *nation* against the abuse of royal power. Rousseau, on the other hand, employed this new sense of the word for a totally different purpose. In his recommendations for systems of government for Corsica and Poland he revealed his conviction that a sense of nationhood is an essential binding force for the people of a country in the modern world.

It was the Abbé Sieyes, however, who constructed the modern French definition of nation and, in so doing, invested it with a clear political meaning inextricably bonded to the concept of citizenship. In August 1788 he wrote:

> Already the patriotic and enlightened citizens, who for so long have looked with sadness and indignation upon all these millions of men heaped together without order or design, give themselves some hope. They believe in the power of circumstances; they finally see the moment arrive for us to become a *nation*.
>
> *(see Forsyth, 1987, p. 69)*

This was a transforming notion and furnished the French Revolution with its political impetus. Exactly a year later the Declaration of the Rights of Man and the Citizen included the assertion that 'The principle of all sovereignty rests essentially in the nation.' *'Patrie'* and *'nation'* became interchangeable; citizenship, patriotism and nationhood were melded into a powerful and emotionally charged political force. The body of citizenry, identified as the nation, was endowed with sovereignty in both its external and internal guises. Nationally defined citizens formed a whole, undivided and integrated state differentiated from all others, the consummation of the post-medieval nation-state and the Westphalian state-system. In Sieyes's words, 'The Nation is prior to everything. It is the source of everything. Its will is always legal; indeed it is the law itself' (Sieyes, 1963, p. 124).

No longer were citizenship, patriotism and nationhood separate ideas. And what of world citizenship? The weakest of the four ideas in any case, it was bound to be squeezed out of existence by this new national-citizenship. Even so, its disappearance in the late eighteenth century was a gradual process. For example, attempts were made by some French revolutionary figures to retain it with their new doctrinal amalgam. Some were temperamentally and intellectually able to accommodate their revolutionary nationalist patriotic zeal with a cosmopolitan idealism by arguing that the French nation's destiny was to rid the world of tyranny. Robespierre, for example, notable for his constant use of *'nation'* rather than *'patrie'*, nevertheless lambasted those who drafted the Declaration of Rights for the (stillborn) 1793 Constitution for having 'utterly forgotten to recall the duties of fraternity which should unite all men and all nations'. The different peoples of the world, he declared, 'must help one another . . . as though they were citizens of one and the same State' (Bouloiseau et al., 1952, pp. 463, 469).

A variation on this theme emerged, too, in Germany, especially in Prussia. The German notion of citizenship remained stuck in the Middle Ages, as the very language indicated: '*Bürger*' had to do service for 'citizen' as well as for a member of the urban middle class, 'burgher'. For, in so far as there was a citizenly role in the eighteenth-century German states, it was performed at the town level. Palmer has suggested that many burghers were straining to achieve a style of citizenship less constricted than this municipal meaning. Lacking a national state, they adopted the term '*Weltbürger*', citizen of the world, to indicate their urge for broader civic horizons (Palmer, 1964, p. 431). Intellectuals, too, naturally absorbed the cosmopolitan ethos of the *Aufklärung*.

But intellectuals – Herder and Fichte are notable examples – were also defining a German style of nationalist thinking. Yet the eighteenth-century harmonious relationship of nationality, cosmopolitanism and citizenship still held its appeal. Fichte, posthumously famous for his nationalistic *Addresses to the German Nation*, delivered in 1807–8, attempted a synthesis (in the Seventh Address) of the three concepts through an effectively devised German civic education. He explained that 'the genuine German art of the state' will produce, by education, 'a firm and certain spirit'; and this political art 'will not turn, as foreign countries do, to the solitary peak, the prince, but to the broad plain which is the nation'. The modern Germans will then become like the Greeks who 'founded citizenship on education and trained such citizens as succeeding ages have never seen' – but with a difference, for the German approach 'will be characterized by a spirit that is . . . universal and cosmopolitan' (Fichte, 1968, p. 99).

But it did not last. The ideological force of nationalism inexorably drew the concept of citizenship into it and made the civic principle part of itself.

It is often observed that this conflation of the two concepts of nation and citizen was a legacy of the French Revolution. True; but the matter is a little more complex than such a bald statement might suggest. The revolutionaries' idea of citizenship rested upon two traditions, not one. The legal language of the Declaration of Rights derived from Lockean contract theory: it concerns the standing and entitlements of the citizen as an individual. The hortatory language to love and defend *la patrie* or *la nation* derived from the civic republican tradition: it views the citizen as a member, a part of the community. It is this latter strand that bound citizen and nation so tightly together. Moreover, by calling on both traditions, modern citizenship became a coherent package containing rights, duties and a sense of tradition, community and identity.

And so, during the past two centuries citizenship and nationhood have become synthesized and have drawn mutual strength from this symbiotic relationship.

Citizenship and nationality synthesized

By *c.*1800, in Britain, the distended French Republic and the USA, citizenship and nationality were to all intents and purposes synonymous, or at the least, two sides of the same political coin. And so they have remained – for the whole world. In diplomatic language citizens of a given state are frequently referred to as 'nationals'; and on a British passport, for example, the bearer finds the description: 'National status/ nationalité: British Citizen'. In academic discourse, one of the most distinguished analysts of nationality and nationalism partly defines a nation as a *'group featuring common citizenship rights'* (Smith, 1971, p. 175).

This much is commonly recognized. However, the details of the connection are often passed over with little comment; yet they most usefully illuminate the questions, What is citizenship? and Who are citizens? The structure of this section is formed by an analysis and interpretation of these details, for readers' consideration. The main thrust of the interpretation is as follows. The collapse of the *ancien régime* in North America and Europe in the eighteenth and nineteenth centuries and of the imperial regimes in Asia and Africa in the twentieth was accompanied by a reformulation of the principles of nationality and citizenship. This reformulation was partly the cause and partly the effect of the revolutionary changes. Moreover, it was a reflection of the transition from the concept of monarchical or imperial government to popular sovereignty, and from a privileged to a mass, democratic style of political legitimacy and activity.

99

In this process of reformulation, citizenship and nationalism mutually profited as political ideas and practices by their being harnessed together for the political shaping of the modern era. The three main benefits were freedom, cohesion and allegiance. We shall examine each of these in turn in order to discover how the proponents of citizenship and nationalism effected their interaction, promotion and achievement.

First, freedom. Nationalism pronounces the right of the nation (however defined) to be free to seek its own destiny – freedom from a stultifying regime, freedom from the colonial condition, freedom to unite with scattered brethren, freedom to secede from culturally or politically uncomfortable union with those who are deemed 'different'. Citizenship too is founded on a basis of freedom, the freedom of citizens to participate in shaping the fortunes of their own state, unhindered by partial interests, partial being understood in both its meanings. This civic freedom is best upheld by the doctrine of the sovereignty of the people.

These two expressions of freedom, interpreted in their own ways by the two ideas of nationalism and citizenship, became amalgamated in the principle of national self-determination. The individual's national identity and citizenly role coincide most obviously when citizens vote in plebiscites to determine the allocation of territory, the possession of which is disputed between two nation-states. The case for the inextricable connection of freedom, citizenship and nationality was expressed with characteristic lucidity by John Stuart Mill. He declared that

> Free institutions are next to impossible in a country made up of different nationalities. Among a people without fellow-feeling, especially if they read and speak different languages, the united public opinion, necessary to the working of representative government cannot exist.
>
> *(Mill, 1910, p. 364)*

Mill is also stressing the need for a coherent populace. This feature of the nationalism–citizenship relationship – the second of what we have called the benefits of the relationship – is more complex than that of freedom, and it is necessary to distinguish four aspects, namely cohesion against divisive privilege, cohesion for equalization and standardization, cohesion by unification and cohesion by cultural homogeneity.

100

Nationalism is incompatible with privileged interest-group identities. In *ancien régime* German states, for example, many aristocrats felt a stronger bond with French aristocrats than with their own peasants. Today a British businessman of a multinational company may feel a stronger bond with his American opposite number than with workers in his British factory or office. Such links strain the sense of national cohesion. Similarly, citizenship, as we have already noticed in this chapter, is predicated on the principle of equality. Marked class divisions are incompatible with this principle and impede the realization of the ideal.

Both nationalism and citizenship therefore require political institutions which enfeeble privilege and enhance cohesion. They were no empty statements when the framers of the French Constitution of 1791, while asserting that all citizens are equal in the eyes of the law, wrote that 'The kingdom is one and indivisible' and that sovereignty 'belongs to the nation; no section of the people nor any individual can attribute its exercise to themselves'. The dissolution of the provincial Estates and *parlements* and the discontinuation of the ancient Estates-General representative system were methods of replacing privilege with national and civic cohesion. Before 1791 only Britain and the American colonies had parliamentary institutions in the elections for which citizens voted for representatives on a territorial rather than a class, estates basis (i.e. clergy, nobility and the bulk of the populace). The victory of the national/citizenship principle of cohesion against privilege ensured that this system rapidly spread.

One particular element in this transition to citizenship-based political institutions requires comment: this is the belief that functional institutions were injurious to the anti-privilege cohesive principle. Rousseau worried that 'sectional associations' would be destructive of the General Will, divert the citizen's attention from his direct connection with the state by the pursuit of private interests (Rousseau, 1968, II.3). During the French Revolution, proposing his law to abolish guilds and corporations and to forbid workers' associations, Le Chapelier voiced similar misgivings and urged that 'No one shall be allowed to induce in citizens an intermediary interest, to separate them from the public good by a corporate spirit' (Thompson, 1948, p. 83). All very logical, but if persisted in, this attitude would have undermined the tradition of civil society. As a consequence, that option for the display

101

of citizenship, the importance of which will be discussed in the next chapter, would have been foreclosed.

Privilege means differentiation by class divisions and provincial particularism, perhaps even group interests; nationalism and citizenship imply equality and standardization – our next aspect of cohesion. In *ancien régime* Europe, law, administration, education were not always standardized throughout the state. Similarly, colonial regimes in Africa did not always provide equal treatment for the component 'tribes' of a given colony.

We may adduce two very different examples where nationalistically conscious new governments invoked the status of citizenship to bolster the cohesion of their states by equalization and standardization. Our first example is drawn from nineteenth-century Europe, our second, from twentieth-century Africa.

In 1868 the government of the newly autonomous Kingdom of Hungary in the Austro-Hungarian Empire issued a Law of Nationalities. It declared that 'all citizens of Hungary, both in virtue of the principles of the Constitution, and from a political point of view, form a single nation . . . and enjoy equal rights.' However, six main languages were spoken in the kingdom, yet 'the demands of administration and the prompt execution of justice' required the use of a single tongue, namely Magyar. A compromise in this case had to be reached between the cohesive efficiency of standardization and 'the equality of rights of all citizens of the country in all other respects' (see Macartney, 1934, pp. 119–20).

Nearly a century later, the Gold Coast became independent under the name of Ghana. Its leader, Nkrumah, concerned at the inheritance of unequally provided provinces of which the new state was composed, made a speech in the run-up to independence in which he explained his policy to meet these circumstances, especially the poorer educational facilities in the Northern Territories.

> I entirely repudiate [he declared] the idea of there being first and second class citizens in the new Ghana. We are determined in the new constitution provision shall be made so that all the people of Ghana, irrespective of whether they come from the Northern Territories, Ashanti, Togoland or the Colony, have the same rights and the same opportunities.
>
> *(Nkrumah, 1961, p. 76)*

102

Nation-creation and building required the construction of coherence through civic and national equality and standardization.

These features are easier to achieve if a country is culturally homogeneous. This is the third of our cohering factors. In spite of the frequent and credible distinction that is made between cultural nationalism and political nationalism, the cultural element in the ideology can never be completely discounted. The force of tradition, ethnicity and language in shaping a nation cannot be gainsaid. These factors, in turn, have an influence on the nature of citizenship. Both psychological and practical considerations that follow from this connection must be taken into account. In other words: Can a person truly be a citizen in an age of nation-states without feeling and behaving as part of the national culture? And can a person perform the necessary functions of a citizen without knowing the language and procedures of the national community? We may usefully remind ourselves of Mill's opinion on this matter which has already been quoted. There are, in consequence, pressures on citizens to conform to the national pattern.

The most famous example of this form of cohering is the USA, which, through successive waves of immigration of epic proportions in the nineteenth century, became, in Walt Whitman's words, 'not merely a nation but a teeming Nation of nations'. While many remained 'hyphenated Americans' – Irish-American, Italian-American, for instance – it was usual for them to feel a pride in their common American citizenship. Immigrants became citizens legally through the process of naturalization and by sentiment through the 'melting-pot' processes of education and the learning of English. And, of course, it goes without saying that the process of cultural homogenization would have been impossible without the operation of the *jus soli* mode of defining nationality/citizenship.

The desire of the nation-state for some cultural homogeneity is also drawn from the feeling that the state needs to be stabilized by being unified. And so we come to the fourth aspect in our list of benefits produced by cohesion. We have already hinted at this factor in the quotation from Dr Nkrumah above. The task in Ghana of effectively unifying a country which had neither ethnic homogeneity nor a tradition of unity was replicated in many former colonies – India, even after partition, and Nigeria are obvious illustrations of this. But the problems of unification have not been confined to post-imperial states:

103

we may cite the examples of Italy, Germany, Czechoslovakia and Yugoslavia in Europe. These European unifications satisfied the nationalist aspirations of the likes of Cavour, Bismarck, Masaryk and Pašić. But how do nationalist unification movements and policies relate to citizenship?

To answer this question it is necessary to understand the term 'unification' in a much more generalized way than the examples already given. The unificatory process of nation-building was occurring, in the eighteenth and nineteenth centuries, even in Britain and France, which could claim to have been nation-states since, say, *c.*1600. Yet a unified sense of Britishness needed the Act of Union between England and Scotland and the wars with France to be cemented (temporarily?) in place; and in France the nationalistic fervour and policies of the Revolutionary and Napoleonic period performed a similar function.

In the modern world, those pushing forward the cohering process of unification so crucial for a consolidated nation-state have no option but to call upon the mass enthusiastic support of the populace, mobilized for civil or military purposes as the case may be. '*Aux armes, citoyens!*' This marshalling of the masses is effected by the creation of emotive symbols and 'invented traditions', by indoctrination or the more gentle socialization functions of the school – and by treating all the people as citizens. By persuading citizens to identify with a unified nation-state, rather than a province (or a previous state in a recently unified state), nationalism secures the cohesion of legitimacy and citizenship secures the cohesion of transmuted and strengthened patriotic virtue.

Mazzini expressed in his own mystical language the notion of citizens legitimizing the political nation. In the new era of national self-determination he saw dawning, he explained, 'Natural divisions, the innate spontaneous tendencies of the peoples will replace the arbitrary divisions of bad government.' However, the unification of Italy could 'only be fulfilled by a NATIONAL CONTRACT, dictated in Rome by a constituent assembly . . . and by all the citizens that Italy contains. The National Contract is the inauguration, the baptism of the nation' (Mazzini, 1961, pp. 52, 236).

The point about patriotic virtue brings us, after the surveys of the benefits of freedom and cohesion, to the last one, namely the benefit of allegiance. As we have seen in chapter 2, a vital strand in the republican tradition of citizenship has been a sense of patriotic commitment and duty. This is a virtue, a mark of the good citizen. The nationalist can argue that the emotionally uplifting love of one's nation adds an intensity which has improved upon the obsolete state patriotism. The distinction was quite clear in Fichte's mind, as he scanned the scene of a German fatherland divided into many states. 'The more . . . anyone was affected and animated by that higher interest [i.e. love of fatherland]', he announced, 'the better citizen also he was for the particular German state, in which his immediate sphere of action lay.' However, 'The dark and confused idea of a separate patriotism is an offspring of lies and clumsy flattery' (see Engelbrecht, 1968, p. 98). What would be described in today's jargon as 'over the top', but there is no escaping the message!

The citizen's loyalty to his nation is especially tested in time of war. And so we have Coleridge – incidentally illustrating the emergence of a British sense of nationhood and citizenship – declaring in 1800, 'Is the nation in danger? Every man is called into play; every man feels his interest as a *citizen* predominating over his individual interests' (see Colley, 1992, p. 313).

But the nation needs the loyalty of its citizens in peace as well as war; moreover, its need is especially pressing if that loyalty is in serious doubt. Symbols and schools are the most common peaceful means of summoning up that loyalty. Take the example of Nigeria after the horrendous war of attempted Biafran secession. One Nigerian educationist has stated that the conflict 'highlighted the role the schools should play in inculcating the values of national consciousness and citizenship education in the youth' (Adeyoyin, 1979, p. 164). And six years after the end of the civil war, the federal government, directly copying US practice, introduced into schools the reciting of a National Pledge and Flag Salute Ceremonies.

However, a more comprehensive survey of the role of education in the making of citizens must be postponed to chapter 5. Meanwhile, we need to continue our focus on nationality by examining the two contrasting policies states have adopted in defining whom they will accept as citizens.

National citizens: made or born

Nationalism as a modern ideology sprang from two distinct sources. And as these two streams of thought mingled with the concept of citizenship, so two main variants of national citizenship have flowed down to our own times.

One tradition defines nationality in political terms. Sieyes posed the question: 'What is a Nation?' He answered: 'A body of associates living under *common* laws and represented by the same *legislative assembly* etc.' (Sieyes, 1963, p. 58). This approach characterized the French style of nationalist thinking: no hint of the need of a common language, tradition or 'race' in the make-up of a nation. In strong contrast, and in parallel with this French Revolutionary interpretation, there emerged the German Romantic notion of the *Volk.* According to this belief individuals are bonded into a *völkisch* nation by a mystical 'essence' related to their natural environment, and by the early nineteenth century German nationalist writers were expressing thoughts about the 'purity' of their language and people.

These distinct views of the nature of nationhood – the one juridico-political and territorial, the other, ethno-cultural and heritable – reinforced by the French preference for *jus soli* and the German, for *jus sanguinis*, shaped the contrasting French and German interpretations of citizenship down to the end of the twentieth century. Thus France has tended to pursue assimilationist policies for immigrants, while Germany has been reluctant to welcome non-German immigrants into the full civic status at all. On the French model citizens can be made; on the German, they must be born.

The key period in France for the consolidation of its policy of assimilation was the 1880s. Non-francophones in the provinces and immigrants of whatever origin were all made French citizens in the fullest sense by teaching the French language and stiffening allegiance to the French nation-state through the institution of compulsory primary education and military service. Furthermore, in 1889 the status of citizenship as allowed by *jus soli*, hitherto unavailable until the third generation, was extended to second-generation immigrants. The French attitude to colonial peoples has reflected the same inclusive view of citizenship, at least, in theory. After the Second World War the Empire was renamed the French Union in the Constitution of the Fourth Republic, and Art. 80 of that document could not have made more manifest its inclusive definition of citizenship: 'All nationals of the overseas territories have the status of citizens, on the same basis as French nationals of Metropolitan France or the overseas territories.'

In contrast with the history of France, Germans became nationally self-conscious before they constituted a state; and then, when that occurred, Bismarck's pragmatism left many of the German *Volk* outside the Hohenzollern Empire. The feeling that these 'outside Germans' should be given due consideration led to a law in 1913 which accorded them and their descendants an indefinite claim to German citizenship, consolidating the German tradition of *jus sanguinis*. The mirror-image of this policy, namely the tendency to deny non-Germans access to German citizenship, was taken to its extreme in the Reich Citizenship Law, promulgated as part of the notorious Nuremberg Laws in 1935. This stated: 'A citizen of the Reich may be only that subject who is of German or kindred blood.' The conscience-stricken post-war German states strove to expunge Nazi racism. However, by the 1990s, with the 1913 law still in place, nearly a tenth of Germany's population were foreigners, many paying taxes but denied the vote.

At the end of the twentieth century, at a time of increased population movement, the persistence of these distinct traditions in two major European states was thrown into sharp relief. The following figures are revealing:

> The overall rate of civic incorporation for immigrants is ten times higher in France than in Germany. . . . A generation of young Franco-Portuguese, Franco-Algerians and Franco-Moroccans is emerging, claiming and exercising the rights of French citizenship. In Germany, by contrast, more than one and a half million Turks – including more than 400,000 who were born in Germany – remain outside the community of citizens. Yet at the same time, newly arrived ethnic German immigrants from Eastern Europe and the Soviet Union – over a million in 1988–91 – are legally defined as Germans and automatically granted full civic and political rights.
>
> *(Brubaker, 1992, p. x)*

Although France and Germany, because of their long distinct traditions, are obvious exemplars of the political and ethnic alternatives to defining national citizenship, three important supplementary observations are essential. One is that other countries have followed each of the two trends. The second is that the 'German' model finds increasing support in an age of renewed heightened ethnic and national consciousness. The third is that, ironically in the light of this observation,

107

a new German government in 1998 planned drastically and controversially to reform the citizenship laws, with the aim of giving some three million of the seven and a half million immigrants full citizenship status. Of particular importance was the proposed concession of dual citizenship, most welcomed by the Turkish people resident in Germany. Because many of those who would be accommodated by the changes are Muslim, the social and cultural implications were far-reaching: the plans cut at the very root of German national self-identity. The scheme aroused considerable hostility and a less radical plan was being considered in 1999.

The most obvious example of the political-assimilationist form of national citizenship is the USA, as we have seen in the previous section of this chapter. Yet even the USA has, on occasions, demonstrated a reluctance to offer citizenship with its customary generosity to those considered to be culturally alien. First, in 1882 the Chinese Exclusion Act both precluded resident Chinese from naturalization and barred that form of trans-Pacific immigration; thus stemming, as it was seen, a source of adulteration of American citizenship. (Australia provides an interesting parallel. Two decades later the 'White Australia' policy was inaugurated, aimed mainly at excluding Asians.) Early in the twentieth century in the USA there quickly followed general laws imposing a literacy test and quotas for non-Western Hemisphere immigrants.

Whereas the USA came partially to close the 'golden door' that had initially been open to the 'tired, poor, huddled masses', the state of Israel, after its creation, opened its portals on a most careful reading of *jus sanguinis*. The 1950 Law of Return gave all Jews the right to migrate to Israel. Two years later, the Law of Citizenship very deliberately conferred on Jewish immigrants Jewish, not Israeli citizenship, and specified that Arabs in the state were of Arab nationality, not Israeli citizens. Since then, the Arabs (Palestinians) living in Israel have remained discriminated against, treated as second-class citizens. It is an awkward, almost apartheid-type anomaly, deriving from the impossibility of reconciling the contradictions in Ben-Gurion's independence speech. In this, while proclaiming Israel a Jewish state, he promised 'complete equality of social and political rights to all its inhabitants, irrespective of religion, race or sex'.

The Jewish Law of Return was a call to the Diaspora to populate Eretz Israel. No similar invitation has been extended to the sixty million people of the Russian diaspora, who, on the disintegration of the Soviet Union, found themselves in the non-Russian successor states. The doubtful civic condition of these minorities in the Baltic states of Estonia and Latvia caused both internal and international friction. For example, in 1993 the Council of Europe protested at Estonia's plan to deny full citizenship rights to its Russian population – 30 per cent of the total populace. In Latvia, 34 per cent of the population are Russian-speakers. From independence in 1991 the law classified these people, who settled in the country after the Soviet annexation in 1940, and their descendants, as 'occupiers', and therefore stateless. However, in 1998 the law was relaxed: children born since 1991 of Russian-speaking parents were accorded full citizenship status.

The intensity of national sentiment has, in all these cases, swung popularly supported governments to definitions of citizenship in the ethno-cultural sense: the USA *v.* Chinese, Jews *v.* Palestinians, Baltics *v.* Russians. Even France, the originator of the alternative political definition of nationality and a bastion of *jus soli*, has experienced a reaction against this tradition. Not only has the racist National Front garnered support for its agenda of stripping the settlers from the francophone Caribbean and Maghreb of full citizenship rights; but such a view has won increasing sympathy in the mainstream Gaullist RPR.

Two hundred years after Sieyes formulated his rational, political definition of a nation and thus delineated the modern French conception of citizenship, that formulation is under challenge from the revived emotional charge of the feelings of ethnicity and cultural nationhood. Moreover, this challenge is being thrown down in so many countries. For a variety of reasons, some of which can be traced back centuries, some of which are very recent, most so-called nation-states are in fact today multicultural communities. This very obvious fact raises questions about the assumption, widely held for two hundred years, that citizenship and nationality are and should be synonymous.

Multiculturalism

Initially, it will be helpful to clarify the various demographic conditions covered by the term 'multicultural'. First, there are the peoples who have become ethnic minorities as a result of conquest. These indigenous

	practical problems	moral issues
competence	no/poor command of official/state language	*either* • assimilation by language-learning – undermining minority culture *or* • responsibility of minorities to learn official language as second language
status	*either* • acceptance of minorities' distinctiveness/problems – differential treatment including 'positive discrimination' *or* • policies of integration/homogenization	*either* • differential treatment – unfair to majority? undermining citizenship principle of equality as same *or* • homogenization – loss of valuable culture/could lead to 'ethnic cleansing' undermining citizenship principle of equality as comparable
identity	stress on cultural identity might undermine integrity of state to point of alienation/rebellion/secession	clash between human rights of cultural identity and citizen duty to protect integrity of state

Figure 3.3

peoples or first nations, as they are called, include the Amerindians of the Western Hemisphere, the Inuits of the Arctic and the Aborigines of Australia. Secondly, minorities exist as a result of migrations, enforced or voluntary. Examples of this category are: the people of African origin in the USA, Britain and France; some of the Hispanics in the USA; Muslims of various geographical provenance in several European countries, notably Britain and France; Chinese in several states of the Pacific rim, including Indonesia and Malaysia. The third category are those peoples who are so geographically and politically consolidated as to render the state truly multinational. For example, the Québécois make Canada an Anglo-French state; Belgium is a Walloon–Flemish state; Bosnia has uncertainly emerged as a Serb–Croat–Muslim state; and many African states contain numerous language and tribal groups.

In some states all three categories exist. Canada is a prime example, containing peoples with strong self-identification as Amerindians or Inuits, as immigrants from a number of countries, European and Asian, and as Québécois.

As the great majority of nation-states are in reality multi-ethnic or multinational states, this condition has an inevitable impact on the nature of citizenship. It places three major question marks over the cohesiveness of the state–citizen bond, relating to the citizen's competence, status and identity. We have seen earlier in this chapter how the concept of nationhood tightened the civic ties. As cultural minorities become increasingly politically conscious and active they imperil the cohesiveness of the nation-state and, in consequence, of citizenship. The existence of distinctive minorities presents both moral issues of justice and practical problems of a socio-political kind. Figure 3.3 provides a summary of these difficulties. A little detail will help to show the reality of this abstract presentation.

Citizens should be treated justly by the courts; they should be able to participate as fully as they wish in the political process; they should be able to take advantage of the educational, employment, welfare and health opportunities and provisions of their state. All these aspects of citizenship require communication. How can individuals be citizens in any true sense if they have no comprehension of the official language as used by the law, by the news media, by the schools, by employers, or by the social services? Conversely, how can members of an ethnic or national minority preserve their cultural identity if they lose their language, the quintessence of that identity? The language requirements of citizenship and ethnic nationhood pull in diametrically opposite directions. Governments, of course, can simply ignore the problem: impose a single language. And if some of the state's legal citizens cannot effectively enjoy that status to the full, so much the worse for them: let them learn the official language. An easy solution; yet surely moral considerations enter here and must complicate policy decisions.

By recalling the three categories of minorities identified at the beginning of this section, we can construct a rough pattern. Governments should feel a moral obligation to protect the languages of indigenous peoples by virtue of the fact that they were the original inhabitants. Yet in practice governments are often hostile to the survival of these tongues. Governments should feel a moral obligation to protect the languages of consolidated national minorities, and pragmatic considerations have generally led to this policy. Immigrants present yet a third scenario. Since they have voluntarily moved to a different country, it can be plausibly argued that the onus is upon them to learn the prevailing language of that state – indeed, that they have a civic duty to integrate in this manner. Furthermore, where, as is frequently the case, the several groups of immigrants have arrived in a country from many lands of origin, the host state might be put to some difficulty to provide all the necessary translation facilities.

A few examples. First, about indigenous peoples. Many North American Indian, Uralic and Siberian languages are rapidly becoming moribund, the American Navajo being a notable exception, supported by its own media network. Secondly, consolidated nations within states. In Canada, English and French, and in Belgium, French and Flemish, have equal status as official languages. Thirdly, on the matter of immigrants' languages, the British welfare Benefits Agency prints most of its documents and supplies interpreters in Arabic, Bengali, Chinese, Greek, Gujarati, Hindi, Punjabi, Somali, Turkish, Urdu and Vietnamese. In the USA, however, the large and increasing Spanish-speaking population presents a particularly complex and contentious problem. Some are well-established families (e.g. Chicanos (Mexicans), Puerto Ricans); others are recent immigrants (e.g. Cubans, legal and illegal Mexican immigrants). Some have no wish to learn English; others are eager. To cope with the problem, some schools have arranged to conduct lessons in Spanish, but this policy has raised the prospect that the USA might become a bilingual state like Canada, for instance – a highly unattractive outcome to many.

Language problems therefore raise the issue not just of competence, but of status. If some citizens are identifiably culturally and ethnically different, should they be treated differently; and, if so, what effect would such a policy have on the principle of equality, which lies at the core of citizenship? Also, on what criteria should some citizens be treated separately? Moreover, if a policy of 'positive discrimination', or 'affirmative action' is employed for the few, is that not unfair on the majority? On the other hand, if recognition of differences is not tolerable, then it follows that a policy of homogenization would be pursued. But that road can lead, indeed so often has led, to 'ethnic cleansing'.

Sometimes the request for special treatment is symbolic. In Britain, Sikh motorcyclists secured the right to wear their turbans, not protective helmets as prescribed by law. In France, Muslim schoolgirls have argued their right to cover their heads in class contrary to established practice. Positive discrimination has been used in the USA to give Afro-Americans preferential employment and educational opportunities to compensate for perceived disadvantages they suffer as a consequence of the prevailing socio-economic system.

At bottom, the problem is this: How can a state balance and reconcile cultural demands for differentiation and citizenship demands for integration, while maintaining – indeed, in order to maintain – its political and moral integrity? Afford group-differentiated forms of citizenship too generously and the civic unity of the state starts to fragment. Refuse such concessions and component ethno-cultural resentment generates alienation, which fragments the state by rebellion or secession in any case. Loyalty in a multicultural state can be frail and fickle, as the disintegration of the USSR and Yugoslavia following the loosening of the grip of Communism has adequately demonstrated.

What can be done? A leading authority on multinational citizenship has distinguished three kinds of demands that are made to resolve tensions:

> self-government rights (the delegation of powers to national minorities, often through some form of federalism);
> polyethnic rights (financial support and legal protection for certain practices associated with ethnic or religious groups); and

113

special representation rights (guaranteed seats for ethnic or national groups within the central institutions of the larger state).

(Kymlicka, 1995, pp. 6–7)

But the will to compromise must be present, and a spirit of toleration. How, for instance, can politicians and community leaders cope with the situation in Belgium, a state that is a culturally artificial outcome of the chance division of the Spanish Netherlands in the sixteenth century and the failure of the brief attempt at reunion in the nineteenth? French-speaking Walloons and Dutch-speaking Flemings live uncomfortably side-by-side in the Belgian state today. Already this small country has six parliaments to cater for different language groups and levels of government, yet still civic harmony proves elusive. Discord has descended into petty bitterness. Here is one extraordinary example, concerning a row over recruitment to the fire service:

Although Brussels is 85 per cent francophone, it is in the Flemish region and Flemings have traditionally been given up to 30 per cent of public sector jobs in the capital. Attempts to change this ended in deadlock until politicians agreed a precise recruiting balance. In future 29.48 per cent of Brussels firemen will be Flemish.

(Guardian, 30 March 1998)

Is it perhaps the very concept of a singular form of citizenship that should be questioned? The posing of this query brings the study of citizenship into line with the fashion of postmodern analysis in sundry fields of humane study, which involves questioning of traditional unified assumptions. Societies and states are no longer viewed as homogeneous; citizenship consequently must be understood and studied as a mosaic of identities, duties and rights rather than a unitary concept.

4

Multiple Citizenship

The idea of multiple citizenship

The assumption that citizenship is a singular, bilateral relationship between the individual and the state is deeply embedded in our understanding of the concept. It is a model common to both classical Greek and modern nationalist thinking on the subject. After all, if the *polis* and the nation-state respectively completely satisfy the individual's requirement for a political identity, then it would appear that there can be neither need of nor room for the complications of other relationships for the enjoyment of rights, the discharge of duties and the expression of loyalty in the political sphere. Yet there are, and to a certain extent always have been, such complications. And unless we accept the validity of a more capacious and flexible definition of citizenship, we shall be denying the evidence of its history, constricting its theoretical investigation and inhibiting its practical development. For, although the idea of a singular mode of citizenship is useful within its own confines – despite never having been more than an oversimplified notion – it cannot today be properly construed without the supplementary idea of multiple citizenship.

A brief explanation of what we mean by 'multiple citizenship' will reveal just how pervasive are its various manifestations. We need initially, by the use of two metaphors, to distinguish between citizenships which coexist in parallel and those which may be described as functioning in layers.

115

parallel	layered

dual	individual $\longrightarrow$ state $\longrightarrow$ State
	(1) federal
	(2) quasi-federal
	  (a) devolution
	  (b) EU [individual $\longrightarrow$ (state) $\longrightarrow$ State $\longrightarrow$ EU]

civil society	individual $\longrightarrow$ municipality $\longrightarrow$ (state) $\longrightarrow$ State
	individual $\longrightarrow$ State $\longrightarrow$ world

Figure 4.1

The first is simply stated: parallel citizenship exists in two forms. It is the condition enjoyed by some individuals of simultaneous citizenship or nationality of (usually) two different states; it may also be used to describe the relationship between membership of a state and membership of civil society.

The existence of the status of citizenship in layers is more complex. We may identify four main kinds. The most obvious instance is the double level of citizenship operating in a federal constitution, so that individuals are citizens of their component state (which we write in the appropriate contexts with a lower-case 's') at the lower level, and of the overarching State (with a capital 'S') at the higher. The arrangement obtains also in a less fully-fledged manner, which we may term quasi-federal systems, where there is devolution of power from the central State to autonomous regions or the building of a supra-State citizenship as is uniquely the case with the European Union. The second instance of layered citizenship recognizes the citizens' additional relationship at the sub-State (and, indeed, sub-state) level, that is, to their town or city. Let us call this municipal citizenship. And, finally, and perhaps a little contentiously, we must cap our layers with the concept of world citizenship at the supra-State level. The above analysis is summarized in tabular form in figure 4.1.

The reader may feel disposed to object to the inclusion of the civil society, devolutionary, municipal and world categories as strictly not being forms of citizenship at all; this is a matter of definition that we shall need to address when we consider these. However, there are, as we shall find, sufficiently strong grounds for attaching the label of citizenship to them to warrant their consideration. That being so, and taken together with the clearer categories of dual, federal and EU forms of citizenship, it is evident that the basic, singular concept of citizenship has burst its bounds. The reasons for this can be succinctly stated and will be more fully treated in the exemplifications of the several categories in the core of the chapter.

A brief conspectus of the categories will be useful here. Dual citizenship arose, even as early as classical times, because of the mobility of individuals, the need to take legal cognizance of multiple identities and, in the case of Rome, the mutual interests of provincial notables and the Roman imperium. Federal systems and quasi-federal systems are political arrangements for coping with the requirements of government in States of more than traditional size or complexity. The definition of citizenship at the two levels (of State and state) is a natural consequence of this constitutional pattern. The municipal and civil society styles of citizenship have derived from pre-nation-state forms of administration and bonding. Moreover, inevitably, such sub-State levels of citizenship are anathema to totalitarians for diverting the citizen's attention from wholehearted commitment to the State/Party and its ideology. By the same token, therefore, it is increasingly recognized that sub-State citizenship, particularly of the civil society variety, has a vital role to play in preventing or undermining the totalitarian subjection of the individual and thus underpinning healthy citizenship at the State level itself. Finally, the concept of world citizenship, almost as venerable as that of State citizenship, has persisted because of the consciousness that humankind is one, inhabiting one planet.

Multiple citizenship is, therefore, a reality. But, even though it evolved and was devised in response to the inadequacies of simple citizenship, we must not assume that, in its various guises, multiple citizenship is free of its own real difficulties.

Parallel citizenships

Let us start with the parallel forms of multiple citizenship. These differ markedly from each other. The one is fully and internationally defined in law; the other might be rated as unworthy of the term citizenship at

117

all. First, then, dual citizenship, the least important of the several forms of multiple citizenship because it involves the smallest number of people. None the less, it does raise interesting questions.

During the century from *c.*50 BC the matter of dual citizenship became a live legal and political issue in Rome and its provinces. As Rome expanded its authority throughout the Mediterranean basin she extended the coveted title of Roman citizen with some generosity. But did this, should this conferment of Roman rights involve the enfranchised man in return renouncing his native civic rights?

A famous test case occurred in 56 BC. Cicero denied the possibility of Cornelius Balbus retaining his status as a citizen of Gades after his enfranchisement by Pompey as a citizen of Rome. The principles of residence and allegiance, key elements in the status of citizenship, could not be shared. In expounding his position with characteristic forensic logic, Cicero nevertheless revealed that Roman practice was not as clear-cut as Roman law, and that, in any case, Roman law was out of line with the laws and practices of neighbouring cities.

> Now all other states would, without hesitation, bestow their citizenship upon our citizens, if we had the same system of law as themselves. . . .
>   Thus we see that citizens of Athens, Rhodes, Sparta, and of other states far and wide, are enrolled as citizens of Greek states, and that the same persons are citizens of many states. And I myself have seen certain ignorant men, citizens of ours, misled by this, sitting at Athens amongst jurymen and members of the Areopagus . . . since they did not know that if they had acquired citizenship there, they had forfeited it here.
>
> *(Cicero, 1958, pp. 29–30)*

By *c.*50 BC distinguished persons were openly flouting this incompatibility rule, especially in Italy; by *c.*AD 50 dual citizenship was being widely practised. The best-known assertion of dual citizenship is the response by St Paul on the occasion of his arrest (*c.*AD 58). While demanding the judicial rights of his Roman citizenship, he yet proudly proclaimed himself 'a Jew of Tarsus, a city in Cilicia, a citizen of no mean city' (Acts 21.39).

The question of dual citizenship under the late Roman Republic, the Principate and early Empire was exceedingly complex. Moreover, we should not be deterred by the simple, strict Ciceronic legal argument of incompatibility from understanding the positive political usefulness of the device. The conferment of citizenship on an alien can be used as a mark of honour; it can be used as a means of cementing the allegiance of aliens to their state of residence; and it can be used to avoid making awkward choices as to which citizenship persons should opt for when the circumstances of their political environment alter. Indeed, although some states preclude the arrangement, it is not uncommon for individuals to acquire this double status – by conferment; by virtue of being born of parents of one nationality on the territory of a different nation; by the attribution at birth of the nationality of both parents in a mixed marriage; or by naturalization in a second state while retaining their original citizenship.

To assert the political reality and utility of dual citizenship must not, however, tempt us to close our minds to continuing practical difficulties. International lawyers have been forced to frame rules for coping with these, for multiple nationality, the usual term in international jurisprudence, is, in fact, a legal inconvenience. What happens if an individual seeks diplomatic protection from state A, of which he is a citizen, against state B, of which he is also a citizen? And if state A requires the individual for military service when he is resident in state B, which has no such requirement, how is the matter to be resolved?

The Hague Convention of 1930 set out some guidelines. Two are of particular importance. One is that 'A State may not afford diplomatic protection to one of its nationals against a State whose nationality such person also possesses' (see Brownlie, 1990, p. 399). The second is the principle of 'effective nationality': the citizenship status of the person's usual state of residence takes precedence over any others. Statesmen have also been reluctant to concede the principle in modern times because, by bifurcation, dual citizenship throws in doubt the loyalty of the person with twin identities.

Reality, however, has supervened. Because of the waves of migration in recent years the numbers of persons with dual citizenship have increased, the policies of states, even so, varying quite considerably. Historical experience goes a long way to explain this divergence. Thus states with traditions of mass immigration (e.g. USA, Canada) or with considerable post-colonial contacts (e.g. UK, France) tend to be relaxed and tolerant on the matter. For example, it is estimated that, by the 1980s, there were in France over one million Franco-Algerians of dual nationality. In contrast, those European countries which either do not have this historical background and/or have been wrestling with the complication of the status of guest-workers (e.g. Germany, Austria, Belgium, Switzerland) are more resistant to the practice of dual citizenship (though, as was recorded in chapter 3, Germany is, at the time of writing, proposing to relax its regulations; so too is Switzerland).

The whole discussion thus far has related to the dual civic status of a relatively limited number of geographically scattered individuals. There is no reason, however, why this device should not be used with whole populations. True, the modern tendency to fuse citizenship with ethnic and cultural nationality raises virtually insuperable obstacles.

Even so, there is one obvious example, namely, the convenient fudging of the civic status of Irish people after the creation of the Irish Free State in 1922. The treaty referred to 'the common citizenship of Ireland and Great Britain'. This position obtained until 1935, though from that date until 1948 Irish citizens remained also Commonwealth citizens, admittedly an extraordinarily vague concept. This status was, in turn, removed with the establishment of the Irish Republic and its withdrawal from the Commonwealth. Yet the Irish still retained a form of dual citizenship. In that same year, 1948, the British Nationality Act granted Irish citizens the privileges of British citizenship. Accordingly, today an Irish citizen resident in the United Kingdom can exercise three sets of citizenship rights (such as voting) – Irish, British and European. This last category takes us on from multiple citizenship in its parallel form into the layered style. However, before moving on, we must examine the second kind of parallel citizenship, namely that which functions through civil society.

Civil society, unlike dual citizenship, is disputed as a form of citizenship in any proper sense of the term. Its claims are none the less sufficiently compelling to justify consideration. Civil society can be interpreted as performing a civic function through its myriad voluntary groupings, organizations, associations and networks, the members of which Burke vividly described as 'the little platoons'. The kinds of memberships that we now recognize as expressions of civil society are trade unions, churches, environmental groups, charities, particularist associations for women and ethnic groups, for example; even families (though these are scarcely voluntary groupings) are now often listed in the category.

120

In its modern meaning civil society is a term used to distinguish the identity and activity of the person in bodies such as these that are separate and distinct from the state. In that sense, therefore, we may classify it as a parallel form of citizenship. Hegel was at pains to correct what he believed to be the traditional conflation of the two sets of institutions in political thinking. For, as he argued, individuals join civil society bodies voluntarily and in order to pursue their particular interests. Therefore, 'If the state is confused with civil society . . . then the interest of the individuals as such becomes the ultimate end of their association, and it follows that membership of the state is something optional' (Hegel, 1967, para. 258, p. 156). But if these bodies are distinct from the institutions of the state (indeed are alternative foci of social identity and activity to those generated and nurtured by the state), how can they be associated with the concept and status of citizenship, the function of which is precisely to connect the individual and the state?

Yet the belief that civil society offers a useful, even indeed a superior option to the traditional state citizenship became widely accepted in the 1980s. Conditions and events in eastern and central Europe drew attention to the notion. Observation of the Communist regimes in these countries made it apparent that conventional citizenship in totalitarian states is a fake citizenship: civil and political rights were so abbreviated by the oppressive security police system. Perhaps, then, civic rights could be demanded by popular mobilization through civil society?

Poland showed the way. In 1980 Solidarity was created as a workers' movement independent of state control and, with notable support from the Catholic Church, extracted sweeping concessions – such as relaxation of censorship, the regular broadcasting of church services and promotion in employment irrespective of Party membership. Then, surely, the Solidarity workers were displaying greater civic consciousness and effectiveness, admittedly of a different kind, than they had previously when going through the motions of voting in elections for Communist Party members or of serving in a Warsaw Pact army. A similar, though less dramatic, story can be told about the role of the civil society associations in helping to effect the smooth conclusion of the Communist era in Hungary in 1990.

Meanwhile, in the West, in Thatcherite Britain conspicuously, doubts arose concerning the continuing vitality of traditional state citizenship.

The doctrines of the New Right and neo-liberalism directly confronted the very concept of social citizenship and seemed intent on dismantling the welfare state. Furthermore, if 'there is no such thing as society' and individualism is all, what price the consciousness of community responsibility that is one of the hallmarks of citizenship? Paradoxically, both Right and Left, discarding and despairing of conventional citizenship respectively, turned to civil society. Thatcherites preached the virtues of 'active citizenship', interpreted as membership of school governing bodies or neighbourhood watch schemes. The Left-inclined young turned Green, forming and joining groups to challenge the immobility and insensitivity of politicians and bureaucrats. Keen supporters of the civil society version of the civic status have even celebrated it as a means of beneficially depoliticizing citizenship.

Is this realistic, is it even desirable? Active membership of civil society organizations reveals an enthusiasm – both as a reason for and a consequence of joining – surpassing the tepid support, even apathy, that has marked attitudes towards state institutions. And by enlarging these enthusiasms, the individuals are, it can be argued, developing the true civic qualities of responsibility, co-operation and participation.

And yet... Do some people join organizations not so much for expansive dutiful reasons, but rather for the pursuit of an enthusiasm, possibly even a selfish desire, utterly blinkered from the holistic needs of the community? If so, then this is not citizenship, which presupposes, ideally, the exercise of judgement and justice in helping to resolve issues affecting not a portion, but the whole of the community. In other words, the very pluralism of civil society detracts from its pretensions to be an alternative school and arena for citizenship.

At the same time, the nature of civil society as a parallel form of citizenship may be seen to be only partially satisfying on the basis of a quite opposite test. The argument proceeds in the following manner. Even when one has acknowledged the civil and social facets of citizenship, the status remains at root political. And in so far as the associations of civil society want to preserve against or accelerate change, they can often achieve their objectives only through the political system. One authority provides a vivid exemplification of this contradiction:

> It is surely highly significant . . . that the Solidarity movement in Poland, the most sensational model of the civil society vision . . . did *not* confine

itself to civil society once the totalitarian state collapsed, but went on to turn itself into a political party, quickly assuming the reins of government. This was not a sellout by Solidarity, but a natural response to the 'built-in' insufficiency of the kind of 'localized' citizenship made available to us at the civil society level alone.

(Beiner, 1995, p. 5)

The parallel lines of civil society and state are in practice therefore sometimes destined to meet.

Federal constitutions

So, from parallel lines to horizontal layers, the clearest example of which is to be found in the federal State.

In the eighteenth century federal forms of constitution were a rarity: one may cite the United Provinces and the Swiss Confederation as examples, but they were anomalies. Today every continent has several examples, and hundreds of millions throughout the world consequently experience the status of citizenship at both the State and state levels (to use the formula adopted earlier in this chapter). The first major nation (if one may use the term without anachronism) to adopt the device was the United States of America, which became something of a laboratory for the federalist structure. Its history therefore provides ample evidence of the difficulties and advantages attendant upon this kind of double-layered citizenship.

In the very process of framing the Constitution, the American draftsmen inscribed an ambiguity at its very heart. The imprecision lies in the apparent discrepancy between the preamble to and Art. 7 of the document. The preamble starts with the well-known words: 'We, the people of the United States'; Art. 7 required the Constitution to be ratified by separate state Conventions. The question thus arose whether the Constitution was the product of the will of the nation acting in unity (the singular 'people' in the preamble), or of the distinct wills of the separate peoples of the participating states. These alternative readings were indicators of different interpretations of the location of sovereignty; or, to put the matter another way, they raised the question whether primacy between the citizenship

123

statuses rested at the local state level or at the level of the overarching State.

In 1857 the Chief Justice gave a ruling in the long-running and controversial Dred Scott case, which underlined the primacy of each state over federal authority in the matter of citizenship. The case was complicated by the fact that Scott had been a slave. However, that aside, the judgment on the conferment of national citizenship was clear. No single state could make a Negro 'a citizen of the United States, and endue him with the full rights of citizenship in every other state without their consent' (see Brock, 1973, p. 154). By implication this meant that citizenship was primarily a state conferment, not national. It took the blood-letting of the Civil War and the subsequent Fourteenth Amendment to reverse this judgment. Henceforth, in law if not in reality, citizenship was a nationwide status beyond the authority of any individual state to abridge.

The relationship of the political and legal powers of the two levels of a federal State is at one and the same time a cardinal issue for the writers of constitutions to decide upon and an intensely delicate one to resolve in practice. For all their wisdom, the American Founding Fathers left a perilous legacy. However, the precision, justice and workability of instruments of constitutional law are only one facet of the intricacies of layered citizenship. The other major question concerns the level to which the citizenry feel themselves the more attached and at which they feel the more able to participate in civic affairs. Here again, the USA provides a prime example of thinking, observation and practice to help us appreciate the nature of layered citizenship.

The two classic commentaries on the US system of government, *The Federalist* papers and Tocqueville's *Democracy in America*, stress the greater reality of the state government for the average citizen. 'Into the administration of these a greater number of individuals will expect to rise', wrote Madison. '. . . With the affairs of these the people will be more familiarly and minutely conversant. And with the members of these will a greater proportion of the people have the ties of personal acquaintance and friendship, and of family and party attachments' (*The Federalist*, no. 46). This excerpt may be compared with Tocqueville's conclusions drawn from his observations in five New England states half a century later. (We may note, incidentally, Tocqueville's admiration for *The Federalist* papers.) He declared that 'The central government of each state, being close to the governed, is continually informed of the needs that arise; every year new plans are put forward . . . and published in the press, exciting universal interest and eagerness among the citizens' (Tocqueville, 1968, p. 199).

The message is clear. A citizen's sense of identity and bonding, his knowledge and civic competence, and his opportunities and inclination to participate are more effectively nurtured at the lower, state level than the higher, federal level. True, these two commentators were writing about a society with strongly established feelings of local community and with much less pervasive national news media than today. None the less, their observations retain a certain resonance both across the generations and in other countries, finding expression, for instance, in the modern principle of subsidiarity, which has been adopted by the European Union and to which we shall refer later.

The relationship of the citizen to the State must, even so, balance this state allegiance and activity, or the federal State would unravel. The centrifugal force of state citizenship must be equalled by the centripetal force of State citizenship. Pairs such as local pride and national patriotism, local traditions and national values, for example, must somehow be kept in harmony if this two-layered citizenship is to be a fruitful device. Sometimes this is not easy. Let us take one final example from the United States.

A tradition of the former slave states of the Deep South has been the separation of whites and blacks, the latter for generations treated as non- or, at best, second-class citizens. A fundamental objective of citizenship is the equality of all those enjoying that status; moreover, the proposition that 'all men are created equal' was written into the American Declaration of Independence. Should, therefore, black children continue to be taught in separate schools in accordance with Southern tradition or should schools be desegregated according to the national principle of equal citizenship? This was a live issue in the mid-twentieth century. In 1954 the Supreme Court ruled that segregation was 'inherently unequal'. Nevertheless, when, three years later, attempts were made to integrate a few black pupils into the Central High School in Little Rock, Arkansas, agitated supporters of segregation prevailed upon the state Governor to prevent this development by deployment of the National Guard. President Eisenhower dispatched federal troops to enforce the Supreme Court ruling. He had upheld not just the law, but also the principles of State citizenship over the traditions of state citizenship.

The European Union

Figure 4.1 identifies two kinds of layered systems which we have termed 'quasi-federalism': the European Union and the distribution of political authority by means of devolution. However, for our purposes, one very important difference distinguishes them from each other. European citizenship is a legally recognized title; residents of a region with devolved powers are 'regional citizens' only, as it were, by courtesy title (if that) – the title has no legal standing. We shall therefore treat the case of devolution in the next section with municipal citizenship as two doubtful attributions of the term. In this section we shall concern ourselves solely with the important and unique topic of citizenship of the European Union.

The European Union (EU) evolved from structures for economic co-operation – the Coal and Steel Community (ECSC) and the European Economic Community (EEC). Why, then, should it have developed a form of supra-national citizenship? From the very beginning, the originators of European unity accepted the need for an elected assembly to monitor the executive bodies. Initially indirectly elected by the constituent members' national legislatures, the European Parliament was first directly elected by the citizenry in nationally drawn European constituencies in 1979.

MEPs (among others) were soon voicing concern about the 'faceless' unaccountability of the European Commission. In 1988 the Commission noted that 'In its resolutions Parliament has laid particular stress on devising a policy which involves European citizens in the creation of a living Community and on transforming the technocrats' Europe into a people's Europe' (see Jones and Robins, 1992, p. 297). It is noteworthy that the phrase rendered into English as 'people's Europe' appears in French as '*Europe des citoyens*'.

Already moves were afoot to build an effective European citizenship. In an effort to encourage individuals to assume a European identity – to think of themselves as 'Europeans' – European passports have been issued, a European flag has been designed and a European anthem

126

adopted. The anthem is Beethoven's version of Schiller's 'Ode to Joy', itself inspired by a reading of the Abbé Saint-Pierre's eighteenth-century Project for European union.

The EU has also struggled with the problem of the stratified nature of the Union by declaring adherence to the principle of subsidiarity. This originated in papal political thinking and the path of its transmission to the EU is somewhat misty. It seems to have been channelled to the European Union from the Italian cleric-politician Don Luigi Sturzo via the Christian Democratic parties. The proposition, as enunciated by Pius XI, is that 'it is an injustice, a grave evil and a disturbance of right order, for a larger and higher association to arrogate to itself functions which can be performed efficiently by smaller and lower societies' (see Oakeshott, 1940, p. 58). In 1990, Delors, President of the Commission, declared that subsidiarity should be the 'watchword' of the European Community (EC).

How does the concept relate to citizenship? Subsidiarity refers to the exercise of power and decision-making at the lowest feasible level in a pyramidal structure. Consequently, if the principle were widely advertised and applied, citizens juggling with their multiple civic identities would know which topics would be handled at which levels; and, furthermore, be assured that their local interests would not be overlooked or overridden by an ignorant or unsympathetic body higher up the scale of authority.

Such ideas and developments (and there were others) were merely tentative steps towards a defined European citizenship. It became a legal status, summarized in figure 4.2, when the Treaty of European Union (usually referred to as the Maastricht Treaty) came into effect in 1993. The treaty also incorporated the principle of subsidiarity (Art. 3b), provided for the appointment by the Parliament of an Ombudsman to receive complaints from citizens (Art. 138e), and enhanced the powers of the Parliament (Arts. 138b, 138c, 189b).

However, citizenship is considered to be not only a civil and political status: there is a social dimension also. The European Union has made some attempt to cater for this. In 1989 the European Community produced its Draft Community Charter of Fundamental Social Rights (the Social Charter). The aim was to provide minimum working conditions throughout the member states. The Maastricht Treaty incorporated these provisions in its Social Chapter. But the contribution of the EU

Art.	General Rights	Art.	Electoral Rights
8a1	Every citizen of the Union shall have the right to move and reside freely within the territory of Member States.	8b1	Every citizen of the Union residing in a Member State of which he is not a national shall have the right to vote and to stand as a candidate at municipal elections in the Member State in which he resides.
8c	Every citizen of the Union shall, in the territory of a third country in which the Member State of which he is a national is not represented, be entitled to protection by the diplomatic or consular authorities of any Member State.	8b2	. . . every citizen of the Union residing in a Member State of which he is not a national shall have the right to vote and to stand as a candidate in elections to the European Parliament in the Member State in which he resides.
8d	Every citizen of the Union shall have the right to petition the Parliament. . . . Every citizen of the Union may apply to the Ombudsman.		

Figure 4.2

to the consolidation of the social rights of the citizen extends beyond the Social Chapter. This process preceded and continues independently of the Maastricht Treaty. European definition of social and employment rights has come about through the issuing of Directives by the Commission and judgments by the European Court of Justice (ECJ). The work of the latter has had a bearing on the status of European citizen since 1963.

In that year the ECJ, in explicating the intention of the Treaty of Rome (which established the EEC), ruled that 'Community law . . . not only imposes obligations upon individuals but is also intended to confer upon them rights which become part of their legal heritage.' Moreover, 'The vigilance of individuals concerned to protect their rights amounts to an effective supervision' of the exercise of power by the Community institutions (see Oliver and Heater, 1994, p. 145). Since then, the Court has built up considerable case law relating to social and especially economic rights, which effectively establishes the superiority of European over national law in the topics covered. The pattern of an evolutionary European citizenship is, in fact, overtly accepted in the Maastricht Treaty. Art. 8e makes it possible for the Council to 'adopt provisions to strengthen or add to the rights' listed in Arts. 8a–d.

The EC/EU has, in practice, been primarily concerned to protect economic rights – understandably because of its mainly economic function. In a complementary manner, the Council of Europe has been primarily concerned to protect civil rights. The rights covered by this organization are defined in the European Convention of Human Rights (ECHR) and are protected by the European Commission of Human Rights and Court of Human Rights. As membership of the Council of Europe far exceeds in number of states the membership of the European Union, the number of 'European citizens' in the sense of people potentially under the protection of the ECHR far exceeds, though of course includes, the number of citizens of the European Union.

But not only are the EU states members of the Council of Europe, the Maastricht Treaty formally recognizes the significance of its setting the standards for the preservation of rights. Art. F of the treaty states that the EU 'shall respect the fundamental rights as guaranteed' by the ECHR 'and as they result from the constitutional traditions common to the Member States, as general principles of Community law'.

Here, then, are the bare bones of European citizenship – the subcontinental quasi-federal system which has been developing during the last decades of the twentieth century. What does it all add up to? Potentially perhaps a sophisticated example of multiple citizenship of the layered kind; at the moment, to be honest, it is a mere shadow of that potential. There is plentiful evidence that the concept and practice of European citizenship is exceedingly weak compared with citizenship as experienced at the national level.

Citizenship is an inert idea if those invested with the status place no value on it or, which is worse, reject it out of hand. Popular support for and identity with the EU, it must be said, has been less than enthusiastic. The very prospect of membership of the Community was greeted with some hostility, notably in Britain and Norway. Even in France, a keen founder-member, the referendum for the ratification of the Maastricht Treaty produced a 'yes' response by the narrowest of margins. Turn-outs in the elections for the European Parliament have been very low in some countries: in 1994 in a third of the twelve member states less than half the electorate voted. Nationalism, xenophobia even, especially in Britain, inhibits the growth of a feeling of co-citizenship with other nationalities.

There is, in addition, an institutional reason for the lukewarmness of European civic identity. The low turn-out in all but a handful of states in Euro-elections is also a reflection of the frailty of the European Parliament. After all, one of the clearest and simplest indicators of citizenship is the casting of one's vote, and the turn-out in an election is often reckoned an index of the strength of a nation's sense of citizenship. But in the case of the EU the relative powerlessness of the Parliament, which has led to complaints about the 'democratic deficit' of the EC/EU, is little incentive to exercise this basic right of political citizenship.

Nor has the EU been at all effective in incorporating the principle of subsidiarity into its procedures. Little wonder when the Maastricht Treaty (Art. 3b) defines the principle as merely refraining from overriding the member states on issues where the states are competent to take the necessary action. This is deference to national sovereignty, not subsidiarity properly speaking. Admittedly, the treaty makes provision for a Committee of the Regions (Arts. 198a–c) to look after local interests; but its members are not elected: consultative, not citizenly subsidiarity.

So, what, at bottom, does European citizenship really mean? To be blunt, there is much vagueness and confusion; and it raises fundamental questions about the nature of citizenship *tout court*. The stress in discussions about European citizenship tends to be placed on the rights which a European citizen can expect to enjoy, the nature of those rights, and the identification of those persons who are eligible to enjoy them. The sphere of political citizenship is clear, laid down in the Maastricht Treaty, which also defines a European citizen as 'a person holding the nationality of a Member State' (Art. 8). The trouble arises when one extends the definition of citizenship into the civil, social and economic spheres. We have dealt with these problems in a generalized way, including the distinction between citizens and denizens, in previous chapters. Suffice it here to place the difficulties succinctly in their European context.

There are four main areas of confusion. One is the existence of a large number of migrant workers in some states of the Union – Algerians in France, Turks in Germany, for example – who are not nationals of EU states. Yet they enjoy welfare and employment rights. Does that make them 'partial European citizens'? Secondly, different member states interpret the rights to social and employment benefits in anything but a uniform way. So, is a resident in a member state with generous regulations 'more of a European citizen' than someone resident in a state with less generous rules?

Thirdly, we have seen that the European Convention of Human Rights, recognized by the Maastricht Treaty, provides a comprehensive definition of rights. But these are rights which adhere to a person *qua* human being, not *qua* citizen. Moreover, individuals in the states of central and eastern Europe, not members of the EU, have the same right to live protected by this code as do citizens of Europe as defined by the Maastricht Treaty. Fourthly and finally, much of the EU discourse about *citizens'* rights is, in truth, about *workers'* rights. Workers' rights concern the relationship between employee and employer; civic rights concern the relationship between citizen and state – or, in this context, the EU standing *in loco civitatis*.

The receptacle that is the concept of citizenship is indeed capacious, but in the case of Europe too much has been poured into it, causing semantic confusion. We would do well, therefore, to keep in mind the unique and experimental nature of the European Union. When Denmark ratified the Maastricht Treaty it appended the following declaration:

> Citizenship of the Union is a political and legal concept entirely different from the concept of citizenship within the meaning of the Constitution of the Kingdom of Denmark. Nothing in the treaty of European Union implies or foresees an undertaking to create a citizenship of the Union in the sense of citizenship of a nation state.
>
> *(see Gardner, n.d., p. 13 n. 26)*

Let the Danish statement stand as an epigraph to this section.

131

Sub-state citizenships

Four years after the coming into effect of the American Constitution, demands, encouraged by this transatlantic event, were voiced in sixty French *départements* for the reduction of Jacobin centralized power by transmuting France into a federal State. This federalist revolt was short-lived. As was observed at the time, it is easier to build up a federation by the gathering together of a number of states, which succeeded in America, than to effect the partial dismantling of an established unitary State, which failed in France.

For, crucially, federation involves the sharing of sovereignty between the two levels. Devolution, on the other hand, stops short of this constitutional step. It was this weaker solution to the centralization-decentralization issue which France did adopt – eventually, 190 years after the abortive federalist revolt. In 1982, the twenty-two already established regional functional bodies were accorded some legislative powers, exercised through elected councils. Spain, too, has a highly developed system of devolution, and Britain started on this road in the last years of the twentieth century.

If the construction of a federation – as is sometimes the case – involves the consolidation of formerly separate states into a new, greater whole, then the major civic task is to create a feeling of and opportunities to exercise the new federal State citizenship. In contrast, devolution – commonly the creation of regional autonomy in a long-established State – involves the fostering of a new civic status at the lower level to complement the national citizenship already in place.

But are the two processes at all comparable? One may argue that the enfranchised inhabitants of, say, Brittany or Catalonia or Scotland are not truly citizens of those regions in the same way as the enfranchised inhabitants of, say, Texas, Bavaria or New South Wales are citizens of their states. In a devolved structure Bretons, Catalans and Scots, for example, are not legally citizens of those provinces. Even so, on at least two key criteria they may be accorded that title: they may well have a deep sense of allegiance to their region, and they certainly have the civic right to vote for and serve in their assemblies.

And if we deny the name of regional citizen, are we also to deny the name of municipal citizen? After all, where regionalism is fully developed, the identity and power of the regions are normally stronger than is the case with municipalities. And yet, the status of citizen has for so much of history been so firmly associated with membership of a town or city that to exclude the municipal layer from our pattern of multiple citizenship would seem perverse.

The city-states of ancient Greece and medieval Germany and Italy, the chartered and free cities of medieval England and Germany were inhabited by men whose social, financial, professional or trading stature placed them in the class of citizen. The very etymology of the word reveals its association with a city – in English, in French (*citoyen*), in Italian (*cittadino*), in German (*Bürger*), for example. A medieval city had its own law and court in the operation of which the citizens participated.

In the nineteenth century the town or city was fully understood to be the cradle of citizenship. Referring to the typical New England township, Tocqueville explained that it was in this local context that the citizen 'learns to rule society . . . and in the end accumulates clear, practical ideas about the nature of his duties and the extent of his rights' (Tocqueville, 1968, p. 85). Do we detect an echo here of Aristotle's famous definition of the nature of citizenship in the city-state as 'ruling and being ruled in turn'?

John Stuart Mill, in his *Representative Government* (chapter 15: 'On Local Representative Bodies'), showed himself to be at one with his French friend. Victorian England in fact provides us with a splendid example of the vigour of municipal citizenship. The growth of industrial cities and the reform of local government led to an extraordinary burgeoning of citizenship at this level. We can cite the extension of the municipal franchise and, at least partly as a consequence of this, a devotion to the creation of civic facilities and the flowering of municipal identity and pride. In 1868 the Municipal Franchise Act enfranchised a larger number of men and (dear to Mill's heart) even some women. As a result, the electorates of Birmingham and Leeds increased to nearly one-fifth of their populations, compared with a figure of about half that for national elections following the Second Reform Act of the preceding year. A leading authority has noted the mood of the age:

> The provincial cities nurtured the sense of loyalty through rivalry with each other and solidarity against the metropolis. They used their status as regional capitals to challenge the claims of the national capital, both

culturally and politically. . . . People felt that they belonged to particular cities, and each with its own identity.

(Briggs, 1968, p. 85)

Birmingham, especially, wonderfully exemplified this style of municipal citizenship. Two men laid respectively the ideological and practical foundations for that city's self-identity and self-esteem. The Baptist minister George Dawson expounded his concept of the municipal or civic gospel. Modelling his combined religious and political zeal on the creed of Mazzini, that arch-exponent of this mode of exultant thinking, Dawson preached a kind of republican civic virtue suited to the municipal layer of multiple citizenship: 'a town is a solemn organism', he declared (see Hennock, 1973, p. 75). At the same time, Joseph Chamberlain, mayor from 1873 to 1876, ensured that Birmingham's claim to be the best-governed city in the world was an expression of pride with much validity.

The emasculation of local government by the centralizing policies of the Thatcherite regime of the 1980s accelerated the decline of the municipal values of the high Victorian era. In other countries, however, municipal citizenship remains a vital bottom level in the layered civic system – and the adjective 'vital' is used in both its senses. Some of the cities and townships of the USA and the communes of France are obvious examples.

We need to imagine a ziggurat. Layers of citizenship are built up starting with a broad foundation stratum of numerous municipalities. On to that layer is constructed a much smaller number of states or regions. Atop that level is the single State, except in the case of the European Union, where the several States are capped by the Union. Each stratum has its own kind of citizenship. But can we stop there? What of the great globe itself?

The idea of cosmopolis

World citizenship is undefinable in theory, non-existent in practice and would be undesirable in any case. Or so it may be, indeed has been, argued. Why, then, devote nearly half of this chapter to the topic? For three reasons. First, the idea that an individual can be a

134

world citizen, or cosmopolite, has survived for two and a half millenia, and is worthy of investigation if only for its staying power. Secondly, the tripartite case against the notion is sufficiently cogent to invite examination in order to test its validity. And thirdly, the positive case is justified on a number of grounds which are becoming increasingly recognized. In this section the history of the concept of world citizenship will be outlined. The following three sections will be devoted to what may be discerned as four main interpretations of the idea.

Dominant as the ideas and practices of the *polis*, Republic and Empire were in Graeco-Roman life and thinking, room was yet found to contemplate the conception of the oneness of mankind and the existence of a universal Natural Law. This was a moral tenet propounded by the Greek and Roman Stoic philosophers in the ancient world, and was later adopted by the Neostoics of the Renaissance. The most famous exponent was the second-century philosopher-Emperor Marcus Aurelius. In one of his characteristic syllogisms he demonstrated the existence of Natural Law and its connection with the idea of world citizenship:

> If the intellectual capacity is common to us all, common too is the reason, which makes us rational creatures. If so, that reason is common which tells us what to do or not to do. If so, law is common. If so, we are citizens. If so, we are fellow-members of an organised community. If so, the Universe is, as it were a state – for of what other single polity can the whole race of mankind be said to be fellow-members? – and from it, this common State, we get the intellectual, the rational, and the legal instinct, or whence do we get it?
>
> *(Marcus Aurelius Antoninus, 1961, IV.4)*

Belief in the moral value of cosmopolitanism was resuscitated by the classical revivals of the Renaissance and Enlightenment. Eighteenth-century writers and intellectuals – the likes of Voltaire, Franklin and Paine – were proud to own the title of 'world citizen'. Schiller created the character of the Marquis Posa in *Don Carlos* to epitomize this frame of mind, and in this play, the King, repenting Posa's death, declares that, 'He lived to serve the world, and humankind' (*Don Carlos*, Act V, Scene ix). Meanwhile, more prosaically, Schiller's German contemporary Kant proposed the principle of a cosmopolitan law, which we shall come to in due course.

Vague ←----------------------------------→ Precise			
Identity	Morality	Law	Politics
Feeling of membership of humankind	Responsibility for planet and its inhabitants	Recognition of natural, international and possible world law	Belief/participation in trans/supra-national forms of political activity/ institutions

Figure 4.3

In the twentieth century the conviction that responsible, thinking people should cultivate a cosmopolitan mentality has been reinvigorated by the horrific tragedies of the two World Wars and the grim threats of nuclear and environmental catastrophe. If the regime of nation-states has brought humanity to this pass, then should not the moral principle of citizenly allegiance to the state in all conscience be complemented, even superseded, by a consciousness of the responsibilities and obligations of world citizenship?

It is quite evident from this survey that the term 'citizenship' in the cosmopolitan sense has been used in a way quite lacking the legal and political exactness of the term when used to describe the status of a person in relation to the state. In fact, if we give full recognition to developments in the twentieth century, it is possible to describe a spectrum of meanings shading from the vague to those of some precision (see figure 4.3). Starting at the vague end, people who have a feeling of identity with the whole of humanity are accorded the title of 'world citizen'. Slightly less vague is the world citizen's acceptance of the moral precept that the individual has some responsibility for the condition of the planet and the rest of its inhabitants, certainly the human ones, even the non-human. Moving to the more precise still, we come to the recognition that one is subject to and should live by the codes of supra- and transnational laws (i.e. natural and international), and possibly, in due time, to a universal world law. Finally, the world citizens who live most precisely up to that title are the ones who believe in the need for supra-national political authority and action, and, the most committed, who involve themselves in some activity of this kind.

World citizenship identity and morality

The feeling of a universal identity and the acceptance of a universal morality are so closely linked that we shall deal with these together in this section.

The word 'cosmopolitan' in general parlance means a person who feels at home in a number of countries. The usefulness of its more specific political connotation of trans- or supra-national has only recently come to be again recognized by scholars. However, in origin it had neither of these meanings. The Greek word '*kosmopolites*' should properly be rendered as 'citizen of the cosmos' or 'universe'. A person thus described was therefore someone conscious of being part of the whole universe, the whole of life, the whole of nature, of which all human beings, let alone just the community of the person's political state, were but tiny portions.

This insight, of course, has been revived in our own times, though in the more restricted, planetary sense. Most akin to the ancient Greek view is the Gaia hypothesis that the entire planet is a living, organic system. More simply, the increasing numbers of people who are concerned about man's impact on the environment not only speak in terms of ecological interdependence, but also in terms of humankind's stewardship of the planet. The massive impact and control that we have must be tempered by respect for other life-forms and for the needs of future human generations. And, concerning other life-forms, animal rights campaigners express this aspect of the issue with particular force.

All this adds up to a moral consciousness which can, perhaps justifiably, use the vocabulary of citizenship. For citizenship entails the ethical element of responsible behaviour towards and obligations to one's fellow citizens and the state or community which provides us with the citizenly status.

Even so, human beings are a special, identifiable part of the total order of nature. And because they are, they must have features which they share in common and which set them apart, as the Greeks saw it, from the gods and beasts. This recognition was a revolutionary step in Greek thought. From the primary human communities of families and clans came the remarkable leaps to the political organization of the state and clustering by cultural affinity. In ancient Greek practice and thought the *polis* provided the political organization; and the sense of distinctiveness from, indeed superiority to, the non-Greek-speaking 'barbarians' provided the sense of a common culture. Yet as early as the eighth century BC the comprehension that the whole of humankind shared something in common was starting to emerge. And slowly the idea gathered strength.

The key to the distinctiveness that humans share and that sets them apart from other animals, as the philosophers explained, was *logos*, the capacity for reasoned speech, which also embraced the capacity to comprehend the universal Divine or Natural Law. All human beings are capable of forming a bond by means of obedience to the common Natural Law and by communication. The possibilities for realizing this potential for the uniting of the human race were limited in the ancient world. Nevertheless, with economic globalization, the spread of English as a lingua franca and the communicative power of the Internet, the dream of Heraclitus, who understood the full implications of *logos* in the sixth century BC, may be nearing realization.

But what of the element of Natural Law in this formulation? The legally minded Romans expounded this. Cicero asserted that 'True law is right reason in agreement with nature; it is of universal application, unchanging and everlasting' (Cicero, 1959, III.22). The link between the concept and human unity was stated unequivocally by Locke seventeen hundred years later: by the law of nature, he wrote, 'common to them all, [a man] and all the rest of mankind are one community, make up one society distinct from all other creatures' (Locke, 1962, IX, para. 128). Through the concept of Natural Law Locke derived the principle of natural rights. These rights, incorporated most distinctly in the eighteenth-century American and French Declarations and in the twentieth-century UN International Bill of Rights, may in a sense be thought of as the world citizen's equivalent of the rights of the citizen *vis-à-vis* the state.

A citizen, however, owes duties as well as enjoying rights; and we must 'think globally'. Let us take three examples of recent proposals to improve humankind's sense of responsibility. First, a modest suggestion. In the 1980s an Australian cabinet minister, Gareth Evans, articulated the idea of 'good international citizenship' as 'an exercise in enlightened self-interest: an expression of idealistic pragmatism' (see Wheeler and Dunne, 1998, pp. 854–5). Andrew Linklater worked on the relationship between the idealism and the pragmatism, drawing the following conclusion:

> Good international citizens are not required to sacrifice their vital security interests out of fidelity to the rules of international society, but they are required 'to put the welfare of international society ahead of the relentless pursuit of [their] own national interests . . . to place the survival of order before the satisfaction of minimal national advantages.
>
> *(see Wheeler and Dunne, 1998, p. 885)*

Secondly, the Commission on Global Governance has urged the adoption of a global civic ethic as the moral foundation for a more effective system of global governance than the current pattern. In addition to reinforcing the established lists of fundamental human rights, it has outlined some half-dozen matching responsibilities. These include: to consider the impact of one's actions on the security and welfare of others, to promote equity, including equality of the sexes, and to protect the interests of future generations (see Commission on Global Governance, 1995, pp. 55–7). Thirdly, a distinguished group of former heads of state and government, calling themselves the InterAction Council, has drawn up a Universal Declaration of Human Responsibilities in a conscious attempt to balance the Universal Declaration of Human Rights.

These lists contain much that is commonsense justice. Even so, it may not be easy always to abide by their precepts, especially in the face of competing loyalties, vested interests and prejudices. Let us none the less hope that today's conscientious world citizens will not need to abide quite so stoically by their principles as Marcus Aurelius suggested. He asserted it was crucial that 'wherever a man live, he live as a citizen of the World-City. Let men look upon thee, cite thee, as a man in very deed that lives according to Nature. If they cannot bear thee, let them slay thee. For it were better so than to live their life' (Marcus Aurelius Antoninus, 1961, X.15).

World law and the citizen

From Locke to the French Revolution the belief that the general notion of Natural Law could be translated into an outline of specific natural human rights became widely accepted. But the protection of those rights was seen to be the responsibility of the state, not of international society; so human rights were closely associated with citizens' rights as explained in chapter 1. What interests us here is how these rights, in expanded form, came to be thought of as universal rights, proclaimed and guarded by the international community of states. For, by this transition, human rights assumed a semblance of the rights of the world citizen. Furthermore, they have the status of law in so far as they are incorporated into documents signed and ratified as treaties.

As early as the revolutionary age, indeed, there was an understanding that in principle the American and French Declarations were being propounded not just for the sake of their own peoples: Jefferson, for instance, wrote about the Declaration of Independence, 'we are acting for all Mankind' (see Schlereth, 1977, p. 106).

What has attracted the attention of scholars more from this period is Kant's conception of a cosmopolitan law or code of right, expounded in 1795 in his *Perpetual Peace*. His image of this form of law is very restricted, merely the right of abode anywhere on earth. The result of its practical application, however, was already an intermingling of people and the opening up of the prospect for 'a universal right [i.e. law] of humanity' – the flowering of world citizenship. 'The peoples of the earth', Kant declared, 'have thus entered in varying degrees into a universal community, and it has developed to the point where a violation of rights in *one* part of the world is felt *everywhere*' (Reiss, 1991, pp. 107–8). From the perspective of the second half of the twentieth century – from the Holocaust to Bosnia, Rwanda and Kosovo – it was a perceptive remark.

However, little was done to draw up the details of such a cosmopolitan law of rights until the mid-twentieth century. The universal protection of human rights assumed unambiguous status in international law through the Charter of the United Nations. Art. 55 states that 'the United Nations shall promote . . . universal respect for, and observance of, human rights and fundamental freedoms for all', while Art. 56 pledges all member states to assist in this task.

These rights were articulated in the Universal Declaration of Human Rights. This document, however, has no legal force. On the other hand, subsequent supporting documents do. These are: the International

Covenant on Economic, Social and Cultural Rights; the International Covenant on Civil and Political Rights; and the Optional Protocol to the latter. These four documents are collectively called the International Bill of Rights. By signing the two Covenants, about half the world's states are party to agreements having the force of international law. And the rights relate to both individuals and groups, notably ethnic groups.

The rights enshrined in these documents are summarized in figure 4.4. So, just as the individual *qua* state citizen is conceived as having civil, political, social and economic rights, so the individual *qua* human being or world citizen is conceived as having a parallel set of rights. It naturally goes without saying that in neither status are these rights necessarily enjoyed and enforced in practice as the ideal documents commend and command.

However, if citizens have rights, they also have concomitant obligations not to infringe the rights of other citizens. Therefore, the same principle of reciprocity must apply to persons in their capacity as world citizens. This precept was made explicit in the Charter of the International Tribunal set up after the Second World War to try German leaders charged with, *inter alia*, crimes against humanity. The Tribunal made it transparently clear that an individual's duty to adhere to this universal moral code transcends his duty of obedience to the state where that state demands the contravention of the higher law. That tenet was, in truth, scarcely novel. Nearly two thousand four hundred years earlier Sophocles understood it well. Antigone, defying King Creon, declared:

> I did not think your edicts strong enough
> To overrule the unwritten unalterable laws
> Of God and heaven, you being only a man.
> *(Sophocles, 1947, p. 138)*

And the principle was still being upheld at the end of the twentieth century AD with the prosecution at The Hague and Arusha of those persons indicted for war crimes in the gruesome Bosnian and Rwandan civil wars respectively.

The work of the Hague tribunal revived interest in the idea that there should be established a permanent world criminal court, accepted,

	Life	Security	Freedom		
			Legal and political — negative	Legal and political — positive	Economic, social and cultural
Rights of the individual	Preservation of life	Not to be tortured or badly treated	From slavery From imprisonment without trial From discrimination because of race, religion or sex	To hold meetings To express political opinions To take part in government To be tried fairly To worship To marry To travel	To work To earn a reasonable wage and to have a reasonable standard of living To own property To education To life of dignity with reasonable leisure
Rights of groups or countries	No mass killing or genocide		From discrimination against whole groups, e.g. religious or racial	To have a nation (i.e. one's own country)	

Figure 4.4

albeit with lukewarm commitment, in 1998. This, in turn, has implications for the creation of a world law and related judicial institutions modelled on national legal systems – an aspiration that is top of the world federalists' agenda. But, of course, world law would be but a pallid replica of municipal (i.e. state) law without enforcement agencies. Such a development inevitably takes us from the realm of cosmopolitan law to that of cosmopolitan politics.

World governance and the citizen

Protection of and obedience to the law is a rather passive form of citizenship, though none the less vital for all that. A potentially stronger form is the exercise of political rights. How does this aspect of the status translate into world citizenship? Three, not mutually exclusive, options are available. One is to participate in civil society organizations with a global reach. A second is to be involved in the supra-national political institutions that already exist. And thirdly, there is the advocacy of new opportunities and institutions to enhance the reality of political world citizenship.

We have already noticed earlier in this chapter that, in a state context, civil society organizations can be effective channels through which to exercise citizenly behaviour and wield influence on government policies. It is becoming increasingly evident that what can be termed global civil society is playing a similar role in a trans-national setting. Many people are now acting as world citizens by participating in organizations which are devoted to publicizing global problems and exerting pressure especially on governments and multinational companies to change their policies and activities. Humanitarian and environmental concerns have generated most support.

Humanitarian organizations include specialist bodies such as Médecins sans Frontières. More generalized humanitarian activities by global civil society relate to two main denials of human rights, economic and civil – through poverty and political persecution respectively. Bodies like Save the Children and Oxfam work in the first field; organizations like Amnesty International work in the second. Amnesty International was established in 1961, the centenary of the emancipation of Russian serfs and the American Civil War, in order to work on behalf of prisoners of conscience. In terms of world citizenship this body is of especial relevance because it is confronting national governments with transgressions against the UN Charter and International Bill of Rights.

Awareness of resource depletion and environmental degradation has spawned a large number of organizations at the national level. Some, however, most conspicuously perhaps, Greenpeace, are global bodies; but many national associations also, by the very nature of their purposes, have global agendas.

In United Nations parlance substantial bodies of this kind are called NGOs or INGOs ((International) Non-Governmental Organizations). These increased in number during the twentieth century: in 1909 there were 176 INGOs; eighty years later there were 4,624. A large proportion of these work on behalf of the planet's environment. In 1992 the UN Conference on Environment and Development met in Rio de Janeiro. Representatives from more than 1,400 NGOs attended and thousands more participated in the unofficial Global Forum which was convened in tandem with the official UN meeting. This NGO collaboration with the UN continued thereafter in conferences on other topics.

Stress has been placed on the world role of individuals who are active participants in the global organizations. Yet very many more behave as world citizens at lower levels of commitment. But then that is true, as well, of state citizens. Signing petitions for and donating charitable contributions to such organizations must surely count as acts of world citizenship.

Finally, and not so obviously, are the influences that are subtly linking individuals into global networks and leading some perhaps to think less nationalistically and xenophobically, even endowing them with a positively cosmopolitan mentality, reminiscent of Kant's cosmopolitan law. To state that trans-national professional, interest-group, financial and commercial links are currently burgeoning to a remarkable degree may be a hackneyed observation. Its truth is none the less incontrovertible: the word 'globalization' has swiftly lodged itself into the vocabularies of journalists and social scientists to describe the phenomenon.

Yet we cannot be sure whether the multiplying webs of globalizing connections are having the moral effect of spreading world civic consciousness, or, instead, facilitating the pursuit of vested interests.

About the second form of political world citizenship – involvement in established institutions of global governance – there is not a great deal to be said. Effectively this means working in or for the United Nations. Perhaps, then, the Secretary-General is the very epitome of the world citizen – though it must be admitted that some who have occupied that office have approximated to the ideal rather less closely than others. Dag Hammarskjöld certainly was conscious of the need to keep the achievement of that goal constantly in mind, and expected the same dedication of his staff. Symbolic of his own conviction was his favourite bedtime reading: Marcus Aurelius' *Meditations*. Concerning the Secretariat staff, he asserted that the implications of Art. 100 of the Charter (demanding exclusive loyalty to the Organization) was that they 'should sever all their ties of interest and loyalty with whatever may be their home country' (see Lash, 1962, p. 286).

Commitment to the UN, support for its work and pressure upon national governments to uphold the spirit of the Charter more whole-heartedly is the collective *raison d'être* of the various national United Nations Associations, loosely federated through the WFUNA. Members of these associations are, naturally, conscious that they are world citizens. For example, in 1990, responding to current worry about global environment problems, the British UNA distributed a Citizens' Charter on the subject. This invited the concerned individual 'as a citizen of the world' to pledge himself or herself to four activities, two of which involved demanding that governments take effective action explicitly through the UN to respond to this critical issue.

But for persons who think of themselves as truly world citizens, the UN is a most frustrating body through which to work, because national interests so often preclude policies and actions for the good of the world as a whole and because individuals have so little access to or leverage on the organization. It is not surprising, then, that schemes to enhance or supplement the UN as a popularly responsive supra-national institution have been forthcoming throughout the whole of its life. And so to our third form of political world citizenship – possible participation through proposed new world bodies.

Most radical have been the programmes of world federalists who, bitterly disappointed with the frailty of the League of Nations and then of the UN, proposed the creation of a world government. For example, in 1945 Robert Sarrazac founded the Front Humain des Citoyens du Monde to campaign for this purpose. Two years later the American Garry Davis launched a World Citizens' Registry, which still exists.

The thrust of this movement is revealed by the following statement: 'Only a world authority deriving its powers directly from the people of the world can give the necessary priority to [the world's] common needs and interests and provide their effective defense and organization' (*Mundialist Summa*, 1977, p. 18).

The immediate post-war movement soon lost its momentum. Some organizations, such as the Association of World Federalists in the UK, survived, and in the 1970s new bodies arose, notably the Mouvement populaire des Citoyens du Monde in France and Planetary Citizens in the USA. Associations which share these views are affiliated to the World Federalist Movement. In 1997 a One World Charter was presented to the UK Parliament requesting the consideration of a number of issues relating to the UN, including the formation of a UN Parliament with a view to its sharing power with the General Assembly.

The felt need for the system of world governance to be rendered more democratic by means of an elected body or bodies brings us, in fact, to the heart of what are widely believed to be both urgent and reasonably practicable proposals at the turn of the century. We need to discuss this general requirement in its two major forms. One is for the creation, as highlighted in the world federalists' agenda, for a second UN assembly; the other, incorporating this scheme in its more ambitious agenda, is the developing concept of cosmopolitan democracy.

'We the peoples of the United Nations . . . have resolved to combine our efforts . . .' These words from the Preamble to the UN Charter have occasioned wry remarks from commentators who bemoan the utter lack of opportunities in the UN's institutions for the peoples to combine their efforts for any purposes at all. The world's states control the Security Council and the General Assembly. Only one tiny loophole exists in the Charter through which the spirit of democratic world citizenship might be able to infiltrate and thus challenge this dominance. The loophole is Art. 22, which makes this provision: 'The General Assembly may establish such subsidiary organs as it deems necessary for the performance of its functions.'

The word 'subsidiary' is a catch, but at least this statement opens up the possibility of transforming the UN into a bicameral institution, with an assembly elected by 'the peoples'. It is an obvious idea. In fact, the shock of the First World War led, especially in the USA, to the composition of plans for world government which included provision for an elected assembly. After the founding of the UN, the British Parliamentary Group for World Government advocated such a plan as early as 1952. The idea has received considerable support in more recent years through specially founded movements for UN reform – the Campaign for a More Democratic United Nations (CAMDUN) and the International Network For a UN Second Assembly (INFUSA).

The creation of an Assembly of Peoples would undoubtedly strengthen the principle of world citizenship. Individuals would be enfranchised, be able to vote for their representatives to a supra-national parliament on a global level just as the citizens of the European Union exercise their right of suffrage at the sub-continental level. Such a constitutional adaptation would also be symbolic: it would signal acceptance that citizens as well as states are entitled to act on the international stage.

There are, of course, very considerable difficulties and obstacles. If Art. 22 were used, the second assembly would be merely consultative to the General Assembly; yet if an attempt were made to endow it with effective powers, the member states would almost certainly block the scheme. Just compare the puny powers of the European Parliament with the powers of the national parliaments of the EU member states. And this in a union with a much more sincere commitment to democracy than may be found in many other countries throughout the continents of the world and which are members of the United Nations. Nevertheless, autocratic and military governments have withered and shoots of democracy, admittedly somewhat tender in some countries, have grown in their place since c.1990 – in central and eastern Europe, Latin America and Africa. These developments have engendered a mood of hopefulness that citizenship with some real civil and political rights is taking root more extensively than ever before. And if democratic national citizenship, why not democratic world citizenship?

The establishment of a UN second assembly, useful as such a step would be, cannot be thought of as a total realization of this objective. Like world peace, in Litvinov's famous adage, world democracy too is indivisible. This understanding of necessary interconnections is the crucial insight of the proponents of the concept of cosmopolitan democracy. If democratic principles are to become truly global, they must undergird the relationships between citizens and their states and the behaviour of states to each other, as well as providing citizens with opportunities to participate in trans- and supra-national political bodies.

The basic justification for such proposals is that many problems affecting ordinary people are no respecters of national boundaries: the issue of global warming is an obvious instance. Democratic citizenship presupposes the right of individuals to have some say about how their lives are affected by factors beyond their immediate personal control. It follows, therefore, that in the contemporary world the individual's voice needs to carry beyond the geographical confines of the state.

The cosmopolitan democracy pattern is envisaged as a gradual evolution of more effective and additional regional institutions and global bodies as well as a reformed UN and the current global civil society networks. This package of enhanced democratic geometry would enable citizens to be protected by improved juridical systems and to participate in a variety of processes – of direct democracy, representative democracy and referendums. In the words of David Held, the leading exponent of the idea, in a cosmopolitan democratic system,

> People can enjoy membership in the diverse communities which significantly affect them and, accordingly, access to a variety of forms of political participation. Citizenship would be extended, in principle, to membership in all cross-cutting political communities, from the local to the global.
>
> *(Held, 1995, p. 272)*

The cosmopolitan democracy thesis is, however, much more complex than just the functioning of the citizen in the proposed web of institutions and activities. It spans legal and economic structures as well as political. In political terms, for example, the arrangements would increase the accountability and therefore legitimacy of decision-making processes at all levels. In terms of the role of the citizen specifically, the model reveals how the principles and practices of multiple citizenship could be knitted together into a rather more coherent pattern of identities, duties and rights than the current, historically *ad hoc*, patchwork outlined in this chapter. Furthermore, the linking of cosmopolitanism with democracy has truly modernized the idea of the cosmopolites, who, in Greek thought, were merely the few furnished with the wisdom to perceive the universal law of nature.

Pros and cons

Multiple citizenship, it is evident, is rapidly becoming a reality. Yet it is complicated and difficult for the individual to cope with. Modern citizens must wear so many civic hats that, if they accept the proper burden of citizenly responsibility, they cannot but feel a variety of strains. Multiple citizenship presents the demands of multiple understanding, multiple identities, multiple loyalties, multiple rights and multiple duties. In the Aristotelian and Rousseauean ideal states the political environment in which the citizen would operate was compact and intimate and possessed of simple sets of participative rules. In today's real world of manifold civic contexts the citizen is required to possess knowledge, acquire understanding and develop skills pertinent to the several citizenly identities outlined in this chapter. Is it not evident that most people have neither the interest nor the time to organize their lives for meeting such a range of civic demands? The conscientious discharge of even a singular citizenship role is difficult enough. Multiple citizenship, to state the obvious, multiplies the difficulties.

We may also question whether multiple citizenship is compatible with the traditional state-centred concept of citizenship at all. What happens to the virtue of patriotism, for example, when a citizen with dual nationality or a citizen of the European Union finds his or her twin allegiances are pulled in opposite directions by irreconcilable differences? We have come full circle and return to Cicero's principle of incompatibility.

Yet it is even more complex today. Now citizens are expected to be loyal to their State. And to their state or region, and to their town, and to the civil society bodies to which they belong. And in Europe to the Union. And to the whole planet? These demands necessitate a most ample sense of allegiance. All very well if the objects of one's loyalty coexist in harmony. But supposing they do not, as in the Little Rock school desegregation incident? How do citizens choose between the competing demands on their loyalty? The citizen may feel overwhelmed, perhaps confused. It is an easy matter to identify with one's nation-state, hence the immense power of nationalism bolstered by the appeal of tradition and the appeal of symbols. It is not so straightforward when one is required to identify with so many different entities which entail one's civic attachment.

The problem is highlighted by the current growing requirement for loyalty to institutions and agendas on supra-national planes, competing with traditional powerful national ties. This consideration leads to compelling objections concerning the building of supra-national layers of citizenship. These may be grouped into two clusters, one concerning individual attitudes, the other concerning the relationship of multi-national/world citizenship to the established state-system.

Many temperamentally find the idea of a supra-national identity uncongenial. Comments uttered in France across two centuries against perceived threats to national identity may be taken as illuminating examples of this standpoint. Reacting against the cosmopolitanism of the *philosophes* in 1772, Rousseau acidly declared: 'Today there are no longer Frenchmen, Germans, Spaniards, or even Englishmen, whatever is said; there are only Europeans. All have the same tastes, the same passions, the same customs. . . . They are at home wherever there is money to steal and women to seduce' (Rousseau, 1969, p. 960). In 1974 the French sociologist Raymond Aron, reacting against the cohering agenda of the European Community, asserted with forthright conviction: 'there are no such animals as "European citizens". There are only French, German or Italian citizens' (Aron, 1974, p. 653).

We may identify some more specific factors behind this general state of mind. The spread of trans-national personal contacts and a pervasive attitude of mind that cosmopolitanism is desirable may lead, in fact, to quite undesirable responses. We must not, for example, be fooled into assuming that, because the word 'understanding' can mean both comprehension and empathy, the first necessarily generates the second. Familiarity, after all, can breed contempt. So, extra knowledge of other peoples, through widespread and frequent travel or foreign domicile, may lead to a hardening rather than a softening of the very nationalistic or ethnic dislikes that inhibit the growth of cosmopolitanism. Even those who pretend to a cosmopolitan heart may in truth have but a hollow commitment to the ideal. Such an insincere cosmopolite, sneered Rousseau, 'loves the Tartars in order to be spared from loving his neighbours' (see Cobban, 1964, p. 106).

If the heart is not deeply touched by the cosmopolitan vision, the reasons can be most readily sought in the power of national binding

150

traditions and the frailty of any comparable global emotional ties. Citizens need to share a sense of community. This consciousness is nurtured most efficaciously by growing up and living in a society that has an identifiable common, especially linguistic, culture, a strong historical narrative and compelling myths. These are features already discussed in chapter 3. And, of course, they are products of centuries, sometimes even millenia, of development. To discard them, even to weaken them, leads to cultural and psychological rootlessness, disorienting for the individual and imperilling of social cohesion.

The problem is that there is no similar culture, history or mythology that is fully universal in scope and in which may be embedded a firm cosmopolitan identity. Even the more plausible efforts to emphasize the common European inheritance of the members of the EU – a kind of cultural highest common factor – is having only limited success.

These problems are compounded by the conflation of culture and politics. If citizens are a reasonably homogeneous group of persons in the cultural sense with a reciprocal set of rights and duties to a state in the political sense, then, as it has often been asserted, world citizenship is undesirable: a homogenized world culture and a world state present a vision of dystopia. Creativity and freedom alike would be seriously impaired; world citizens would be too punily motivated and organized to act as guardians of the quality and liberties of human life.

We must, indeed, recognize the very real differences between the ancient Stoics' imagined cosmopolis and the modern blueprints for a world state. The Stoics could manage to balance their loyalty to the state and their adherence to a universal morality by separating them into virtually distinct public and private spheres. A fully-fledged modern world state, in contrast, might well require a transfer of civic allegiance from the state to the universal polity.

However, this is to wander into the realms of unbridled speculation, into the world of H. G. Wells's *The Open Conspiracy*, *A Modern Utopia* and *The Shape of Things to Come*. What should more properly attract our attention is the set of concerns that have been aired (e.g. by Aron (1974) and Green (1987)) about the relationship between any form of trans-national citizenship and the nation-state as can be currently observed.

States wield *de jure* and *de facto* power. States are recognized by international law as sovereign entities, and since post-feudal times have become the sole repositories of the legal means for the exercise of force. It can be argued from these starting-points that political citizenship is and must properly be confined to the state. There are two reasons for this. One is the international law stress on citizenship as a status conferred by a state (admittedly geographically partially weakened by the Maastricht Treaty). The second reason derives from the state's monopoly on the use of just force and the connection between that factor and the nature of citizenship as a notional contract of reciprocal rights and duties. Civil and political rights are useless if they are not honoured and protected. The state has the power negatively to infringe these rights or positively to uphold them. By the argument of reciprocity citizens consequently rely on the obligation of the state to exercise that power justly: to guarantee the rights against internal injustice or lawlessness and external attack. In return, citizens have the duty to support the civil forces of law and order and the military forces of defence. The duty of defence, by patriotic civic republican tradition, as explained in chapter 2, or by the pragmatic need for self-preservation *in extremis*, includes military service in person. Is this not incompatible with any other citizenly allegiance?

Moreover, the exercise of power in both the internal and external domains is the mark of sovereignty. And, however much sovereignty is being diluted in the contemporary world, there is little likelihood that these key attributes will be readily relinquished. Accordingly, political citizenship, so intimately reliant on the possession of the means of force by the state, must remain absorbed in the state as the necessary catalyst for its vitality.

Yet, despite such cogent arguments against multiple citizenship, the developments outlined in this chapter are really not going to wither. Indeed, for those who welcome the phenomenon of plural citizenships, there are ways of supporting the trend, at both individual and institutional levels.

We may start by appreciating that, like it or not, much of life is a good deal more complicated now than it used to be. Human beings are adaptable; so if people are adjusting to increasingly complex lifestyles and employment patterns, perhaps there are grounds for believing that adaptation to the complex role of multiple citizenship is not impossible. The assertion of one academic points in the same direction: 'many psychologists would argue that an individual's potential for loyalty and identity can be enhanced in an almost limitless fashion by participation in different groups rather than being "used up" by relationship with one' (Torney-Purta, 1981, p. 258). It is a matter of an expansion of moral awareness, in particular emancipation from the moral tunnel-vision of nationalism. The communications media and the schools, of course (as we shall see in chapter 5), have crucial responsibilities in helping to achieve this objective.

In addition to the question of the individual's sense of identity and loyalty, one of the most cogent contrary arguments already presented is the matter of state sovereignty. This relates most strongly to the political facet of citizenship. If, however, we look at the social and economic features of citizenship, it is evident that multiple citizenship is easier both to conceive and to concede in these fields. For example, the universal right to travel to, trade with and settle in countries other than one's own has long been recognized. Kant's cosmopolitan law, for example, starts with the proposition that 'all men . . . [have a] right to communal possession of the earth's surface' (Reiss, 1991, p. 106).

And what is the Single European Act, laying the foundations for the Single Market, if not a contract among the signatories to codify and fully realize this basic precept over that portion of the earth that is the EC/EU? Indeed, the EU as a whole, its more prosperous regions particularly, has acted as a powerful magnet to aliens seeking employment. These persons have commonly been granted the welfare and economic rights that have become associated with citizenship. In other words, millions of immigrants are treated as members of the socio-economic civil society, a kind of quasi-citizenship. Most commentators, therefore, concede that trans-national socio-economic rights, however classified, exist and are justified.

The institutions through which the status of citizenship is performed also have an important function to play in clarifying and justifying the multiple citizen's roles. We have already seen how international law has tackled dual citizenship; how the Maastricht Treaty and the European Court of Justice case law have been defining European citizenship; and how too the EU has accepted the principle of subsidiarity. This principle for the apportionment of decision-making could be more widely adopted – for example, to help ease the problems associated with the sense of world citizenship. For we must remember that Pope John XXIII, in his Encyclical *Pacem in Terris*, built on his predecessor's enunciation of subsidiarity by using the term with the global dimension very much in mind.

A good deal of this section indicates that there are weighty arguments against the principle and practice of multiple citizenship. Nevertheless, they do not, surely, more than dent the body of the chapter. The conventions of international law and state sovereignty, it is true, supply robust underpinning for the traditional uni-dimensional concept of citizenship; yet both are flexing beneath the intricate realities of a world being transformed for the twenty-first century.

5

Problems and Resolutions

Inherent problems and tensions

Is citizenship really worth bothering about? Maybe it is a 'myth' (Ignatieff, 1995); maybe it is 'an unnatural practice' (Oldfield, 1990b); and maybe the citizen today is effectively 'disenfranchised' (Horsman and Marshall, 1994). Article- and chapter-titles raise such basic doubts. However, readers have not been brought to this final chapter in order maliciously to inform them that the subject-matter of the book has so tenuous an existence as to be unworthy of study. Citizenship unquestionably presents plenty of problems; however, it is the very importance of the status and activity of being a citizen that commands us, not to neglect the subject, but, on the contrary, to understand the complexities and tensions that do exist and worry them to resolutions. This is the purpose of the present chapter.

The root difficulty lies in the enormous scale of the changes that citizenship has undergone since the age of the classical city-state. The contexts in which the rights of citizenship are claimed and enjoyed and its duties discharged would be unrecognizable to, not to mention disapproved by, Aristotle. Moreover, what these rights are have become more extensive and the proportion of the population embraced by full civic membership has vastly expanded. In short, the concept and practice of citizenship have been struggling to encompass ideas, attitudes and activities for which it was not originally designed. So present-day critics of citizenship reviewing its shortcomings, incompatibilities and

155

inconsistencies are, in effect, wondering whether its remarkable elasticity has not at last reached its limit.

Of the three ways in which citizenship has been stretched – geographical context, legal/constitutional content and demographic quota – it is the last of these that we should dwell upon. In the Greek city-states and the Roman Republic the numbers of citizens as a proportion of the total population was quite small. This was true, too, of the modern nation-state until the liberalizing and democratizing reforms that flowed from the late eighteenth-century revolutions. Citizenship was formulated as an elite status; the expectation today is that it should be universally conferred.

This distinction leads to a dichotomous Left–Right response. The Left argue the justice of universal citizenship: it is unfair, illogical and even inefficient to bar any portion of a society from full membership. Commentators on the Right challenge this view by arguing that the system cannot cope. This position has been summarized from an American perspective as follows:

> The problem is that certain groups that were marginal and generally uninvolved in politics in the past, including blacks and women, are now involved in politics and making demands for government resources. This risks overloading the democratic process.
>
> *(Sinopoli, 1992, p. 160)*

Such a proposition leads to the argument that an ample measure of apathy is essential – either as an ingredient for good governance, or for supine acceptance of complacent governance, depending on one's position on the political spectrum. It was once said of a languid British politician that he went around the country stirring up apathy! Was he doing good by this, and was it a difficult task? If it can be convincingly argued that a country a-bubble with millions of active citizens conscious of their entitlements is unhealthy, it can equally be argued that it is unlikely to happen: politics is a minority game; most citizens are, in their normal state, passive. And surely the clinching consideration is that if citizens behave in a manner proper to their status, they should be constantly and responsibly checking that their activities are not 'overloading the process': citizenly activity that endangers the common weal is a contradiction in terms.

156

'Too much' citizenship manifests itself either as the selfish pursuit of entitlements, which has just been countered, or as zealotry. Here is another problem: the urge to display your commitment to the ideal of civic virtue and to persuade, by perhaps questionable means, the less politically devoted citizens to follow your example. Nathaniel Hawthorne's *Scarlet Letter* may be taken as a parable on this. Writing in mid-nineteenth-century America about the pillory, he explained: 'this scaffold . . . was held, in the old time, to be as effectual an agent in the promotion of good citizenship as ever was the guillotine among the terrorists of France' (Hawthorne, 1992, p. 74).

Reference to the French Revolution is a useful reminder that it is in revolutionary times that citizenly ardour can become so enflamed as to be an awful portent of the potential intensity of feeling in citizenship. Like all good things – and let us not be deflected from the truth that citizenship is good – you can have too much of it. It is possible for civic enthusiasm to lead, in its unbridled mood, to an intolerant suffocation of the private life. An American historian has provided a colourful analogy: 'The Germans have a consoling proverb: "The soup is never eaten as hot as it's cooked." But certainly in the crisis period of revolutions there is an effort to force it steaming down the throat of the ordinary citizen' (Brinton, 1952, pp. 200–1). Just look at the record of the French Jacobins, the Russian Bolsheviks and the Chinese Red Guards.

But even if the problems attendant upon expansion can be avoided and of zealotry be guarded against, there are still the difficulties of internal contradictions. These have been touched upon in earlier chapters, but it is useful to gather them all together at this point.

That two distinct styles of theorizing about citizenship exist – the civic republican and the liberal – might suggest that there is an underlying fault-line in the very concept. How can citizenship entail simultaneously an insistence on the primacy of public life over the private, the basic tenet of civic republicanism, while preaching the exact reverse in its liberal mode? How can the deep commitment to duties of the one be reconciled with the casual acceptance of duties in favour of rights of the other?

One answer could be that reconciliation is only possible if we shift our sights from the hardened positions of idealistic theory to the softer compromises of reality. The republican ideal of citizenship has been described as 'noble myth' and the liberal as 'fanciful lie' (Ignatieff,

1995, p. 53). Republican theorists devoutly wish the truly civically virtuous citizen to exist, but he cannot; liberal theorists urgently wish the economic consumer to engulf the politically active citizen, but he should not. It is the liberal distortion that is the more relevant and therefore the more necessary to resolve today because, even if citizenship be a lie, it is one of 'the basic fictions which sustain our democracy' (R. Dore, see Roche, 1992, p. 224).

If the edifice of citizenship is undermined by the cleavage between and frailty of its two main theoretical supports, it is also weakened by tensions within the structure itself. These strains are of two kinds: between the different geographical loci of commitment, and between the social and economic and civil and political facets of citizenship.

The first of these has been discussed in chapter 4 and merely needs recapitulation here. To be a citizen in a *polis* gave a man a simple, straightforward, easily comprehended station in life; and as the modern form of citizenship developed in the nation-state, a similar simplicity applied. But with the proliferation of multiple citizen identities – municipal, regional/state, national, dual, European, world – the classical, Aristotelian model was steadily overwhelmed. Rules, rights, duties and loyalties for the different levels could well be in tension. And if the basic form of relationship for which citizenship was devised no longer obtains, does citizenship in any authentic sense still obtain? A citizen was, as originally conceived, a full member of a *polis* or *civitas*, a single, coherent political body. Because the environment in which the citizen has been expected to operate has been dramatically diversified, has citizenship perforce so adaptively evolved that it has lost its true essence? Has Aristotle's 'political animal' become a different species?

But even avoiding this radical line of thought, there can be little doubt that holding the first and second generation of citizens' rights together in a coherent package presents considerable difficulties. The very principle of economic citizenship is at loggerheads with the principle of civil and political citizenship. The exercise of the right to economic freedom leads to inequality; civil and political forms of citizenship exist to treat individuals as equals. Social and political citizenships are also at variance. Social rights are necessarily vague; political rights must be legally precise. 'Welfare stresses the right to receive; democracy the duty to participate' (T. H. Marshall, see Roche, 1992, p. 36). Social rights, it has been argued, therefore tend to be given with no expectation of moral obligation – they are entitlements; political rights are given in the expectation that they are used with due responsibility.

The incorporation of social rights into the meaning of citizenship changed its character. For centuries citizenship was clearly a juridico-political concept and status. Socio-economic standing or condition were relevant only in three qualifying senses. One was freedom from constant toil so that the citizen had time to perform his duties. The second was the belief that only 'fit and proper persons', with a stake in the country's welfare, should have the civic status. The third was the belief that it would be imprudent to allow the uneducated masses to tamper with civic affairs. A person's socio-economic standing was an entrance ticket into the status of citizenship, not a set of rights acquired on entry.

In any case, those conditions are now obsolete. The first argument, central to citizenship in the *polis*, is scarcely pertinent to the modern state. The second was a combination of snobbery and the truism that people do not behave responsibly if they are not given responsibility. The third could only be held with conviction in ages of restricted access to education and the press. The abolition or decline of class distinctions, the processes of economic and educational levelling-up and the proliferation of the news media have seriously blunted the second and third arguments.

The question is now, therefore, whether the modern state that is relatively egalitarian and democratic requires the addition of the social dimension to citizenship in order to support those two desirable qualities. Marshall, famously and influentially, believed the case to be incontrovertible. Most commentators follow his basic argument. But is the case so crucial that it is worth all the tensions and incompatibilities it has introduced into the hitherto uncomplicated concept of a state juridico-political citizenship? Granting the desirability and justice of an inclusive citizenship based on this simple, traditional model, could not the necessary social and economic levelling-up be accomplished without turning the arrangements into an integral part of citizenship? Can they not be categorized as *human* rather than citizenship rights? Indeed, are they not in any case so classified in international documents and in some states in practice (as will be shown in the next section)? The state would still be obligated to provide the basic employment, welfare and educational standards, which would then again be considered the entrance ticket to citizenship, but now universally issued.

159

The relationship between citizenship rights and human rights, the underlying matter of the relationship between social and political rights, and the question of apathy are proving to be significant current issues.

Current issues

Has citizenship as a *state*-defined status outlived its usefulness? Students of International Relations refer to the emergence of the post-Westphalian state, a style of polity that, they suggest, is superseding the sovereign territorial state recognized by those mid-seventeenth-century treaties. Can this new, less autonomous state, moulded by migratory, sub-national and trans-national forces, still support a form of citizenship designed in and for different conditions? The influences of two trans-national forces in particular cast doubt on the sustainability of citizen-ship in its traditional form. One is the increasingly accepted validity of universal human rights; the other is the globalization of trade, com-munications and, most importantly, financial transactions.

The 1789 French Declaration listed both the rights of man and the rights of the citizen. Are these two sets of rights still distinguishable – the rights that an individual should expect to enjoy *qua* citizen and *qua* human being? The answer is that they are, in the following limited ways. In the first place, the two sets of rights have different sources of legitimacy, the one deriving from state constitutions, the other from international treaties and conventions. Secondly, some constitutional lists are less comprehensive than the human rights documents, which therefore perform a useful supplementary function. Thirdly, citizens' rights, naturally, cover only citizens; aliens must therefore rely on the protection of international human rights. And fourthly, *protection* is indeed the prime function of human rights. A British authority on international law explains:

> the rights which uniquely concern citizenship are those which involve a duty and responsibility on both the citizen and the State. By contrast human rights . . . impose limitations on the powers of the State in order to enjoy minimum freedoms. . . .
> . . . citizenship provides a basis for State action.
>
> *(Gardner, n.d., pp. 197–8)*

160

Diplomatic intervention on behalf of citizens is an obvious instance of the principle of state action, enunciated most famously for Britons in Palmerston's *Civis Romanus sum* speech.

However, these differences are residual, for, generally speaking, the distinction between the two kinds of rights is rapidly losing its clarity. The sections of modern constitutions devoted to rights do not mention any differentiation; moreover, international lists, notably the constituent documents of the International Bill of Human Rights, bear a remarkable resemblance to those in recent national documents.

Even more notably, in the states of the European Union, non-nationals enjoy on a par with national citizens the social and economic rights which are statutorily accorded to the latter, though – and here is this dichotomy again – not the political rights (unless the non-nationals possess these as European citizens under the terms of the Maastricht Treaty). This is a development of cardinal importance to our theme and needs to be dwelt upon. An extended quotation from a report on citizenship in a number of EU states will explain the situation.

> in the light of rights given to everyone under the European Convention on Human Rights and rights given to EC nationals under European Community law it now seems futile to try to identify a clearly defined set of rights given only to those having the status of nationals, since so many rights are now given to those without that status. . . .
>
> This is most strikingly illustrated in relation to entitlement to welfare benefits and the right to education. . . .
>
> This leads us to conclude that the 'old' concept of citizenship (that regulated by nationality) is indeed redundant and that there is now need for a new definition of citizenship. . . . New citizenship should be made up of those rights and obligations conferred on all persons with some kind of link with the conferring State. . . .
>
> . . . the question should be asked whether . . . it is right that there are still certain, albeit few, rights and obligations which are regulated according to nationality-citizenship.
>
> *(Gardner, n.d., pp. 43–4)*

The willingness of some European states to extend rights to non-nationals and the existence of the status of citizen of the European Union make the confusion in the EU states somewhat peculiar on a global scale. Nevertheless, the EU is a geographically expanding

161

community and it serves to highlight the world-wide problem of the dubiety of separating citizen and human rights. Indeed, a much more dramatic example than the confusion in the EU supports this point with particular force. That the Universal Declaration of Human Rights exists and has been universally agreed has been used as a justification for foreign intervention to protect citizens against their governments. The imposition of no-fly zones in Iraq and intervention on behalf of the Albanian Kosovars are notable examples. The implication of these developments is that state sovereignty may be infringed if a government infringes the rights of its citizens tested against the benchmark of universal human rights.

So, it can no longer be assumed that the relationship between state and citizens is immune from outside intervention if the state has malign intentions towards some of its citizens. But nor can a state that wishes to treat its citizens beneficently necessarily protect them from the fluctuating effects of the global economy. Globalization, therefore, also raises questions about the nature of citizenship in our own times. If a government is reckoned legitimate in so far as it can be held accountable to the citizenry (and this is the democratic principle), then legitimacy is weakened as accountability is undermined. In the words of a British political scientist,

> just as more and more people today are . . . asserting that they should control their destinies and that government must operate on their behalf if it is to be legitimate government – the very scope and relevance of this principle is . . . being contested by processes of global restructuring.
>
> *(Held, 1991, p. 226)*

To be concrete and relevant: if a government can blame the failure of businesses and unemployment on trans-national financial difficulties or manipulations over which it truly has no control, then what price national citizenship? The state has failed to honour one element of its side in the reciprocal relationship – namely, to ensure its citizens' economic rights; yet it cannot be held responsible for this dereliction. Accountability is impossible; legitimacy and citizenship are consequently impaired.

This example is apposite precisely because it is drawn from the field of economics and therefore affects living standards. This is what most people are interested in. A state that transparently fails to maintain living standards soon loses legitimacy, that is, the committed adherence of its citizens, no matter how conscientious it is in upholding civil and political rights and freedoms. Weimar Germany and, perhaps, the perilous trends in post-Soviet Russia are awful witnesses to this pattern. Nothing breeds civic disillusion and apathy more than the belief that a government or a regime is impotent before the pressure of forces inimical to its citizens' core interests.

We return, therefore, to the question of apathy. If the body of citizens is too apathetic, the whole state-citizenship structure is in danger of collapsing. A happy medium must be struck between deep and pervasive apathy and intolerant zealotry. Is the *fin-de-siècle* nation-state facing a public mood that has swung dangerously towards apathy for reasons that assuredly include disillusion leading, in turn, to an erosion in the credibility of the citizenship contract between individual and state?

Listen to the evidence and opinion of a British political scientist concerning attitudes in the United Kingdom:

> At the General Election in May [1997] the turnout was 71.4 per cent, which was 6 per cent down on 1992, and the lowest since 1935. In many inner-city constituencies the turnout barely exceeded 50 per cent. . . .
> . . . not to vote should be interpreted . . . not as *exclusion* but as *disengagement* from the rest of society.
>
> *(I. Crewe, in Jowell and Park, 1998, p. 3)*

The speaker could have added that even the figure of 71 per cent was inflated because it masked the large numbers who had not even registered for enlistment on the electoral roll. There has been little agreement about either the cause of this 'disengagement', which includes evidence of positive cynicism and disrespect for politicians, or how significant were the research findings about the especially politically passive and alienated young adults.

Be that as it may, some British politicians and academics became worried by this kind of evidence and sought for methods of stimulating greater interest, commitment and involvement in public affairs. In 1998 the Lord Chancellor declared: 'We should not, must not, *dare not*, be complacent about the health and future of British democracy. Unless we become a nation of engaged citizens, our democracy is not secure' (see Advisory Group on Citizenship, 1998, p. 8).

A House of Commons Select Committee even considered the possibility of making voting compulsory. Others placed their faith in more effective citizenship education in schools. An Advisory Group, convened to improve and consolidate education for citizenship, expressed its purpose with determined immodesty: 'we aim at no less than a change in the political culture of this country both nationally and locally' (Advisory Group on Citizenship, 1998, p. 7). One recognizes the tone of confidence of the most famous belief in the power of education: *'L'éducation peut tout'*. At least it is refreshing to find more than a modicum of Helvétius's Enlightenment optimism in an age notorious for its amorality and cynicism. But can education really accomplish everything?

The roles of education

Education has a twofold purpose: to develop individuals for their own sakes and to fit them for life in the society into which they were born. The process raises three absolutely fundamental questions. These are: What should be the proper balance and connections between personal and social education? What distinguishes education for independent thinking and indoctrination? And what pedagogical methods and at what ages are various types of education most apt?

All these questions are highly germane to citizenship for the very simple and obvious reason that being a citizen is a role that, somehow or other, has to be learned. Citizens need knowledge and understanding of the social, legal and political system(s) in which they live and operate. They need skills and aptitudes to make use of that knowledge and understanding. And they need to be endowed with values and dispositions to put their knowledge and skills to beneficial use. The trouble is, 'beneficial' is a subjective ideal in a political context. Different states and regimes have different priorities and consequently different notions of what they expect from their citizens. This is true, too, of political theorists who have considered the role of citizens and how they should be educated. In practice, however, although educationists have occasionally shaped citizenship education in schools, more often than not it has been the state that has determined the prevailing style.

164

Defining principle	Focus	Purpose
Related to the two citizenship styles	Civic republican	Producing participant and patriotic citizens
	Liberal	Support for democracy
Moulding for particular socio-political purpose	Indoctrination	Producing 'robotic citizens'
	Separate education for different classes	Training elite citizens
Geographical level	National identity for all	Nation-building
	European	Create sense of EU identity
	World	Combat xenophobia, war, environmental degradation

Figure 5.1

It is possible to identify seven kinds of education for citizenship, each defined by its focus and its purpose. Figure 5.1 displays these and the subsequent paragraphs will briefly explain and exemplify them.

The differences between the republican and liberal modes of thinking about citizenship admirably illustrate the tension between the alternatives of civic and private objectives of education. To take the republican view first. Just as civic republicanism urges the priority of the public life over the private, so it must require education to have a mainly civic purpose in preference to a philosophy of education that seeks personal development as its prime objective. Or to put the republican belief with a coherence of the purest interpretation: since individuals are only true to their own human nature when they are behaving as citizens, education for citizenship is in any case the finest way of encouraging the development of the individual being's personality and potential.

Rousseau understood the distinction, indeed the potential gulf, between personal and civic education. In *Émile*, his treatise on education, he wrote: 'Forced to combat either nature or society, you must make your choice between the man and the citizen, you cannot train both' (Rousseau, 1911, p. 7). And although in *Émile* he favours objectives to

165

educate the person, in other works he reveals his commitment to the civic republican ideal. Rousseau had one eye on the ancient Spartan system of education, which was uncompromisingly geared to inculcating an unsullied and unrelenting civic virtue, while he focused the other on the needs of the nation-state of his own times. He accordingly recommended state control of education and the infusing of a common civic spirit from the earliest age:

> If children are brought up in the bosom of equality; if they are imbued with the laws of the state and the precepts of the general will; if they are taught to respect these above all things . . . we cannot doubt that they will learn to cherish one another mutually as brothers, to will nothing contrary to the will of society.
>
> *(see Oldfield, 1990a, pp. 70–1)*

Binding schools so tightly to the purposes of the state makes the liberal feel somewhat uneasy. It strikes at the rights and autonomy of both parents and pupils. Parents have the right to a say in the kind of school their children attend and the curriculum they follow, and pupils have a right to a full personal education undistorted by political considerations. On the other hand, the liberal democratic state needs democratically educated pupils in both senses: to be educated, in Rousseau's words 'in the bosom of equality', and to an understanding and appreciation of democratic processes involved in being a citizen. There are numerous problems here, which are currently recognized and being widely debated. The matter therefore needs separate treatment later.

What we must give our attention to next are two other kinds of citizenship education, each of which bears a relationship to the republican and liberal forms respectively. These are indoctrination and education according to social class.

Indoctrination, it has been said, is going on in a classroom

> . . . whenever one of a number of points of view is presented as though it were the only one possible; whenever questions are suppressed rather than answered; whenever certain areas of questioning are taboo; and whenever the educator is psychologically unable to tolerate the expression of dissenting views.
>
> *(Cohen, 1969, p. 180)*

166

How well one can recognize the educational practices of totalitarian states such as Nazi Germany and the Stalinist Soviet Union. Citizenship education was conducted in these countries for the mobilization of young minds in unquestioning support of the ideologies and the regimes that were built upon them.

But were the young people who were successfully programmed in this manner really citizens? For, this educational process is qualitatively different from the republican mode, which does not, except in its extreme Spartan form, totally preclude independent thought. Rousseau had no wish to produce robots. So, if indoctrinatory schooling is a production-line for 'robotic citizens', devoid of the faculty of personal judgement, these products are lacking a crucial component in the citizen design. One may thus classify totalitarian indoctrination as deformed civic republican education.

It can also be argued, in a much less sinister context, that a school system organized to produce an elite class of citizens distinct from other citizens is not an inherent feature of the civic republican ideal. Nevertheless and most famously, Plato reserved for his Guardian class in the *Republic* an education specially designed for first-class citizenship. We may find a parallel in modern England. The Public Schools, following the reforms of Arnold of Rugby in the early nineteenth century, plunged their privileged pupils into a classical education of Latin grammar and syntax and the grandeur of Roman Republican and Imperial history. The purpose? To create an elite citizenry, drawn largely from the wealthy upper-middle class as well as the hereditary aristocracy. This purpose, reflected in the curriculum, had civic republican overtones: the elite was being trained as a kind of senatorial cadre of politicians and bureaucrats for domestic government and of proconsuls for the British Empire, great successor to the Roman: *noblesse oblige* as civic virtue.

So unlike the civic education commended for the lower orders. The 1909–10 Board of Education handbook of suggestions for teachers in state schools urged teachers to develop in their pupils 'loyalty to comrades, loyalty to institutions' and to teach 'Thirty-five lessons on citizenship, local and national'. However, this sort of expected advice was overshadowed by the twenty pages devoted to the prime virtue of temperance (see Brennan, 1981, p. 34). Even as late as 1949 the Ministry of Education sent the following message to teachers:

There are forward-looking minds in every section of the teaching profession ready to reinterpret the old and simple virtues of humility, service, restraint and respect for personality. If schools can encourage qualities of this kind in their pupils, we may fulfil the conditions of a healthy democratic society.

(Ministry of Education, 1949, p. 41)

'*Forward-looking* minds' were commending '*humility*' for democracy, notice: not an understanding of rights or the need to monitor government policies.

What the private and state sectors of English education did share was an education in patriotism. This was an essentially political sensation and virtue, with very little of the cultural and ethnic overtones of national identity. Citizenship education in this latter sense – the conscious creation of a cohesive nation by means of the schools – has nevertheless been a very common policy. Rousseau and Fichte are notable thinkers who placed great emphasis on this need. Schools were part of the 'melting-pot' experience of the USA. More recently the countries of sub-Saharan Africa, the ethnically artificial inheritors of colonial cartography, have invoked the aid of schools to consolidate their identities as nation-states.

Expressing a simple statement that the schools can be used to meld disparate peoples into a nation of citizens should not lure the reader into assuming that this is a simple process. The example of the severe problems facing Israeli teachers should dispel any complacent thoughts. Israel is a deeply divided society. The rifts between orthodox and non-orthodox Jews are culturally and politically uncomfortable; so also, and more painfully, is the coexistence with Jews of an understandably resentful minority of Muslim Arab people. In the words of one Israeli educationist, Orit Ichilov: 'Educating the younger generation for citizenship where little consensus exists regarding a vision of what Israeli society should be, and what binds citizens together, is an extremely difficult task' (Ichilov, 1998, p. 69). In 1985, in a directive on education for democracy, the Ministry of Education and Culture tried to resolve the dilemma presented by any clash between the 'principle of universalism' and 'an expression of Jewish-Zionist national values and culture' by giving priority to the former (Ichilov, 1998, p. 77). This involved downplaying the traditional Zionist message in Israeli schools in favour of human, individual rights. All very well; but in the face of bitter

168

internal hatreds the teaching profession is presented with a task of herculean proportions to help forge a homogeneous nation of Israeli citizens.

In the meantime, while there are pedagogical attempts in so many countries to create citizenly identity as nationhood, in the states of the European Union teachers are presented with the novel undertaking of explaining to their pupils that they are at one and the same time national and EU citizens. For how can the EU effectively exist as an integrated community if young people grow up ignorant of, even antipathetic to, their twin identities? The European Commission indicated in 1989 that it was becoming aware of the need to encourage schools to participate in the enterprise of further European integration. In a Communication it asserted 'the importance of preparing young people for citizenship which involves the Community dimension in addition to their national, regional and local affiliations' (see Heater, 1992, p. 56). Two years later, signature of the Maastricht Treaty, with its establishment of the legal status of citizen of the Union, rendered schools' involvement both more relevant and more urgent. Yet the problems were, and still are, legion.

What has been quoted above about the situation in Israel (and could be replicated about many states in the world today) concerning the lack of consensus on what that society should be is even more true of the European Union. Certainly, one can teach children the facts of their future citizenly status under the Maastricht terms, and one can teach them the facts about the history and institutional structures of the Union. But beyond that, there is a grey uncertainty. EU assistance to the teaching profession is helpful in various sectors, for language teaching, for instance; but it is negligible when it comes to sharply focused citizenship education. It is a delicate area, of course: the very national sensitivities, xenophobia even, that the European unity project is designed to blunt would be further sharpened at any hint of the Commission's exerting pressure on the schools of the member states to shape little European citizens. Even so, the teaching profession itself in many member states contains a growing number of enthusiasts for the task – for good or ill! For, as one British academic has concluded from his researches, 'The range of activity which relates to education for European citizenship is staggeringly diffuse' (I. Davies, in Davies and Sobisch, 1997, p. 115).

If education for European citizenship eludes authoritative and crisp definition, how much greater is the task of educating world citizens. Our survey of the notion of world citizenship in chapter 4 has demonstrated just what an extraordinarily broad spectrum of meanings the term has acquired. No wonder that teachers have interpreted their responsibility to educate for world-mindedness in widely disparate ways. Education for International Understanding, World Studies, Global Studies are some of the umbrella terms; UNESCO even devised the excessively clumsy portmanteau term Education for International Understanding, Co-operation and Peace and Education relating to Human Rights and Fundamental Freedoms. The vast potential subject-matter has often been unpicked: World History, Disarmament Education, Peace Studies, Environmental Studies, Development Education and Human Rights Education reflect the attempts at more manageably specific programmes.

The word 'citizenship', the reader will have noticed, does not appear in any of these. The term Education for World Citizenship seems to have originated in Britain in the inter-war years, and by 1939–40 the teacher-support organization, the Council for Education in World Citizenship (CEWC) had evolved. The name it adopted immediately provoked consternation. A Junior Education Minister referred to CEWC's 'humbug and false piety', while the *Times Educational Supplement* laid about it with some vigour:

> It sometimes seems that adults, exasperated at the failure of their own generation to achieve the ideal society, get at the children and impose on them the ideas which they think will produce it. Fundamentally their claim is not different from that of the Nazis and Communists.
>
> *(see Heater, 1984, p. 56)*

The criticisms were grossly distorted calumnies. Unfair too were similar comments made when World Studies courses blossomed in English (and indeed US) schools in the 1980s. However, the nervous fears so evident in the 1940s and 1980s that a global dimension to some teaching would become a concerted political campaign to undermine the younger generation's loyalty to the nation had subsided by the 1990s. Nevertheless, pedagogical objectives and methods still require extremely careful devising; at the same time clarity of purpose is extraordinarily difficult to achieve because the concept of world citizenship is itself so befogged.

Although education for supra-national forms of citizenship presents difficulties that are particularly hard to resolve, the very principle of citizenship education even at state level has been the subject of doubt and debate throughout history. As so often, Aristotle makes a splendid starting-point for our discussion. Expanding on the brief comments about his views presented in chapter 2, we can garner from his thinking on the matter three fundamental considerations.

First, he believed that the academic study of politics was unsuitable for young people. He pronounced:

> political science is not a proper study for the young. The young man is not versed in the practical business of life from which politics draws its premises and data. He is, besides, swayed by his feelings, with the result that he will make no headway and derive no benefit from a study the end of which is not knowing but doing.
>
> *(Aristotle, 1955, I.3)*

But he drew a distinction between the study of political science and preparation for citizenship. The latter Aristotle held to be of cardinal importance; this is his second consideration. He describes education as '*the* means of making [a *polis*] a community and giving it unity' (Aristotle, 1948, 1263b). Schools should prepare young people for participative life in the *polis*, which signifies, above all, that they should be 'able to do good acts' (Aristotle, 1948, 1333b). The means to forming such a noble citizenly character is aesthetic, especially musical, education.

Aristotle's third message is that 'The citizens of a state should always be educated to suit the constitution of their state' (Aristotle, 1948, 1337aII). By this he meant that the educational programme in a democracy should be designed to uphold democracy, and in an oligarchical state to uphold oligarchy. The purpose of education should be to support social as well as political stability; for we must remember that Aristotle embraced in the term 'constitution' both way of life and political institutions and arrangements.

These propositions may be nearly two and a half millennia old, but they still have relevance, even if not universally favoured. The case

171

against teaching academic politics has sometimes been presented along the following lines. Teaching constitutional 'nuts and bolts' is dull and by itself has little meaning. However, enlivening such a syllabus with a study of political issues can lead to the pupils, who are inexperienced in adult affairs, either making premature judgements of their own or accepting uncritically those foisted upon them by their teachers.

Heuristic learning experiences are better, that is, learning by practical activities such as participation in school councils and committees, or involvement in community work. The first reveals that not all problems have simple solutions and teaches the virtues of give-and-take; the second instils consideration for others – Aristotle's ability 'to do good acts'. And his third requirement – namely, that education should be consonant with the political and social style of the state – clearly happens: no one would suggest that programmes of teaching for civic purposes in the USA, China and Iran, for instance, are by any means identical. In fact, an Israeli professor of education has asserted quite bluntly that 'it is impossible to engage in citizenship education in isolation from its social and political context. Citizenship education mirrors the social, political and value changes within society' (Ichilov, 1998, p. 80).

Thus far, we have been considering some of the general issues relating to education for citizenship in schools. Yet it is utterly artificial to treat the civic educative process as a school responsibility in isolation from the community at large and from the individual's experience as a citizen over his or her whole lifetime. Pupils grow to be citizens under the influences, consciously aware or not, of their parents, peer-friendships, the news media, the entertainment industry and whatever groups, clubs or churches to which they might belong. Moreover, some of these influences will persist into adulthood. And in some states, of course, news communication, symbols and the mobilization of opinion is centrally encouraged. Indeed, the history of citizenship in the civic republican mode is replete with examples in both theory and practice of this kind of citizenship education, as we have seen in chapter 2. In many states today, however, 'the mobilization of opinion' means control through censorship, thus impairing the crucial citizenship function of framing and passing judgements.

A form of adult civic education that does not depend on these kinds of manipulative devices is a version of the heuristic style of school learning, namely participation in local affairs. The most notable exposition of this idea is John Stuart Mill's famous passage in *Representative Government*. He regretted that Victorian England could not match the educative experience of participation in public affairs enjoyed by Athenian citizens in that city's democratic era. The whole of a man's life, he argued, is elevated by such activity. The involvement of those who are able to do so in jury service or parochial duties, for example, 'must make them ... very different beings, in range of ideas and development of faculties, from those who have done nothing in their lives but drive a quill, or sell goods over a counter'.

Indeed, three kinds of benefit derive from engagement in local affairs. One is that it is a form of general education: 'If circumstances allow the amount of public duty assigned [the citizen] to be considerable,' Mill wrote, 'it makes him an educated man.' Secondly, participation makes a man a more virtuous citizen:

> Still more salutary [than the general educative benefit] is the moral part of the instruction afforded by the participation of the private citizen, if even rarely, in public functions. He is called upon, while so engaged, to weigh interests not his own. ... Where this school of public spirit does not exist, scarcely any sense is entertained that private persons, in no eminent social situation, owe any duties to society, except to obey the laws and submit to the government.

And thirdly, without opportunities to participate, an individual is not only a worse citizen but a worse human being. In these circumstances,

> Every thought or feeling, either of interest or duty, is absorbed in the individual and in the family. ... A neighbour, not being an ally or associate ... is therefore a rival. Thus even private morality suffers, while public is actually extinct.
>
> *(Mill, 1910, pp. 216–17)*

Mill was over-optimistic in thinking that any meaningful number of citizens in Victorian Britain could possibly participate in public affairs and exaggerated the potential effect on the person of participation in any case. This does not, however, necessarily mean that his thesis is worthless. Surely, since he wrote, considerable numbers have

173

been educated somewhat in the manner he contemplated through membership of trade unions and single-issue political movements, the bodies of which civil society is composed – though with the imporant caveat that, having specific agendas, they lack the potential for purveying the entirely altruistic public morality Mill envisaged.

It would be foolish to dissent from the views that citizenship education is and should be an adult, indeed lifelong, process, and that its content, methods and objectives vary according to the polity and society in which the people act out their citizenly functions. Nevertheless, of prime concern today is how schools can educate their pupils as novice-citizens in states that are or have the desire to be liberal democracies. It is necessary, therefore, to identify the fundamental problems that underlie the discharge of this responsibility and to examine one recent set of suggestions as to how in practical terms schools might with reasonable efficiency make the attempt to turn pupils into citizens.

The basic problem for schools rests in the essence of democratic citizenship itself. For, at the heart of the concept lies a, perhaps insoluble, contradiction. Eamonn Callan, a Canadian professor of education, has explained the conundrum in the following words:

> The pluralism of free societies makes urgent the task of creating citizens who share a sufficiently cohesive political identity. At the same time, the sheer range and power of pluralism make it hard to see how reasoned agreement on the content of that identity and the educational practices that would make it safe for the future could be more than an idle wish.
>
> *(Callan, 1997, p. 221)*

Why the pessimism? By extracting the salient arguments from this book we can produce a rough sketch of some of the dilemmas facing schools. These are made particularly acute because five elements need to be juggled into reciprocally acceptable place.

First, the state. It requires a stably coherent population, not one over-strained by antagonisms arising from party political, class, religious or ethnic differences. Potential divisiveness can be abated if citizens display the virtues of empathy and tolerance. The obvious place for cultivating these virtues is the school. So, school is the second element in the pattern. But what kind of school? Clearly, pupils are best able to understand and come to terms with all the diversity of the society in which they are growing up if the school population is as near as possible a microcosm

174

of that society. Common or comprehensive schools provide this; private, selective or special schools do not. But if all children are required to attend schools of the comprehensive kind, the rights of parents – the third element – are abridged. Should they not, as free citizens, be able to choose where to send their offspring for education and with whom, therefore, they shall mix? However, the children themselves form the fourth element. They surely also have rights, not least as budding citizens. They have the right to be given the best possible education to ensure that they grow up to be good citizens.

Then, fifthly, of course, there are the teachers. Individually and as a collective body they have the ultimate responsibility of creating the right moral tone or ethos in the school (the 'hidden curriculum', as it is sometimes called) and of teaching appropriate material in their classrooms so that their pupils emerge as good citizens at the end of this experience. Yet teaching attitudes is the most delicate of all pedagogical tasks. Too little revealed enthusiasm on the part of the teacher and the pupils remain unmoved and unconvinced; too much, and the teacher in a liberal democracy will be charged, not least by the parents, with the professional crime of indoctrination.

Yet, for all the hazards and impediments, liberal democratic states need their citizens to be educated in their civic role, and some countries have made commendable efforts to achieve this objective. The task has been approached with extreme, almost unique, casualness in England – until, that is, 1998, when a government-appointed Advisory Group on Citizenship published a report providing authoritative guidelines. It is a document, therefore, worthy of some consideration here as an exemplar of what is thought both desirable and practicable for, to quote its title, 'education for citizenship and the teaching of democracy in schools'.

It is not our purpose here to investigate curricula and teaching methods. Our interest in the report lies rather in what this expert body has considered that schools can achieve; and this reflects an image of how young citizens ought to be readied for their mature lives. The Advisory Group decided that effective education for citizenship should comprise three interrelated components, moral, social and political:

> Firstly, children learning from the very beginning self-confidence and socially and morally responsible behaviour both in and beyond the classroom, both towards those in authority and towards each other. . . .

175

Secondly, learning about and becoming helpfully involved in the life of their communities, including learning through community involvement and service to the community. . . .

Thirdly, pupils learning about and how to make themselves effective in public life through knowledge, skills and values.

(Advisory Group on Citizenship, 1998, pp. 11–13)

The types of 'learning outcomes' expected from the school programmes once under way also indicate what is meant by being an educated citizen. These 'learning outcomes' are of four kinds. The citizen should comprehend key concepts (e.g. 'democracy and autocracy'); have acquired values and dispositions (e.g. 'concern for the common good'); be equipped with skills and aptitudes (e.g. 'ability to make a reasoned argument both verbally and in writing'); and be possessed of knowledge and understanding (e.g. 'topical and contemporary issues and events at local, national, EU, Commonwealth and international levels') (Advisory Group on Citizenship, 1998, p. 44).

The English Advisory Group were presented with a practical task. Debating the various styles, forms and contents of citizenship would have been an intellectual indulgence well beyond their remit. They framed a most serviceable definition and worked to that. We, however, cannot leave the matter there. The preceding chapters have shown how convoluted the concept of citizenship and arguments about its true nature have been. Is it possible, we must therefore finally ask, to connect up the disparate interpretations and reveal the quintessence of citizenship?

Connections and essence

When the human mind is presented with a plethora of data it tries to cluster them into patterns for greater comprehension. Citizenship has been subjected to constant interpretation and reinterpretation of this sort, partly to reflect changing conditions and partly to reveal new insights. It is not possible to survey all the interpretations and models that have recently been published. We conclude our survey, therefore, with a summary of two particularly illuminating recent suggestions and a simplified presentation of citizenship's component parts.

Studies of the subject have very often asserted or taken for granted that an absolute dichotomy exists between the civic republican and liberal forms of the concept and status. Here is a firmly worded example:

> Citizenship in the republican tradition . . . is undergirded throughout its ancient and modern history by patriarchialism. As such, a civic paradigm was bound to come into eventual conflict with a rights-based paradigm of political community. There is a clear contradiction between the restrictive property-based citizenship implied in the classical republican model and the universal adult citizenship that follows necessarily from any conception of human beings as equal rights-based creatures.
>
> *(Ignatieff, 1995, p. 57)*

Chapters 1 and 2 of the present book reflect this distinction. Yet is it not possible to achieve some kind of conjunction between these two traditions, which, after all, are talking about the same subject? An American scholar, Richard Dagger, has accomplished this through his concept of 'republican liberalism' (Dagger, 1997).

Dagger believes that, as long as the liberal rights version of citizenship is not interpreted as selfish individualism, then a marriage with the republican tradition is feasible. Indeed, he shows that a number of political theorists in the past, without systematically thinking through their positions in this respect, were in fact working astride the two styles. Locke, Madison, Kant, T. H. Green, for example – and J. S. Mill. We have, indeed, already seen how Mill argued that, by being a virtuous, community-conscious participant in civic affairs (a republican requirement), a citizen benefits by enhancing his or her own individual development (a liberal objective). Citizenship does not involve an either/or choice.

Dagger sees republican liberalism as promising 'to strengthen the appeal of duty, community, and the common good while preserving the appeal of rights' (Dagger, 1997, p. 5). His argument, in extreme skeletal form, proceeds as follows. Citizenship incorporates three elements, namely, autonomy, virtue and rights, which should be regarded, not as in tension, but as complementary. For autonomy is the fundamental right. But, as everyone is an autonomous being, all are morally equal. Therefore, each must respect the other's autonomy, and so rights involve reciprocity: I enjoy my rights and must allow you to enjoy yours. Thus,

177

the belief that liberalism, in safeguarding the individual, should eschew precepts of social morality can be discarded. In defending the enjoyment of individual rights liberalism should accept the moral obligation to respect the rights of all members of the community. In its turn, republican civic virtue need not ignore the individual by requiring commitment to the community, because respecting the rights of other individuals is itself a virtue. And so, by concentrating on the true subtlety of the two traditions, we witness their convergence.

All this has practical application in an age when constant pressure for making citizens' rights more effectively available has led to a backlash demand for citizens to comprehend their moral responsibilities and obligations to the state and the community. In the words of Dagger, summarizing his case, 'To appreciate rights is to understand that they are as valuable for the way they connect us to as for the way they protect us from one another' (Dagger, 1997, p. 201). Republican liberalism need not be a perverse contradiction in terms; it can be a most helpful theoretical and pragmatic integration of the splintered concept of citizenship.

Our second novel interpretation is taken from a British scholar, Geraint Parry (Parry, 1991). Instead of the conventional republican–liberal divide, he presents for our consideration three recently established schools of thought, all of which contain useful principles, but also drawbacks.

One, which he associates with Michael Oakeshott, he describes as the minimalist or civil association model. This is a desperately thin conception of citizenship involving little more than acceptance of and obedience to the law and, in Oakeshott's own inimitable term, a 'watery fidelity' (see Parry, 1991, p. 170). The second is the human rights model, for which Parry draws on the work of Alan Gewirth, who has argued that citizenship rights derive in essence from human rights and have no other ultimate justification. Consequently, as we have already seen, citizenship rights themselves may be regarded as almost redundant. Parry's third model is the communitarian, already outlined in chapter 1. Depending on its particular interpretation, this might undervalue individual identity and rights. And so Parry produces his own preference, a fourth, 'mutual society' model. This, by relating rights and obligations, has some affinity with Dagger's republican liberalism, though built on different arguments.

Parry explains his metaphor: 'The principle of the mutual society might be "from each according to his or her ability, to each according to his or her need for the conditions of agency"' (Parry, 1991, p. 186). The twist at the end of the slogan is crucial: citizens must be able to do, not just to be; they must be able to act. Moreover, the distribution of goods is arranged by citizens, defined by three features, namely, impartiality, communal awareness and relationship by a common historical background and awareness.

Mutuality, of course, is the essence, that is, all citizens need to be aware of the total interconnection between receipts and payments, between rights and obligations. Parry explains:

> Citizens would be regarded as belonging to a network of rights and duties around which they formed certain expectations and build their lives. In this way the mutual society would shape the lives of its members and force them to recognise that the possibility of their own agency rests, in part, on what others have contributed and on whom they thus rely.
>
> *(Parry, 1991, p. 187)*

Although the concept is most readily understood and could most readily be implemented within the framework of the state (the American 'workfare' project is an obvious example), other contexts are possible, even desirable. Local initiatives, EU-wide welfare, global environmental protection fit into the mutual society model. It is therefore applicable – and this is important for any credible model – to the notion and increasing reality of multiple citizenship.

Our third example of pattern-making is quite different from the other two. It is a simple, visual presentation of the network of interconnections that relates the various components of citizenship, however defined and whatever the nuances. One of the problems confronting the student of the subject is that written descriptions are necessarily expounded in linear fashion, they are one-dimensional. And so, figure 5.2 is offered to the reader as a two-dimensional diagrammatic presentation of the quintessence of citizenship. Only by appreciating the connections thus displayed can we see the concept whole. Except, we must remember to imagine it in three dimensions because multiple citizenship needs to be accommodated.

Rarely has the word 'citizenship' been so pervasive. It reaches us from the lips of politicians and broadcasting journalists and from the

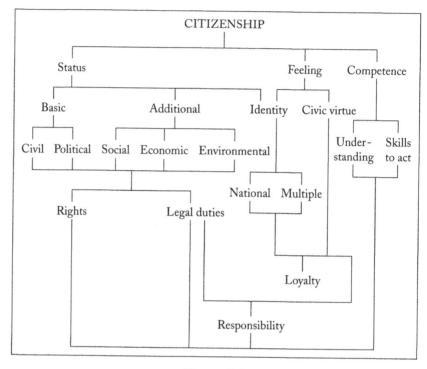

Figure 5.2

printed pages of newspapers, books and journals. Yet, even though the legal status has percolated from its origins in Europe to all the continents of the world, the full understanding and enjoyment of that status are anything but universal. The study of citizenship is consequently not just topical, but a large, variegated, ever-changing subject. What has been presented in this book is therefore just one picture, which, it is hoped, will be sufficiently illuminating to encourage the reader to deeper and continuing interest.

References

Adeyoyin, F. A. 1979: The Role of the School as a Politicizing Agent Through Citizenship Education. *International Journal of Political Education*, 2.

Advisory Group on Citizenship 1998: *Education for Citizenship and the Teaching of Democracy in Schools*. London: Qualifications and Assessment Authority.

Andrews, G. (ed.) 1991: *Citizenship*. London: Lawrence & Wishart.

Arendt, H. 1973: *On Revolution*. Harmondsworth: Penguin.

Aristotle (trans. and ed. E. Barker) 1948: *Politics*. Oxford: Clarendon Press.

Aristotle (trans. J. A. K. Thomson) 1955: *The Ethics of Aristotle*. Harmondsworth: Penguin.

Aron, R. 1974: Is Multinational Citizenship Possible? *Social Research*, 41.

Beiner, R. 1983: *Political Judgment*. London: Methuen.

Beiner, R. (ed.) 1995: *Theorizing Citizenship*. Albany, NY: State University of New York Press.

Benyon, J. and Edwards, A. 1997: Crime and Public Order. In P. Dunleavy et al. (eds), *Developments in British Politics 5*. Basingstoke: Macmillan.

Bouloiseau, M. et al. (eds) 1952: *Oeuvres de Maximilien Robespierre*, vol. 9. Paris: Presses Universitaires de France.

Brennan, T. 1981: *Political Education and Democracy*. Cambridge: Cambridge University Press.

Briggs, A. 1968: *Victorian Cities*. Harmondsworth: Penguin.

Brinton, C. 1952: *The Anatomy of Revolution*. New York: Prentice-Hall.

Brock, W. R. 1973: *Conflict and Transformation*. Harmondsworth: Penguin.

Brownlie, I. 1990: *Principles of Public International Law*. Oxford: Clarendon Press, 4th edn.

Brubaker, W. R. (ed.) 1989: *Immigration and the Politics of Citizenship in Europe and North America*. Lanham, MD, and London: University Press of America.

Brubaker, W. R. 1992: *Citizenship and Nationhood in France and Germany.* Cambridge, MA and London: Harvard University Press.

Buck, P. W. (ed.) 1975: *How Conservatives Think.* Harmondsworth: Penguin.

Bulmer, M. and Rees, A. M. 1996: *Citizenship Today: The Contemporary Relevance of T. H. Marshall.* London and Bristol, PA: University College London Press.

Callan, E. 1997: *Creating Citizens: Political Education and Liberal Democracy.* Oxford: Clarendon Press.

Cicero (trans. R. Gardner) 1958: Pro Balbo. In *The Speeches.* London: Heinemann and Cambridge, MA: Harvard University Press.

Cicero (trans. C. W. Keyes) 1959: *De Re Publica.* London: Heinemann and Cambridge, MA: Harvard University Press.

Clarke, P. B. 1994: *Citizenship.* London: Pluto Press.

Cobban, A. 1964: *Rousseau and the Modern State.* London: Allen & Unwin, 2nd edn.

Cohen, B. 1969: The Problem of Bias, in Heater, D. (ed.), *The Teaching of Politics.* London: Methuen.

Colley, L. 1992: *Britons: Forging the Nation 1707–1837.* New Haven, CT, and London: Yale University Press.

Commission on Citizenship 1990: *Encouraging Citizenship.* London: HMSO.

Commission on Global Governance 1995: *Our Global Neighbourhood.* Oxford: Oxford University Press.

Dagger, R. 1997: *Civic Virtues: Rights, Citizenship and Republican Liberalism.* New York and Oxford: Oxford University Press.

Davies, I. and Sobisch, A. 1997: *Developing European Citizens.* Sheffield: Sheffield Hallam University Press.

de Burgh, W. G. 1953: *The Legacy of the Ancient World.* Harmondsworth: Penguin.

Dickinson, H. T. 1977: *Liberty and Property: Political Ideology in Eighteenth-century Britain.* London: Methuen.

Engelbrecht, H. C. 1968: *Johann Gottlieb Fichte: A Study of his Political Writings with Special Reference to his Nationalism.* New York: AMS Press.

Etzioni, A. 1993: *The Spirit of Community.* New York: Simon & Schuster.

Faulks, K. 1998: *Citizenship in Modern Britain.* Edinburgh: Edinburgh University Press.

Fichte, J. G. (ed. G. A. Kelly) 1968: *Addresses to the German Nation.* New York: Harper & Row.

Forsyth, M. 1987: *Reason and Revolution: The Political Thought of the Abbé Sieyes.* Leicester: Leicester University Press and New York: Holmes & Meyer.

Fraser, A. 1984: *The Weaker Vessel.* London: Methuen.

The Federalist 1787: various edns.

Fukuyama, F. 1992: *The End of History and the Last Man*. Harmondsworth: Penguin.

Gardner, J. P. (ed.) n.d.: *Hallmarks of Citizenship: A Green Paper*. London: British Institute of International and Comparative Law.

Green, L. C. 1987: Is World Citizenship a Legal Practicability? *Canadian Yearbook of International Law*, 25.

Hawthorne, N. 1992: *The Scarlet Letter*. Ware, Herts.: Wordsworth Classics.

Heater, D. 1984: *Peace Through Education: The Contribution of the Council for Education in World Citizenship*. Lewes: Falmer Press.

Heater, D. 1991: Citizenship: A Remarkable Case of Sudden Interest. *Parliamentary Affairs*, 44.

Heater, D. 1992: Education for European Citizenship. *Westminster Studies in Education*, 15.

Hegel, G. W. F. (trans. T. M. Knox) 1967: *Hegel's Philosophy of Right*. London: Oxford University Press.

Held, D. 1989: *Political Theory and the Modern State*. Cambridge: Polity Press.

Held, D. (ed.) 1991: *Political Theory Today*. Cambridge: Polity Press.

Held, D. 1995: *Democracy and the Global Order*. Cambridge: Polity Press.

Hennock, E. P. 1973: *Fit and Proper Persons*. London: Arnold.

Horsman, M. and Marshall, A. 1994: The Disenfranchised Citizen, pt. 3 ch. 3, *After the Nation State: Citizens, Tribalism and the New World Order*. London: HarperCollins.

Ichilov, O. (ed.) 1998: *Citizenship and Citizenship Education in a Changing World*. London and Portland, OR: Woburn Press.

Ignatieff, M. 1995: The Myth of Citizenship. In Beiner, 1995.

Janowitz, M. 1988: The Good Citizen – A Threatened Species? In W. K. Cummings, S. Gopinathan and Y. Tomoda (eds), *The Revival of Values Education in Asia and the West*. Oxford: Pergamon Press.

Jones, B. and Robins, L. (eds) 1992: *Two Decades of British Politics*. Manchester: Manchester University Press.

Joseph, K. and Sumption, J. 1979: *Equality*. London: Murray.

Jowell, R. and Park, A. (eds) 1998: *Young People, Politics and Citizenship: A Disengaged Generation?* London: Citizenship Foundation.

Kane-Berman, J. n.d.: Let us be clear about the role of the Bill of Rights. London: South African High Commission, mimeo.

Kennedy, E. 1989: *A Cultural History of the French Revolution*. New Haven, CT, and London: Yale University Press.

Kymlicka, W. 1995: *Multicultural Citizenship: A Liberal Theory of Minority Rights*. Oxford: Clarendon Press.

183

Lash, J. P. 1962: *Dag Hammarskjöld*. London: Cassell.

Lister, R. 1997: *Citizenship: Feminist Perspectives*. Basingstoke: Macmillan.

Livy (trans. A. de Sélincourt) 1960: *The Early History of Rome*. Harmondsworth: Penguin.

Locke, J. 1962: *Two Treatises of Civil Government*. London: Dent.

Lutz, D. S. 1992: *A Preface to American Political Theory*. Lawrence, KS: University Press of Kansas.

Macartney, C. A. 1934: *National States and National Minorities*. London: Oxford University Press.

Macedo, S. 1990: *Liberal Virtues*. Oxford: Clarendon Press.

Machiavelli, N. (ed. B. Crick) 1998: *The Discourses*. Harmondsworth: Penguin.

McLellan, D. 1977: *Karl Marx: Selected Writings*. Oxford: Oxford University Press.

MacNeill, J., Winsemius, P., and Yakushiji, T. 1991: *Beyond Interdependence*. New York: Oxford University Press.

Marcus Aurelius Antoninus (trans. C. R. Haines) 1961: *The Communings with Himself* [i.e. Meditations]. London: Heinemann and Cambridge, MA: Harvard University Press.

Marshall, T. H. and Bottomore, T. 1992: *Citizenship and Social Class*. London and Concord, MA: Pluto Press.

Mazzini, J. 1961: *The Duties of Man and Other Essays*. London: Dent.

Mead, L. 1986: *Beyond Entitlement: The Social Obligation of Citizenship*. New York: Free Press.

Mill, J. S. 1910: *Utilitarianism, On Liberty, and Considerations on Representative Government*. London: Dent.

Ministry of Education 1949: *Citizens Growing Up*. London: HMSO.

Montesquieu, Baron de (trans. T. Nugent) 1949: *The Spirit of the Laws*. New York: Hafner.

Mundialist Summa, vol. 1: *A World of Reason* 1977. Paris: Club Humaniste.

Nkrumah, K. 1961: *I Speak of Freedom*. London: Heinemann.

Oakeshott, M. (ed.) 1940: *Social and Political Doctrines of Contemporary Europe*. London: Basis Books.

Oldfield, A. 1990a: *Citizenship and Community: Civic Republicanism and the Modern World*. London: Routledge.

Oldfield, A. 1990b: Citizenship: An Unnatural Practice? *Political Quarterly*, 61.

Oliver, D. and Heater, D. 1994: *The Foundations of Citizenship*. Hemel Hempstead: Harvester Wheatsheaf.

Pakendorf, H., 1995: Social rights as basic rights. London: South African High Commission, mimeo.

Palmer, R. R. 1964: *The Age of the Democratic Revolution*, vol. 2. Princeton, NJ: Princeton University Press.

Parry, G. 1991: Conclusion: Paths to Citizenship. In U. Vogel and M. Moran (eds), *The Frontiers of Citizenship*. Basingstoke: Macmillan.

Plant, R. and Barry, N. 1990: *Citizenship and Rights in Thatcher's Britain: Two Views*. London: IEA Health and Welfare Unit.

Plato (trans. F. M. Cornford) 1941: *The Republic of Plato*. Oxford: Clarendon Press.

Plato (trans. T. J. Saunders) 1970: *Laws*. Harmondsworth: Penguin.

Reiss, H. (ed.) 1991: *Kant: Political Writings*. Cambridge: Cambridge University Press.

Riesenberg, P. 1992: *Citizenship in the Western Tradition: Plato to Rousseau*. Chapel Hill, NC, and London: University of North Carolina Press.

Roche, M. 1992: *Rethinking Citizenship: Welfare, Ideology and Change in Modern Society*. Cambridge: Polity Press.

Rousseau, J.-J. 1911: *Émile*. London: Dent.

Rousseau, J.-J. (ed. M. Cranston) 1968: *The Social Contract*. Harmondsworth: Penguin.

Rousseau, J.-J. 1969: *Oeuvres complètes*, vol. 4. Dijon: Gallimard.

Rudé, G., 1975: *Robespierre*. London: Collins.

Sampson, A. 1998: Men of the renaissance. *Guardian*, 3 January.

Schapiro, L. 1977: *The Government and Politics of the Soviet Union*. London: Hutchinson, 6th edn.

Schlereth, T. J. 1977: *The Cosmopolitan Ideal in Enlightenment Thought*. Notre Dame, IN: University of Notre Dame Press.

Sherwin-White, A. N. 1973: *The Roman Citizenship*. Oxford: Clarendon Press, 2nd edn.

Shklar, J. 1969: *Men and Citizens: A Study of Rousseau's Social Theory*. Cambridge: Cambridge University Press.

Sieyes, E. J. (ed. S. E. Finer) 1963: *Emmanuel Joseph Sieyes, What is the Third Estate?* London: Pall Mall.

Sinopoli, R. C. 1992: *The Foundations of American Citizenship and Civic Virtue*. New York: Oxford University Press.

Smith, A. D. 1971: *Theories of Nationalism*. London: Duckworth.

Sophocles (trans. E. F. Watling) 1947: *The Theban Plays*. Harmondsworth: Penguin.

Stockton, D. 1986: The Founding of the Empire. In J. Boardman, J. Griffin, O. Murray (eds), *The Oxford History of the Classical World*. Oxford: Oxford University Press.

Thompson, J. M. 1948: *French Revolution Documents*. Oxford: Blackwell.

Tocqueville, A. de (ed. J. P. Mayer and M. Lerner) 1968: *Democracy in America*. London: Collins.

Torney-Purta, J. 1981: Applying Perspectives of History and of Psychology to Three Models of International Education. In D. Heater and J. A. Gillespie (eds), *Political Education in Flux*. London and Beverly Hills: Sage.

Turner, B. S. 1986: *Citizenship and Capitalism*. London: Allen & Unwin.

Wheeler, N. J. and Dunne, T. 1998: Good international citizenship: a third way for British foreign policy. *International Affairs*, 74.

Wollstonecraft, M. (ed. M. B. Kramnick) 1975: *Vindication of the Rights of Woman*. Harmondsworth: Penguin.

Wootton, D. 1986: *Divine Right and Democracy*. Harmondsworth: Penguin.

Select Reading List

Andrews, G. (ed.) 1991: *Citizenship*. London: Lawrence & Wishart.

Barbalet, J. M. 1988: *Citizenship*. Milton Keynes: Open University Press.

Beiner, R. (ed.) 1995: *Theorizing Citizenship*. Albany, NY: State University of New York Press.

Brubaker, W. R. (ed.) 1989: *Immigration and the Politics of Citizenship in Europe and North America* (Lanham, MD, and London: University Press of America.

Clarke, P. B. 1994: *Citizenship*. London: Pluto Press.

Demaine, J. and Entwistle, H. (eds) 1996: *Beyond Communitarianism: Citizenship, Politics and Education*. Basingstoke: Macmillan.

Faulks, K. 1998: *Citizenship in Modern Britain*. Edinburgh: Edinburgh University Press.

Gardner, J. P. (ed.) n.d.: *Hallmarks of Citizenship: A Green Paper*. London: British Institute of International and Comparative Law.

Heater, D. 1990: *Citizenship: The Civic Ideal in World History, Politics and Education*. London: Longman.

Heater, D. 1996: *World Citizenship and Government: Cosmopolitan Ideas in the History of Western Political Thought*. Basingstoke: Macmillan.

Ichilov, O. (ed.) 1998: *Citizenship and Citizenship Education in a Changing World*. London and Portland, OR: Woburn Press.

Kymlicka, W. 1995: *Multicultural Citizenship: A Liberal Theory of Minority Rights*. Oxford: Clarendon Press.

Lister, R. 1997: *Citizenship: Feminist Perspectives*. Basingstoke: Macmillan.

Marshall, T. H. and Bottomore, T. 1992: *Citizenship and Social Class*. London and Concord, MA: Pluto Press.

Meehan, E. 1993: *Citizenship and the European Community*. London: Sage.

187

Mouffe, C. (ed.) 1992: *Dimensions of Radical Democracy: Pluralism, Citizenship, Community*. London: Verso.

Oldfield, A. 1990: *Citizenship and Community: Civic Republicanism and the Modern World*. London: Routledge.

Riesenberg, P. 1992: *Citizenship in the Western Tradition: Plato to Rousseau*. Chapel Hill, NC, and London: University of North Carolina Press.

Roche, M. 1992: *Rethinking Citizenship: Welfare, Ideology and Change in Modern Society*. Cambridge: Polity Press.

Turner, B. and Hamilton, P. (eds) 1994: *Citizenship: Critical Concepts*, 2 vols. London: Routledge.

van Steenbergen, B. (ed.) 1994: *The Condition of Citizenship*. London: Sage.

Index

accountability/monitoring of government 52, 54, 65, 162
Addresses to the German Nation 98
Advisory Group on Citizenship (England) 164, 175–6
Africa 2, 33, 94, 99, 102, 147, 168
  see also South Africa
alienation 42, 43, 76, 84, 113, 163
America, 18th-century 1, 4–5, 6, 55, 58, 68, 101, 123
  see also USA
American Revolution/War of Independence 5, 7, 40, 49, 69, 83
Americans, Native 87, 111, 112
Amnesty International 143–4
Anarchy, State, and Utopia 27
apartheid *see* South Africa
apathy 32, 43, 45, 84, 87, 156, 160, 163
Arendt, H. 69–70
Aristophanes 88
Aristotle 44–8, 50, 53–8, 60, 62, 63, 65–7, 71, 72, 83, 88, 89, 133, 149, 155, 158, 171, 172
Aron, R. 150, 151

Athens 1, 44–5, 47, 65, 66, 83, 84, 85, 88, 173
attitudes/dispositions 164, 176
  empathy 33, 139, 150, 174
  moderation 33
  motivation/commitment 31, 45, 47, 49, 50, 60, 61, 64, 66, 74–5
  mutuality 56, 70, 72, 78, 178–9
  tolerance 32
  see also virtue(s)
Augustus 67
Australia 108, 111

Baltic states 109
Barber, B. 70
Barry, N. 28
Belgium 111, 112, 114, 120
Ben-Gurion, D. 108
Beyond Entitlement: The Social Obligations of Citizenship 28
Bill of Rights, 1689 40
Birmingham 133–4
Bismarck, von, O. 22, 104, 107
Blackstone, W. 90
Blair, A. 79

Board/Ministry of Education
    (England) 167–8
Breaking the Spell of the Welfare State
    27
Brown, G. 79
Brutus, L. J. 59–60
Burke, E. 30, 120

Callan, E. 174
Canada 2, 81, 111, 112–13, 119
capitalism 7–12, 13, 21, 24, 85
    environmental citizenship and 31
    figure 1.1 8
    origins of liberal citizenship 7–9
    social citizenship and 2, 10, 11,
        13, 15–17, 20
    support for citizenship 7–9, 11,
        14
    undermining of citizenship 9–12,
        14, 16–17, 24, 158
Chamberlain, J. 134
Cicero 44, 46, 48, 60, 72, 118, 138,
    149
Cincinnatus 60
Citizen's Charter 10
citizenship
    'active' (UK) 77
    active and passive, 1791 86, 122
    best context for: compactness 45,
        50, 54, 61, 69, 124–5, 149;
        local 17, 61, 69–70, 94; mixed
        constitution/republic 48, 53–5;
        organic community 72
    capitalism relations *see* capitalism
    civic republican 4, ch. 2, 95–6,
        99, 152, 157–8, 165–7,
        177: figure 2.1 52; neo-
        republicanism 70
    civil *passim*
    dual 116, 117, 118–20, 149,
        158

economic 15, 16, 21, 35, 37–8,
        41, 43, 89, 91: European
        Union 128–9, 130–1, 153,
        158–9
    environmental 3, 29–32, 38–9,
        94, 120, 122, 137, 143–4, 179
    European *see* European Union
    figure 5.2 180
    'good international' 138–9
    gradations of 87
    'horizontal'/citizens' relations 37,
        137, 141, 177–8
    industrial *see* citizenship,
        economic
    lack of 3
    'layered' 116, 120, 123–48
    liberal ch. 1, 157–8
    Marshall's three 'bundles' 13, 18,
        19, 21, 24, 27, 29
    multiple 3, 78, ch. 4, 158, 179:
        figure 4.1 116
    municipal 8, 55, 61, 69, 116,
        117, 126, 132–4, 158
    'mutual society' 178–9
    national *see* nationality
    'new' 161
    parallel 116, 117–23
    political *passim*
    purpose of 52–5
    'republican liberalism' 177–8
    second class/partial 20, 23, 87,
        91, 102: minorities 20, 23, 78,
        84, 86–7, 110–14, 120, 131;
        'underclass' 20, 26, 28, 87
    social 2, 13, 15–17, 19, 20,
        24–8, 35, 37–8, 41, 91,
        128–31, 153, 158–60:
        capitalism, relationship with
        see capitalism; civil/political,
        relationship with 14–15, 21,
        43, 158–9, 161; imprecision

of 16; inclusion in citizenship, arguments against 11, 24–5, 43; inclusion in citizenship, arguments for 2, 11, 14, 18, 24–5; New Right, attitude of 2, 10, 21, 24–8, 122; origins 10, 13–15, 22

world 95–8, 116, 117, 134–48, 158, 179: figure 4.3 136; identity 136–9; law 136, 139–43; morality 136–9; politics 136, 143–8; *see also* Council for Education in World Citizenship

Citizenship and Community 52

Citizenship and Social Class 12–17, 18

civil society 8, 9, 31, 37, 73–4, 85, 101–2, 116, 117, 120–3, 143–4, 153, 172, 174

Civil War, English 4, 5, 7, 58–9

civitas sine suffragio 86

class, social
   capitalism, effects of 8, 9, 10, 28, 84–5
   elite, citizenship restricted to 46, 58, 73, 86, 133, 156, 159, 167
   equality principle undermined 101, 102, 159
   Marshall's interpretation 12–15, 17, 20–1, 23–4, 43
   persistence 28, 43
   professional 7

Coke, E. 88

Coleridge, S. T. 105

Commission on Global Governance 139

Commonwealth 22, 120, 176

Commonwealthmen 59

Communism 2, 11, 22, 33, 75, 113, 121, 167

communitarianism 70, 77–9, 178

community service 76, 77, 172, 176

competence/skills 66, 100, 102, 110–12, 125, 133, 149, 164, 176

deliberation 62

judgement 52, 60, 61, 62–3, 73, 74

concord/harmony/fraternity 28, 33, 45, 52, 55–7, 62, 69, 72, 73, 84, 97–8

consumer, citizen as 10–11

cosmopolitanism *see* citizenship, world

Council for Education in World Citizenship 170

Dagger, R. 177–8

Dahrendorf, R. 18

Dawson, G. 134

declarations of/constitutional rights 34–9, 90, 160, 161
   American 6, 90, 138, 140
   French 5, 6, 9, 34, 35, 36, 51, 90–1, 97, 98, 138, 140, 160
   German 36
   Indian 35–6
   South African 34, 35, 36–9, 43
   Soviet 41

Defoe, D. 59

democracy 2, 33–4, 84, 99, 130, 146, 156, 158, 159, 162, 163, 166, 168, 171, 173, 174
   Athenian 44, 65, 84
   cosmopolitan 146, 147–8

Democracy in America 124

denizens 87, 131

Denmark 131

devolution 116, 126, 132

Discourses 49, 64

dispositions *see* attitudes/dispositions

Don Carlos 135
Dred Scott case 124
duties/obligations *passim*

education
    citizenship 52, 66–7, 72, 73, 75,
        76, 98, 104, 105, 153, 164–76
    European citizenship 169
    figure 5.1 165
    right 14, 16, 17, 19, 90, 111,
        161, 175
    state provision 10, 11, 14, 16, 17,
        19, 20, 26, 27, 46, 49, 52,
        66–8, 98, 103, 106, 113, 125,
        159, 164, 167–8, 171, 174–5
    teaching methods/curriculum
        171–2
    world citizenship 170–1
Eisenhower, D. D. 125–6
Émile 165–6
empathy *see* attitudes/dispositions
England *see* United Kingdom
Enlightenment 46, 49, 95, 98, 135
entitlements 21–2, 28, 98, 156,
    159
equality 1, 9, 10, 13, 15, 20, 25–8,
    43, 81–8, 94, 96, 100, 102–3,
    110, 113, 125, 159
    figure 3.2 82
    legal 6, 14, 21, 84, 85, 92, 158
    moral 14, 83, 166
    political 35–6, 58, 84, 158
    social/of opportunity 2, 16, 20,
        25, 35–6, 92
    tabulation 82
Etzioni, A. 77–9
European Commission 126, 169
European Convention of Human
    Rights 40, 129, 131, 161
European Court of Justice 128–9,
    153

European Parliament 126, 127,
    128, 130
European Union (EC/EU) 3, 126,
    150, 151, 153, 161, 176, 179
    citizenship in 18, 94–5, 161, 169
    citizenship of 3, 116, 117, 120,
        126–31, 134, 147, 149, 153,
        158, 161, 169: figure 4.2 128
Evans, G. 138

federalism 55, 61, 69, 115, 117,
    123–6, 132
Federalist, The 124
feminism *see* women
feudalism *see* pre-capitalist society
Fichte, J. G. 98, 105, 168
Florence 1, 48
France 35, 36, 75, 81, 96, 104, 106,
    107, 111, 113, 119–20, 131,
    134
    see also French Revolution
fraternity *see* concord
freedom 28, 52, 53, 55, 72, 73, 77,
    96
    Aristotle 53
    economic 9, 13
    equality and 83–4
    moral qualities needed 32
    nationalism and 100
    political system, as 2, 34–5, 41,
        68
    right, natural/citizenship 5, 6,
        13, 25, 27
    Rousseau 50–1, 53
    state, against 25, 27, 160
    Tocqueville 68
    women 91
French Revolution 1, 4, 5, 6, 7,
    35, 40, 51, 56–7, 83, 86, 89,
    97, 98, 101, 106, 132, 139,
    157

General Will 50–1, 53, 54, 63, 66, 101, 166
Germany 22, 36, 81, 98, 104, 105, 106–8, 120, 131, 133
Gewirth, A. 178
Ghana 102, 103
globalization 144, 160, 162
Great Britain *see* United Kingdom
Greece 44–6, 55, 60, 64, 73, 85, 98, 115, 118, 133, 135, 137–8, 148, 156, 158, 159
  see also Athens

Habeas Corpus Act 5
Hague Convention, 1930 119
Hamilton, A. 55
Hammarskjöld, D. 145
Hawthorne, N. 157
Hayek, F. A. 25
Hegel, G. W. F. 52, 121
Held, D. 148
Hobbes, T. 71
Hobhouse, L. 18
Human Condition, The 69
human/natural rights 4–5, 14, 138, 140, 143, 159–62, 178
  figure 4.4 142
  rights of citizen, distinction 5, 7, 34, 159–62, 178
  see also declarations of/ constitutional rights; United Nations International Bill of Rights
Hungary 102, 121

Ichilov, O. 168
identity
  bonding 9, 14, 17, 124
  complications 2, 124–5, 127, 149–50, 169, 174

consciousness of status 1, 2, 8
European 127, 130, 132, 169
liberal tradition 6, 17
world 136
see also nationality
immigration/immigrants 2, 22, 81, 85, 103, 106–8, 112, 119, 131, 160
India 35–6, 103
indoctrination 166–7, 175
Ireland 120
Islam/Muslims 75, 108, 111, 113, 168
Israel/Jews 2, 108, 168–9

Janowitz, M. 76–7
Jefferson, T. 69–70, 74, 140
Jews *see* Israel
John XXIII 153–4
Johnson, S. 61–2
Joseph, K. 27
judgement *see* competence/skills
jury service 45, 62, 65
jus sanguinis 80, 106, 107, 108
jus soli 80, 103, 106, 109

Kant, I. 135, 140, 144, 153, 177
knowledge/information/ understanding 66, 74, 125, 138, 149, 164
  experiential 46, 61, 62, 64, 66, 76, 150, 176
  media, news 74, 125
  school 46, 169, 176
Kymlicka, W. 18

Latin America 2, 33, 43, 147
law(s)
  figure 3.1 81
  see also citizenship, civil *passim*; *jus sanguinis*; *jus soli*;

law(s) (*cont'd*)
    nationality, legal definitions;
    Natural Law
Liberal Virtues 32–3
Linklater, A. 138–9
Little Rock school desegregation
    125–6, 149
Livy 48–9, 50, 59–60
Locke, J. 5, 6, 7, 38, 98, 138, 139,
    177
loyalty/allegiance 115, 149–50,
    151–3
    see also nationality; patriotism;
    virtue(s)

Maastricht Treaty 127–30, 131,
    152, 153, 161, 169
Macedo, L. 28
Machiavelli, N. 46, 48–50, 54, 56,
    60, 61, 63, 67–8, 72
Madison, J. 124, 177
Marcus Aurelius 135, 139, 145
market (forces) *see* capitalism
Marshall, A. 12
Marshall, T. H. 12–24, 25, 27, 29,
    43, 159
    analysis of 12–17
    criticism of 18–23
    praise/defence of 17–18, 23–4
Marx, K./Marxism 5, 7, 9, 11, 67,
    84–5, 90, 91
Mazzini, G. 104, 134
Mead, L. 28
media, news 32, 74, 121, 125, 153,
    159, 172, 180
Middle East 39–40
Mill, J. S. 90, 91, 100, 103, 133,
    173–4, 177
military service/discipline 34, 52,
    62, 64, 74, 75, 76, 92, 104,
    106, 152

Aristotle 46, 58, 60
Greece 45, 64, 65
Machiavelli 49, 50, 60, 61, 63,
    64–5
Rome 60–1, 65
Rousseau 50, 60, 64, 65
minorities *see* citizenship, second
    class/partial; nationality,
    multiethnic/multinational
    states
monitoring of government *see*
    accountability/monitoring
Montesquieu, Baron de 55, 61, 66,
    96
multiculturalism *see* nationality,
    multiethnic/multinational
    states
Muslims *see* Islam

nationality 95–114, 125
    cultural/political, distinction 85,
    96, 103, 105–9
    identity/loyalty/cohesion 2, 14,
    51, 96, 99–105, 110, 111,
    149–51, 168, 169
    legal definitions 80, 99, 116, 119,
    130, 151–2: *see also jus*
    sanguinis; *jus soli*
    multiethnic/multinational states
    2, 109–14, 174: figure 3.3
    110
    nationalism 9, 95–105, 109, 130,
    149, 153
    national self-determination 100,
    104
    origins, citizenship connection
    95–9, 158
    unification of states 103–4
Nationality Acts, British 81, 120
naturalization 85, 119
Natural Law 135, 138, 139, 148

neo-liberalism *see* New Right
New Right 2, 10, 21, 24–8, 79, 92, 122
Nicomachean Ethics 45, 55, 66
Nigeria 103, 105
Nkrumah, K. 102, 103
Non-Governmental Organizations (International) 144
Norman, W. 18
Nozick, R. 25, 27
Nuremberg Laws 107

Oakeshott, M. 178
Oldfield, A. 52, 63, 74
Orwell, G. 58

Paine, T. 6, 135
Palestinians 2, 108
Palmer, R. R. 98
Palmerston, Lord 140
parents 67, 79, 166, 172, 175
Parry, G. 178–9
participation/action
  Aristotle 45, 53, 54, 56, 62, 65, 66
  conditions for 56, 58, 62, 66, 76, 100, 148, 149, 173–4
  duty 17, 42, 52, 64–5
  Machiavelli 49, 64–5
  Mill 173–4
  Plato 66
  practice, in 36–7, 45, 57, 65, 66, 74, 76, 90, 94–5, 156, 174
  right 25, 38, 69–70, 84, 90
  Rousseau 54, 64, 65
  Stoics 47
  Tocqueville 65
patriarchialism 91, 92–4, 177
patriotism 14, 52, 60–2, 72, 95–7, 104–5, 125, 149, 152, 168
  Machiavelli 49, 61

Rousseau 51, 61
  Tocqueville 61, 68
Perpetual Peace 140
Phillips, W. 65
Plato 66, 67, 88, 167
pluralism 33, 109–14, 174
Plutarch 50
Pocock, J. G. A. 49–50
Poland 51, 65, 96, 121, 122–3
Politics, The 45, 66
positive discrimination 110–13
pre-capitalist/feudal society 7–8, 14
Prince, The 64–5
private and public spheres 6–7, 72, 73, 89–90, 92–3, 157, 165, 173
  Cicero 47
  Machiavelli 49
  Montesquieu 61
  Rousseau 53
property 6, 9, 21, 35, 38, 46, 52, 57–9, 85, 88–9, 177

Quebec *see* Canada

Rainborough, Colonel 5
Reagan, R. 10, 25, 27
regions/provinces 125, 126, 127, 130, 132
religion 72, 73, 75, 79, 108, 120, 134, 174
  ancient 67–8
  Christianity 49, 68, 89, 121
  modern civic 49, 50, 56, 57, 60, 61, 63, 66, 68, 75
Renaissance 46, 48–9, 135
Representative Government 133, 173
Republic, The 88, 167
revolutions 4, 6, 7, 8, 53, 83, 89, 99, 140, 157

revolutions (*cont'd*)
see also American Revolution;
French Revolution
rights, civic *passim*
*Right to Welfare and Other Essays,
The* 18
Robespierre, M. 51, 68, 97–8
Rome 1, 44, 46–50, 64, 65, 67–8,
85, 86, 117, 118, 135, 138,
156
Rousseau, J.-J.
education 67, 165–6, 167, 168
politics 46, 50, 53, 54, 56, 58,
60, 61, 63–6, 68, 72, 75, 83,
96, 101, 149, 150
Russia 42, 43, 108–9, 112

St Paul 118
Sandel, M. 70, 77
Scandinavia 90, 91
Scarlet Letter, The 157
Schiller, J. C. F. 135
Sieyes, Abbé 86, 89, 97, 106, 109
single-issue politics *see* civil society
skills *see* competence/skills
slavery 36, 40, 73, 86
Social Chapter (EU) 127–8
social citizenship *see* citizenship,
social
social class *see* class
Social Contract, The 50–1, 68
social contract theory 4, 50–1, 83,
98
Sophocles 141
South Africa 2, 33, 34, 35, 36–9,
43
Spain 132
Sparta 44–5, 46, 50, 54, 65, 166,
167
Spirit of the Community, The 78
Spirit of the Laws 55

Stoicism 46–7, 135, 151
Subjection of Women 90
subsidiarity 125, 127, 130, 153–4
suffrage 35, 38, 39, 86, 147
female *see* women
male 6, 22
Switzerland 91, 120, 123

Tacitus 85
taxation 6, 10, 20, 21, 26, 28, 34
Tebbit, N. 27
Thatcher, M. 10, 25, 27, 121–2,
134
'Third Way', the 79
Tocqueville, A. de 52, 55, 61, 65,
68, 69, 75, 79, 124–5, 133
trade unions 16, 21, 22, 73, 120,
174
Turner, B. 9, 11–12

understanding *see* knowledge
UNESCO 170
United Kingdom/Great Britain/
England 13, 22, 24, 40, 74,
88, 89, 104, 133
eighteenth-century 4, 14, 58–9,
101, 105
nineteenth-century 14, 15, 86,
90, 133–4
seventeenth-century 5, 7, 14,
58–9, 88
twentieth-century 19, 20, 76, 81,
86, 90: nineteen-eighties/
nineties 2, 10, 18, 21, 25, 27,
40, 77, 79, 112, 121–2, 132,
163–4, 170, 175; post-war 16,
17, 18, 19, 111, 113, 119,
130
United Nations Associations 145
United Nations Charter 140, 144,
145

United Nations International Bill of
  Rights 83, 138, 139, 140–1,
  144, 161, 162
United Nations, reform of 145–8
Universal Declaration of Human
  Responsibilities 139
Universal Declaration of Human
  Rights *see* United Nations
  International Bill of Rights
USA, nineteenth-century
  Afro-Americans/blacks 86–7
  constitution 6, 55, 61, 86–7,
  125
  practice 55, 61, 76, 90, 103, 108,
  119, 124–5, 133, 157, 168
USA, twentieth-century
  Afro-Americans/blacks 23, 113,
  125–6
  constitution/law 23, 81, 85, 87,
  90, 108, 125–6
  practice 2, 10, 25, 27–8, 76, 78,
  79, 85, 87, 90, 111, 112–13,
  119
USSR 2, 41–2, 113, 167

*Vindication of the Rights of
  Woman* 89
virtue(s)/morality 29, 32–3, 42,
  ch. 2, 104–5, 134, 149,

157–8, 166, 168, 173–5,
  177–8
Volk, German concept of 106–8

Walzer, M. 71
war crimes tribunals 141
War of Independence *see* American
  Revolution
welfare state 2, 10, 11, 15–21,
  25–8, 72, 78, 84, 92, 94, 111,
  159
Wells, H. G. 151
Whitman, W. 103
Wollstonecraft, M. 89–90, 91
women 19–20, 36, 78, 88–95, 120
  civil rights 20, 90
  feminist theory 74, 78, 88–95
  role in reform 90, 91, 92–4
  suffrage 20, 36, 39–40, 88–9,
  90–1
'workfare' 28, 179
world citizenship *see* citizenship,
  world
world criminal court 141, 143
world federalists 143, 145–6

Yugoslavia 2, 104, 113

zealotry, civic 157, 163

Lightning Source UK Ltd.
Milton Keynes UK
UKOW06f0959070315

247453UK00001B/65/P